Praise for *Thriving in Leadership*

"This is a very good book, a helpful book. It carries the additional authenticity of the authors' experiences—they have practiced what they preach in challenging times."

> —**Max Depree**, former CEO of Herman Miller; best-selling author of *Leadership Is an Art*, *Leadership Jazz*, *Called to Serve*, and *Leading without Power*

"Here is a book on leadership that is practical *and* spiritual, grounded *and* inspiring. These essays by seasoned leaders in the academy shed light on 'secrets hidden in plain sight' that all academic leaders should find of lasting value: the importance of 'showing up' as a whole person; the centrality of tenacious relationships; the vital role of rich, transformative conversations with all stakeholders; and the courage it takes to lead in ways that do not always conform to our cultural model assumptions about how leaders should act. I hope this book will gain a wide audience in and out of Christian higher education. Its hardwon and well-tested insights can help campus leaders of every sort navigate the tricky terrain that higher education travels today."

> —**Parker J. Palmer**, author of *Healing the Heart of Democracy*, *The Courage to Teach*, and *Let Your Life Speak*

"If you are drawn to the topic of leadership, especially in the context of a Christian serving in higher education, this book is a must read. I am challenged by these amazing authors and feel short-changed in not having their insights earlier in my career. I will call upon this deep well of scholarship, theory, practice, and stories many times in my work with diverse leaders."

> —**Robert C. Andringa**, president emeritus of the Council for Christian Colleges & Universities and managing partner of The Andringa Group

"*Thriving in Leadership* is an engaging conversation about the complexities, pressures, and joys of senior leadership in Christian higher education. The authors draw on their vast professional experience and the latest leadership literature to offer insights into the best practices in organizational leadership."

> —**Alec Hill**, president of InterVarsity Christian Fellowship USA

"*Thriving in Leadership* is indispensable for anyone committed to leadership excellence in Christian higher education. If you seek best practices in leadership for yourself and your organization that offer a collegial, collaborative, and empowering approach that fosters transformation, start here. Those who have contributed to this remarkable effort are gifted and accomplished leaders in their own right. I respect their wisdom, I seek their advice, and I recommend their scholarship in this book."

—**Jon R. Wallace**, president of Azusa Pacific University

"In these challenging times, institutions of higher education need leaders who possess the vision, proficiencies, and sense of calling to navigate a complex array of urgent and transcendent issues facing our educational communities. In *Thriving in Leadership*, an impressive assembly of authors provides thoughtful and practical counsel for guiding our institutions in a way that honors both their present realities and future promise. Rooted in lived experience, these leaders have shaped a compelling narrative of what leadership has been, is now, and should be in the future. This volume, which contributes greatly to the field of higher educational leadership, will be an invaluable resource for my own leadership team."

—**Kim S. Phipps**, president of Messiah College and chair of the Board of the Council for Christian Colleges & Universities

"For those of us who have been praying for more women to join the leadership ranks of Christian higher education, this book is an answer to prayer. It shows that not only has a new generation arrived, but that its members also have much wisdom to teach all of us about Kingdom leadership!"

—**Richard J. Mouw**, president of Fuller Theological Seminary

"Karen Longman has assembled an impressive group of leaders who have contributed significantly to Christ-centered higher education with this collection of theory-based, research-laced essays loaded with anecdotal stories and practical advice ready for real-life application. This volume should become a well-worn reference book in the libraries of leaders and students of leadership alike."

—**Paul Corts,** president emeritus of the Council for Christian Colleges & Universities

"Inspiring and compelling, these authors deftly introduce research and perspectives on leaders and organizations while telling their stories, inviting the reader to join them in the worthy calling of Christian higher education leadership. Collectively, these authors provide insight and fresh ways of understanding faithful leadership, filling a gap in the literature focused on college administration. This volume is destined to be valuable for seasoned, newly appointed, or aspiring leaders. Readers will, like me, keep a pad and pen available while reading, eager to follow-up on ideas that confront and encourage. This is a remarkable book that I will have my team read over and over! BRAVO!!"

—**Steven Timmermans**, president of Trinity Christian College

"This volume is compelling entrée into discussions of both leadership and Christian higher education. Every chapter in its own way probes how both overarching perspectives and daily decisions either contribute to or erode the elusive dynamic of trust that is so essential to vital, flourishing institutions. The resulting mosaic portrays Christian higher education with the kind of frank realism and resilient optimism that is ultimately far more compelling than high gloss college admission ads. The volume will be invaluable for current and prospective administrators, for student leaders on college campuses, for anyone considering enrolling themselves or their children in a Christian college, and for anyone looking for reflections about leadership that are grounded in the daily struggles and opportunities of institutional life."

—**John D. Witvliet**, director of the Calvin Institute of Christian Worship, Calvin College

"*Thriving in Leadership* offers perspectives on leadership that have been largely muted in business theory publications. Though it is written from the perspective of Christian college and university administrators, the book offers practical applications for those of us called to be servant leaders in the business world. The common thread that weaves through each chapter is that leadership begins with an acute self-awareness and requires an exchange of energy between the leader and their teams, fueled by a personal investment that emanates from deep within. If we approach leadership from the inside out, as a 'calling,' then we become transformational rather than transactional leaders."

—**Michelle VanDyke**, regional president of Fifth Third Bank

"The challenges of our country and our world call for gifted individuals to provide insightful and competent leadership. This encouraging yet provocative book draws from the leadership well of such gifted leaders, offering fresh insights that can benefit readers across the non-profit and for-profit spectrum. The role of Christian higher education can and should model the way for exemplary mission-driven leadership. Reading this book will give you practical lessons that will benefit the kingdom in all your spheres of influence."

—**Rick Warren**, founding pastor of Saddleback Church

"Written from the heart and from the trenches, Thriving in Leadership will benefit anyone thinking about accepting the responsibilities of leadership in higher education. The wisdom, the experience, the pain, and the joy resonate for those of us who have served in these roles. I wish I had read this book before I accepted a presidency. Relationships, story, body, place, and metaphor provide creative channels for influence, forming vision and culture as calling emerges. This kind of leadership offers hope for the future of Christian higher education."

—**Walter C. Wright, Jr.**, Senior Fellow and former executive director, Max De Pree Center for Leadership, Fuller Theological Seminary

"Karen Longman, an established and well-respected leader in the field of Christian higher education, has assembled an interesting and diverse team of contributors, drawing upon years of various experiences, to reflect upon their understandings of and approaches to leadership. A few of the chapters reflect more traditional approaches to the challenges of leadership, others are more intuitive and creative, and some take on the form of celebratory exhortation. Taken as a whole, these essays offer insights worthy of reflection for both seasoned and prospective leaders in the world of Christian higher education."

—**David S. Dockery**, president of Union University

Thriving

in

Leadership

Thriving
in
Leadership

Strategies for Making a Difference
in Christian Higher Education

Karen A. Longman

general editor

Abilene Christian University Press

THRIVING IN LEADERSHIP
Strategies for Making a Difference in Christian Higher Education

ACU PRESS

Copyright 2012 by Karen A. Longman

ISBN 978-0-89112-229-6
LCCN 2012016284

Printed in the United States of America

LIBRARY OF CONGRESS CATALOGING-IN-PUBLICATION DATA
Thriving in leadership : strategies for making a difference in Christian higher education / Karen Longman, general editor.
    p. cm.
Includes bibliographical references (p.   ).
ISBN 978-0-89112-229-6
1. Church and college--United States. 2. Christian universities and colleges--United States--Administration. 3. Eduational leadership--United States--Handbooks, manuals, etc. I. Longman, Karen.
LC383.T57 2012
378'.070973--dc23

2012016284

Cover design by Jennette Munger
Interior text design by Sandy Armstrong

For information contact:
Abilene Christian University Press
1626 Campus Court
Abilene, Texas 79601

1-877-816-4455 toll free
www.abilenechristianuniversitypress.com

Table of Contents

ACKNOWLEDGMENTS

The dream of launching a multi-tiered program for leadership development within Christian higher education emerged from my providential meeting nearly twenty years ago with Barry Hawes at a Peter Drucker seminar. With more than four hundred participants having benefited from subsequent leadership institutes for newer presidents, chief academic officers, and emerging leaders sponsored by the Council for Christian Colleges & Universities, Barry and his wife Sharon deserve special thanks for their significant personal and financial support for that dream. CCCU presidents Bob Andringa and Paul Corts, along with vice presidents Ron Mahurin and Mimi Barnard, have advocated for these leadership initiatives and personally invested themselves in various offerings.

The authors of this volume have all served as Resource Leaders for the Women's Leadership Development Institutes and the Women's Advanced Leadership Institutes. The "sacred space" for this life-changing work has been Cedar Springs Christian Retreat Center, near the Canadian border in Washington State. Dubbed by some as the prettiest place on the planet, this prayed-over setting has contributed to life-giving networking among more than two hundred and fifty women across Christian higher education—resulting in "constellations of developmental relationships" that have enriched our lives and enhanced our work. Special thanks to owners John and Jeannie Bargen, as well as Doris Rempel, who have welcomed our groups each June with open arms and hearts.

Our authors have been supported by their home institutions for time away from campus as they contributed expertise to the Women's Leadership Development Institutes. Azusa Pacific University, in particular, has invested significantly in terms of personnel and finances to ensure that the transformative work of leadership development continues. For that support, we are deeply grateful.

We also express appreciation to Leonard Allen, Director of Abilene Christian University Press, who has been enthusiastic about this book project since our earliest conversations. Our editor, Heidi Nobles, has modeled a level of approachable professionalism that contributed greatly to the enjoyment of this collaborative project and the quality of the final product. Ultimately, all of us give thanks to the Father of Lights, who has showered us with so many good gifts, among them deep friendships and meaningful Kingdom service.

Karen A. Longman

FOREWORD

Since first authoring the book *Courage and Calling* over ten years ago, I have had the privilege of interacting with people in business, the arts, religious leadership, and of course, higher education, about the role of calling as they seek to be obedient to God's work in and through their lives. Given my own background as a faculty member and academic administrative leader at a number of institutions, including Regent College in Vancouver and then over the last decade as an advisor to theological schools in the global south, the role of calling in the context of Christian higher education has been a special focus of my reflection—particularly for those called into the leadership of academic institutions. I have interacted with some of the authors in this volume during campus speaking engagements and as we served together as resource leaders for leadership institutes sponsored by the Council for Christian Colleges & Universities at Cedar Springs Christian Retreat Center, near Sumas, Washington. Indeed, these authors have been called to significant roles of leadership within Christian higher education, and they offer prophetic insights into an array of topics that have both challenged and encouraged me.

To speak of academic leadership and administration as a calling requires an appreciation of how this vocation finds its interplay with the work of research and teaching—the work, in other words, that is the heart and soul of an academic institution.

The faculty—those who are in the classroom and who lead the process of teaching, learning, and research—embody the university's values, ethos, and defining commitments. They are the *college*, one might say. With this understanding, how do we then speak of the work of academic leadership?

First, we recognize that administration is *not* a higher or more noble calling. Within the academy, what could be a higher calling than the work of research and the work of teaching? The classroom door is closed at the appointed time for the course session to begin, and this is sacred time, this is the sacrosanct time and space. One is not "promoted" to an administrative post from the responsibility of teaching.

I recently read the biographical reflections of Stanley Hauerwas, and with particular interest, I followed the narration of his academic pilgrimage, undergraduate and graduate and postgraduate. And all along there is no mention, through his years as a student, of deans or presidents. Later, as a faculty member himself, most assuredly he was working with administrators, but those who left their mark upon him when he was a student were, invariably, his teachers. This is as it should be.

Yet while saying that administration is not a higher calling, we also take note that it is not a lower calling. Administration is a necessary evil—this is surely the perspective of some academics. They have no doubt that it is not a promotion to move into administration; they are almost inclined to think of it as a demotion! One could easily get the sense that it is a *lesser* calling, not true academic work.

But what this volume profiles is how academic leadership merits our attention as good, noble, and necessary work—necessary and welcomed, for the sake of the quality and character of academic institutions. It is neither a higher calling nor a lower calling nor a mere necessary chore. It is an avenue for shaping the contours of the teaching-learning process.

Academic leadership fosters institutional vitality and effectiveness. What will become apparent to the reader is that each contributor is convinced that institutions matter, for they house the academic process. And academic leadership means that we learn how to think institutionally.

Good administrative leaders care about people! And they care about good scholarship. And they care about teaching and learning. But their work is inherently *institutional*; their academic discipline, one might say, is the college or university. Their mental and emotional energy—critical thinking, creativity, problem solving, nuanced and complex understanding—is focused on the phenomenon of an institution.

Institutions and people should not be pitted against each other. Not for a moment. People suffer when administration is carried out poorly, and they thrive when it is executed well. The very best institutional leadership is evident, in part, in the quality of concern that is manifested for the people who make up that institution. And yet, the essence of academic leadership is institutional: thinking about mission and all that it will take for that mission to be accomplished.

Administrative leadership is not easy work. We recognize that the work of research and writing and teaching and grading is difficult and deeply challenging. And yet, those who have moved from the work of the classroom to the work of administration, know that the complexities of academic leadership—the social, emotional, political, and economic challenges—will stress us like few other demands we will face in our lives. I am not trying to be melodramatic or to glorify the administrator's role; what I want to do is recommend that if you sense you are called—indeed, if you have a holy ambition for this work—you not go into it with any illusions. This is no easy ride; it will test your mettle. Don't be shy; if this is not your "cross," try another line of work. No one will give you grief if you decide it is really not for you.

So why do it? Because these institutions matter. And the people who make up these institutions matter. And those with a true calling to academic leadership know this profoundly. They do their work not for any glory; not for the chance to exercise power (as though they had much of that!); not so they can be the "boss," whatever that means, but so they can foster institutions that effectively fulfill a mission that matters. They work so that the collective wisdom, influence, talent, and calling of the people who make up the institution are engaged in a common cause, with shared values and commitments. It is this mission that consumes the hearts and souls and minds of academic leaders.

The urgency of institutional mission suggests that the calling to academic administration is always particular, rather than generic: leaders are called to specific institutions, at specific times, for specific chapters in history. As a result, any learning we might glean from the experience of a fellow administrator in another college or university can only be learning that is borrowed and adapted, never copied. Nothing is gained by going from leadership in one institution to another, and reminding your new colleagues how back at "'whatever' university," we always did it this way, and it worked for us there. Leadership must always respond to a unique set of circumstances and challenges.

The writers in this volume also demonstrate that academic leadership is for a season—we are in our roles or responsibilities for a while, not for an infinite amount of time. We are contributors in a relay race, where we carry the baton. We carry it well and run the race well when we know how to pass the baton on to those who follow us. Knowing when to let go is an essential dimension of good leadership. Leaving well is a matter of professional integrity. The institutions we lead do not belong to us; we are stewards, only stewards. We are not institutionalized into our roles. And yet, while we have the baton in hand, we hold it firmly and run hard. When we are in these roles, we certainly are not heroes; but we contribute and we can make a difference. Academic administration *does* provide the potential for meaningful leverage and influence within an academic institution; yet presidents, deans, and other leaders are aware of both the potential and the limits of their roles.

This dichotomy means that one of the deep imperatives for effective leadership is a capacity for prudence and discernment. We read the situation and name the reality; we recognize what needs to be done; we discern who will partner with us and how we will work together to do what needs to be done. We discern how our involvement as leaders will be appropriate and fitting for this institution, at this time. We discern both the limits of our influence and the potential for positive influence. And knowing the real limits also means recognizing false limits, contrived and assumed limits, that need to be challenged.

Readers of the fine essays that follow will recognize at least two things. First, that it is so very important that we attend to—and foster, and encourage—the *craft* of administration. It is a calling, and it is good work. It can and needs to be done well. And we can learn from others who are colleagues and fellow academic leaders. And second: this collection of essays rightly gives profile to the interior life of the academic leader. The work of administration will necessarily force you to draw on your deepest spiritual reserves. In many respects, the reading of these essays is a spiritual journey of reflection on the journey of faith within academic leadership and how one can grow in faith, hope, and love through the grace-filled challenges that one faces in the roles and responsibilities to which one is called.

Gordon T. Smith
President of Ambrose University College and Seminary and
Professor of Systematic Theology
May 2012

LEADERSHIP LITERATURE
Implications for Christian Higher Education

KAREN A. LONGMAN

*"Leadership is the ability to make a difference
through influencing others."*

—Roberta Hestenes

Things were going well on the campus of a small Midwest liberal arts university. Hopeful anticipation prevailed as preparations were made for the inauguration of a new president on a Friday morning in April. Given the incoming leader's former position as the president of a nearby institution and as a ten-year CEO of a respected nonprofit organization with international ties, the ceremony would draw participants from across the country and around the world. On Wednesday evening, an out-of-control semitruck sent the idyllic world of this university into turmoil. As student workers and food service staff were returning from inaugural preparations on an extension campus, the semi crossed the median and slammed into the university van, sheering off its side and ejecting several occupants. Five from the university community were killed; four were injured.

As news spread on the home campus, the leadership team immediately began making plans for a memorial service on Thursday morning. Simultaneously, the president faced a weighty decision: How should the campus handle the inauguration? Should it be delayed? Clearly the community needed to come together in the face of great loss and to begin the long process of individual and collective healing. If the inauguration proceeded on schedule, the president would need to consider the tone that his inaugural message should set in light of the somber mood of the community.

The inauguration was held on that Friday morning. All of us sitting in the large crowd that assembled for the service probably wondered what the president would choose to say, given his physical and emotional exhaustion, and the level of personal and institutional grief, while many from afar had come to celebrate this inauguration. In my mind, the opening minutes of this inaugural address stand out as a "great moment" in institutional leadership.

After being introduced by the university's board chair with words of warm affirmation, the incoming president rose to speak. He commented that, given the circumstances of this inauguration, he had been unsure of the message he should communicate. In prefacing his remarks, the president briefly explained for the guests the tremendous loss that the community had experienced. He cited his awareness of how much the students and employees needed to find comfort, and he then embraced those assembled with these words: "How like God, that just when we need to be reminded of his love and comfort, he would send all of you to look into our students' eyes and to give them a hug, reminding them that there is a family of faith surrounding them in this time of loss."[1] He then challenged the guests to be the hands and heart of Christ during their day on campus for those who were grieving. By taking the focus off himself and reframing the day's inaugural activities as an opportunity for those gathered to reflect Christ's love for the students, he allowed that service—even in the midst of tragedy—to be a holy moment in leadership, a service of consecration aimed toward the university's brighter future.

Educators frequently speak of "teachable moments" that are particularly powerful in the learning experience of students. As an observer of faith-based higher education for the past three decades, I have been privileged to witness an array of impressive "leadership moments." During nearly twenty years as the vice president for professional development and research with the Council for Christian Colleges & Universities (CCCU), I interacted on an annual basis with hundreds of administrative leaders from across higher education, as well as "cream of the crop" faculty who took the initiative to apply for participation in various CCCU professional development offerings. I also had opportunities to spend time on some eighty CCCU campuses as a speaker or resource leader. Over the years, I watched the movement of Christian higher education mature into a visible and better-respected force within the broader community of North American higher education, with the CCCU member campuses currently serving nearly 325,000 students, having sent out 1.6 million alumni, and with total operating budgets of $4.5 billion.

Even as numerous books and media references bemoan the fraying of American higher education, the Christian college sector has retained and sharpened its potential to deliver a distinctive and holistic education to hundreds of thousands of students. Indeed, the recent publication edited by Samuel Joeckel and Thomas Chesnes titled *The Christian College Phenomenon* carries the engaging subtitle *Inside America's Fastest Growing Institutions of Higher Education.*[2]

An overarching characteristic of these campuses—large and small—comes from the passion, competence, and sacrificial investment that many people are making because they view the strategic mission of Christian higher education as being a highly effective instrument for bringing "salt and light" into every sphere of influence across our broken world. Carol Taylor's chapter in this volume on the turn-around unfolding at Vanguard University recounts movingly how the alumni of that institution are making powerful contributions for good. Those stories are multiplied across every CCCU campus in ways that provide encouragement and inspiration to leaders who carry heavy loads on a daily basis. I have observed gifted leaders move a team toward stated goals, elevate the sense of *esprit d'corps* across a campus, and mobilize others throughout an institution to enthusiastically invest themselves in this shared mission. The opening vignette of this chapter also illustrates how words of encouragement or a prophetic challenge from a Spirit-led leader can change the tenor of a meeting and reinvigorate a community for holy purposes through Christian higher education.

An Inclusive Perspective on Leadership

While this book is primarily oriented toward senior-level administrative leaders, I have come to value deeply the definition of leadership offered by Roberta Hestenes, who chaired the board of World Vision International and served on the faculty of Fuller Theological Seminary prior to a ten-year presidency of Eastern University in Pennsylvania. I love the inclusivity of her definition: "Leadership is the ability to make a difference through influencing others."[3] In a keynote address in 1999, Hestenes commented that some people write themselves out of leadership because they do not hold positional power. However, Hestenes argued that every Christian, regardless of position, should have identified passions and burdens in certain areas as we seek to make this world a better place. Intentionality and persistence are important components as we seek to influence others regarding these areas of concern.

Hestenes described the advantages of leading from "above" (a term she acknowledges is co-opted from the world's perspective), where access to resources and decision-making authority can expedite progress on matters of import. However, leadership through influence can equally be effective when leading from "alongside" or even leading from "below." What matters is how we use the opportunities around us to build relationships and mobilize others for the causes that God has placed on our hearts. On Christian college and university campuses, we all know people of great influence who do not hold positional power. These are often the people in unlikely roles who have the ability to bring people together, swing a vote, or mobilize a campus for some greater good. Carolyn Dirksen's chapter titled "Inside Faculty Culture" makes the point that influence from the faculty perspective does not always equate to roles held by those with positional power within the administrative structure. Thus, being a person of influence may have greater potential significance for kingdom purposes than serving in a role of positional power. In amplifying her understanding of effective leadership, Hestenes acknowledges the importance of relationships to accomplish God's work:

> Leadership is about people—influencing people, listening to people, understanding what makes them tick, forming networks, relationships, and alliances. There's a cynical saying, "It's not *what* you know, it's *who* you know." Guess what! The universe is personal and it *is* who you know. God made it that way. . . . The challenge is to take what you know and who you know and put them together productively.

So pay attention to people, where they are, what's happening to them, both men and women. Consider more than your agenda, but the needs and concerns of the people that you relate to. This is a very important part of leadership. . . . You can be the most effective person in the room if you pay attention to these kinds of dynamics and then master the skills of learning how to ride the wave of relationships in those interactions and decision-making kinds of processes.[4]

This book brings together the work of seventeen seasoned senior-level college and university administrators who have experienced the power of relational leadership. While bringing effective leadership to their campuses, the authors have also benefited from networks of mutual support within and beyond Christian higher education that have sustained them when the going has gotten rough. All of the writers have served as resource leaders for the CCCU's Leadership Development Institutes, held since 1998 at Cedar Springs Christian Retreat Center in Sumas, Washington. The friendships that began and subsequently developed among all of us—as well as with the high-potential emerging leaders who participated—have been life-giving, with ripple effects we believe benefit our home institutions as well.

The power of placing highly competent individuals into relational leadership roles has been emphasized throughout recent leadership literature. As ten-year president Lee Snyder notes in her chapter, "Leadership in the Fifth Dimension," effective leadership depends less on a single "star" and more on developing a constellation of talented individuals who are passionately committed to a worthy cause. Similarly, researcher Sharon Gibson has referenced the importance of having a constellation of developmental relationships to sustain and encourage us during the ebbs and flows of senior-level leadership.[5]

The chapters of this book provide fresh perspectives on what is required to thrive in leadership and to shape institutions where both employees and students flourish. Indeed, much recent leadership literature focuses less on individual performance and more on the importance of emotional and social intelligence, strategies for effective collaboration, and what Richard E. Boyatzis and Annie McKee refer to as "resonant leadership."[6] Similarly, researchers Connie Gersick, Jean Bartunek, and Jane Dutton have written on "The Importance of Relationships in Professional Life."[7]

This chapter offers a brief historical overview of various theories that have dominated the leadership field over the last century and addresses the importance of having diverse perspectives around the leadership table. In short, generational differences, the impact of the civil rights movements of the 1960s and 1970s, and the "flattening" of our world through technology have contributed to a generation of up-and-comers who expect to be taken seriously, who want their lives to matter, and who are eager to invest themselves in worthy causes. Old models of leadership have been replaced by approaches that emphasize empowerment, collaboration, and respect for all persons. For Christian believers, many of the tenets of newer leadership theories described below, such as transformational leadership, authentic leadership, relational leadership, and strengths-based leadership, resonate as consistent with biblical principles. That's good news.

Yet Christian higher education lags significantly behind other sectors in reaping the benefits of having diverse perspectives around the leadership table. Goshen College's Center for Intercultural Teaching and Learning (CITL) issued a report in 2011 showing that the percentage of ethnic minorities in 2005 at all administrative ranks was 5.77 percent; in 2009 that percentage had increased to 6.24 percent.[8] In contrast, CITL also reported that the overall percentage of students of color at CCCU institutions stood at 19.9 percent in 2009.[9] Similarly, a 2010 demographic analysis of senior leadership in the CCCU's 108 U.S. member institutions revealed that of those holding vice president or higher titles, the average number of men per campus was 4.9; the average number of women was .99.[10] These statistics—showing that approximately 17 percent of senior leaders are female—are particularly troubling given that the CCCU's undergraduate student body is approximately 60 percent female. The world is changing, and Christian higher education loses credibility when old patterns of leadership prevail.

In light of the increased challenges facing leaders in today's complex world, this book offers perspectives on several aspects of leadership that relate to individual and institutional thriving. The chapters that follow are divided into three sections: The first focuses on the interior life of the leader, the second contains several chapters around the social intelligence needed to lead effectively, and the third addresses how leaders can shape a thriving organizational culture.

The Importance of Effective Leadership

This opening chapter, and indeed this entire book, is written out of a concern that Christian higher education must have exceptional leadership if the complex challenges facing today's colleges and universities are to be effectively addressed. In fact, much of higher education has not done a good job of spotting high-potential future leaders, equipping and mentoring them, and providing the kind of executive coaching that ensures the success of those moving into higher levels of campus leadership. Results of a 2010 survey of senior and mid-level managers in higher education reported by *Academic Impressions* titled "Rethinking Higher Education's Leadership Crisis" concluded that colleges and universities were largely "underprepared" to replace a rapidly graying senior-leadership cadre, with only one third of the 176 respondents indicating that their campus offered any kind of in-house leadership development program. Notable in the report was this statement:

> Perhaps the starkest finding from our survey, 48 percent of respondents graded their institution with a C, D, or F letter grade when assessing the level of commitment they felt their institution has toward their development as a leader.
>
> Similarly, when asked an open-ended question, "How is your institution responding to the waves of faculty and administrators who will be retiring in the next five years?" 40 percent of those responding indicated that, to their knowledge, nothing was being done. Responses included comments such as "No institution-wide strategy, not doing anything, and seat-of-pants approach."[11]

The importance of identifying and preparing emerging leaders for Christian higher education was spotlighted two decades ago, in part due to several CCCU presidential transitions that went awry, resulting in embarrassment to the individuals involved and pain for the institutions affected by a failed presidency. Championed by Canadian philanthropists Barry and Sharon Hawes and launched by the CCCU in the mid-1990s, the Executive Leadership Development Initiative (ELDI) has offered regular summer institutes, shadowing, and mentoring to presidents and chief academic officers with less than three years of service. Biannual offerings of both the "mixed" (men's and women's) cohorts and the Women's Leadership Development Institutes have been offered since 1998; in total, the ELDI programs have served more than four hundred participants from over seventy-five CCCU member institutions.

One program component for these leadership institutes over the years has been introducing participants to the latest leadership literature and research findings about "best practices" for leadership effectiveness. Much has been written on the subject; indeed, some have noted that there are more books about leadership than there are good leaders. The following brief overview provides insights from leadership theory and practice that may have implications for those holding responsibility for leading Christ-centered colleges and universities.

Trends in Leadership Literature

First, it should be noted that what constitutes "good leadership" has varied widely over time. In their 2006 volume *Rethinking the "L" Word in Higher Education: The Revolution of Research on Leadership*, Adrianna Kezar, Rozana Carducci, and Melissa Contreras-McGavin have masterfully summarized the unfolding array of theories that have shaped our understanding of leadership theory and practice. Noting that leadership has been studied for at least two thousand years, these authors describe much of the early literature as hierarchical in nature, with an emphasis on social control.

In the late 1800s, leader-centered "great man" theories were highly popular and were based on assumptions that leadership qualities were inherited (especially by people in the upper class); thus, leaders were considered to be born, rather than made. By the early twentieth century, the "great man" theories had evolved to encompass broader traits such as height, courage, and self-confidence. Although trait theories gradually fell into disfavor, leadership research more recently has returned to the conviction that certain characteristics do set effective leaders apart, among them intelligence, the ability to formulate and communicate a compelling vision, and effective goal setting. Gary Yukl's summary of findings from recent trait research, in fact, concluded that effective leaders do differ from followers in eight ways. Among those qualities noted as typical in effective leaders are higher levels of energy and higher tolerance for stress, a strong internal locus of control, low affiliation needs, and high emotional stability.[12]

A gradual movement away from trait theory led to the development of transactional leadership—an approach that emphasized outcomes and was based on "social exchange," or the exchange of rewards for goods and services. Thus, the leader (or employer) had the ability to exchange higher wages or other benefits for exemplary levels of production or performance. Scholars Adrianna Kezar and Jaime Lester have described transactional leadership as being consistent with the orientation of the "veteran generation" (i.e., those born between 1922 and 1943), who typically felt comfortable with the directive leadership and well-defined hierarchy, rules, and systems of the military and the corporate setting, in which loyalty to the organization was assumed.[13] This transactional approach to workplace dynamics was similarly evident in research by Warren G. Bennis and Robert J. Thomas on exemplary "Geezer" leaders (those over age seventy). For these leaders, the influence of World War II and the Great Depression instilled a desire for stability and security, a value for hard work and loyalty, and an honoring of a "command and control" leadership style.[14] Notably, an ASHE-ERIC Higher Education Report published in 1989 by Estela Bensimon, Anna Neumann, and Robert Birnbaum suggested that transactional leadership based upon social exchange theory may still characterize the leadership approach within higher education: " . . . college and university presidents can accumulate and exert power by controlling access to information, controlling the budgetary process, allocating resources to preferred projects, and assessing major faculty and administrative appointments"[15]—even within the context of shared governance.

A shift in leadership literature from a *transactional* to *transformational* model as the leading paradigm for leadership today has significant implications for Christian higher education. Transformational leadership emerged from the work of James McGregor Burns, a Pulitzer Prize winner who has been termed the "patriarch" of leadership studies. Burns' classic book, *Leadership*, released in 1978, advocated for a shift from the outcomes orientation of transactional leadership to a relational style of leadership. In short, Burns encouraged readers to "see power—and leadership—as not things but as relationships."[16] His subsequent work outlined a model for transformational leadership that emphasized four dimensions: (1) idealized influence/charisma; (2) inspirational motivation; (3) intellectual stimulation; and (4) individualized consideration.

Transformational leadership typically is based on influence rather than hierarchy, with the leader appealing to higher needs or causes for the well-being of the organization. This approach incorporates a commitment to empowerment, relational skills, shared respect, consensus-building, and mutual collaboration between leaders and followers. Followers are moved toward a particular shared purpose, often undergirded by a moral purpose. Numerous studies over the past twenty years confirm the effectiveness of a transformational leadership approach. Notably, the characteristics of transformational leadership are consistent with the workplace environment sought by the baby boomer generation (those born between 1944 and 1960), which prefers a collegial and consensual approach to leadership, with shared responsibility; the generation Xers (those born between 1961 and 1980), which tends to disregard institutional authority and prefers an egalitarian leadership style; and the "Nexter" generation (those born between 1981 and 2000), which values flat organizational structures and attentiveness to workplace quality.[17]

In a period when collaborative leadership within the workplace has largely become the expectation of the college graduates who will shape our nation's future, researchers and practitioners have recognized the emergence of other non-hierarchical forms and theories of leadership such as authentic leadership, servant leadership, social constructivism, and strengths-based leadership. Such models typically emphasize context-based and process-oriented approaches involving empowerment, social responsibility, and collaboration. In fact, *Rethinking the "L" Word in Higher Education* opens with a recognition of the "incredible complexity of organizations and global societies where contemporary leadership takes place, underscoring the need for more adaptive, systems-oriented approaches to leadership."[18] The newer approaches to "best practices" in leadership thus align well with Christian commitments to valuing individuals, honoring the diversity of gifts within the body of Christ, and seeking to discern where God's spirit is at work on our campuses and in our world, investing energy and resources accordingly.

Diverse Perspectives around the Leadership Table

Numerous studies over the past twenty years confirm the effectiveness of a transformational leadership approach. Research by Northwestern University's Alice Eagly and related work with a variety of her colleagues have documented that transformational leadership can enhance both organizational culture and organizational effectiveness.[19] Yet research has also suggested that exemplary leadership may be perceived differently based in part on leaders' racial or gender backgrounds and by the backgrounds of those evaluating the leaders.[20] With regard to the latter, Rebecca Hernandez describes in her chapter titled "Beyond Hospitality" the expectations of first-generation student of color—expectations that leaders will shape organizational cultures able to affirm and respect, for example, the kind of supportive interdependence Hernandez had experienced from her "close-knit Mexican-American family and community."

In seeking transformational models of leadership, many experts are looking to women, who more typically use this approach—with verifiable success. In a 2007 meta-analysis of research regarding leadership effectiveness, Alice H. Eagly and Linda L. Carli offered this summary statement, "In the United States, women are increasingly praised for having excellent skills for leadership and, in fact, women, more than men, manifest leadership styles associated with effective performance as leaders."[21] Similarly, a 2009 *Harvard Business Review* article by Herminia Ibarra and Otilia Obodaru that synthesized findings from 360 reviews of 2,816 organizational leaders worldwide concluded that women were viewed as having superior abilities in a majority of leadership categories.[22]

Interestingly, women were rated lower by male evaluators (but not by female evaluators) on one dimension—their capabilities in "envisioning." Given that the ability to articulate a compelling vision and move the organization in that direction is widely understood to be a key criterion of effective leadership, this perceived deficit in envisioning may be problematic even for highly gifted females. In fact, the article suggests that women may intentionally downplay their own role in casting vision and emphasize a collaborative approach that moves the organization forward equally well, doing so through shared ownership rather than individual recognition.[23]

Despite the effectiveness of a transformational leadership style, *Rethinking the "L" Word in Higher Education* emphasizes that not all organizations embrace this collaborative approach. Organizational culture itself can influence the emergence of leadership styles, and higher education is known to be a hierarchical culture. William Bergquist and Kenneth Pawlak, in their 2009 *Engaging the Six Cultures of the Academy,* describe the deep and even "pernicious" aspect of the collegiate culture, noting the "often subtle yet nevertheless quite powerful competition and striving for prestige and dominance" distracting from the organizational mission and undermining necessary collegiality.[24] In 2008, Deborah O'Neil, Margaret Hopkins, and Diana Bilimoria published a summary of nearly twenty years of leadership literature from the business field, concluding that hierarchical structures and policies continued to influence organizational research and practice.[25]

Yet as college and university leaders seek to bring their best to the task of educating the next generation, full representation by those who have been previously excluded—ethnic minority and female leaders among them—is important at the leadership table. Furthermore, a single representative in senior-level leadership faces the likelihood of being viewed as a token, with that individual remaining an anomaly, rather than being heard and respected as an equal partner in leadership. Harvard's Rosabeth Moss Kanter coined the term tokenism in the 1970s, describing it as the negative impact of an environment on individuals who represent a particular demographic category within a different dominant culture. In general, research suggests that a tipping point of approximately one-third representation is needed for an environment to be truly welcoming of minority perspectives. Yet the majority of CCCU member institutions have either no women or one woman and even fewer ethnic minorities in vice presidential or higher administrative roles.[26]

Clearly, our campuses miss important perspectives when the senior-level team is essentially homogeneous in terms of gender and race/ethnicity. Does the 60 percent female student population feel that their perspectives and voices are heard if women do not represent them at the table? Does the 20 percent ethnic-minority student population across the CCCU sense that they are valued and that their perspectives are sought after if no one on the leadership team has walked in their shoes as a person of color on a predominantly white campus?

Allow me to conclude this opening chapter on a personal note. I was frequently inspired during my nineteen years of working on the staff of the CCCU in Washington, DC, by members of our board of reference who championed the work of Christian higher education in their spheres of influence. Among these was Richard C. Halverson, Senate Chaplain, who often identified Christian colleges and universities as the church's "best hope" for the future. He believed deeply, as do those who have contributed to this volume, that educating the next generation in ways that combine intellectual engagement with hearts passionate for the work of Christ in our world is a worthy calling. As I have read through various drafts of the chapters that follow, I have been brought to tears by several of the stories that have emerged from these leadership journeys, and brought to laughter by others. I am inspired by these sixteen fellow sojourners—including Gordon T. Smith and William P. Robinson—who have literally invested their lives, far beyond a forty-hour workweek, in institutions and a cause that they love. Through their words, I am impressed afresh by the potential of Christian higher education to lead the way in terms of offering a model of institutional thriving that other sectors of higher education might wish to emulate. Our hope is that readers of this volume will find similar inspiration and encouragement to keep our eyes on the high calling before us.

Notes to the Introduction

1. This story relates to the inauguration of President Gene B. Habecker at Taylor University in April 2006. Five weeks later, the same tragedy resulted in an even broader story about mistaken identity that resulted in national news coverage.

2. Samuel Joeckel and Thomas Chesnes, *The Christian College Phenomenon.*

3. Roberta Hestenes, "Leadership and the Christian Woman," plenary address, Christians for Biblical Equality conference, San Diego, 1999.

4. Ibid.

5. Sharon K. Gibson, "The Developmental Relationships of Women Leaders in Career Transition."

6. Richard E. Boyatzis and Annie McKee, *Resonant Leadership.*

7. Connie Gersick, Jean Bartunek, and Jane Dutton, "Learning from Academia."

8. Robert Reyes and Kimberly F. Case, "National Profile."

9. Ibid.

10. Karen A. Longman and Patricia Anderson, "Gender Trends in Senior-Level Leadership."

11. Douglas Fusch and Amit Mrig, "Rethinking Higher Education's Leadership Crisis," 7.

12. Gary Yukl, *Leadership in Organizations.*

13. Adrianna Kezar and Jaime Lester, "Leadership in a World of Divided Feminism."

14. Warren G. Bennis and Robert J. Thomas, *Leading for a Lifetime.*

15. Estela Bensimon, Anna Neumann, and Robert Birnbaum, "Making Sense of Administrative Leadership."

16. James MacGregor Burns, *Leadership.*

17. Kezar and Lester, 52–54.

18. Adrianna Kezar, Rozana Carducci, and Melissa Contreras-McGavin, *Rethinking the "L" Word in Higher Education*, ix.

19. Alice H. Eagly and Linda L. Carli, *Through the Labyrinth.*

20. See for examples, Adrianna Kezar, "Expanding Notions of Leadership to Capture Pluralistic Voices" and Roya Ayman, Karen Korabik, and Scott Morris, "Is Transformational Leadership Always Perceived as Effective?"

21. Eagly and Carli, *Through the Labyrinth.*

22. Herminia Ibarra and Otilia Obodaru, "Women and the Vision Thing."

23. Ibid.

24. William H. Bergquist and Kenneth Pawlak, *Engaging the Six Cultures of the Academy,* 33.

25. Deborah O'Neil, Margaret Hopkins, and Diana Bilimoria, "Women's Careers at the Start of the 21st Century."

26. Longman and Anderson, "Gender Trends in Senior-level Leadership."

For Discussion

1. Consider the vignette that opened this chapter. Have people on your leadership team faced a similar campus crisis at some point in their career? If so, what "leadership moments" emerged in response to that situation?

2. Thinking about the Hestenes definition of leadership ("the ability to make a difference through influencing others"), what exemplars come to mind on your campus of individuals leading effectively either from "alongside" or from "below"?

3. To what extent, and in what ways, would you say that the leadership team closest to you models various aspects of transformational leadership?

4. To what extent are elements of transactional leadership viewed to be "the norm" and/or desired by the senior-leadership team on your campus?

5. Numerous researchers make the case that organizational cultures are predominately hierarchical. In what ways, if any, do you believe that to be the case on your campus? Can you think of any specific proposal that those in leadership might consider to make the "norms" more inclusive of multiple perspectives?

6. Can you think of examples where someone from a non-dominant group has offered a valuable insight to a discussion or debate that changed the direction taken by a leadership team? In what ways are such voices and perspectives made to feel welcome on your campus?

PART I

The Interior Life of Thriving Leaders

Chapter One

THRIVING AS A LEADER
The Role of Resilience and Relationships

LAURIE A. SCHREINER

*"In the middle of winter I at last discovered that there
was in me an invincible summer."*

—ALBERT CAMUS, "Return to Tipasa"

Sitting around a table of university leaders fifteen years ago, the stories I heard had a common theme: unexpected challenges that erupted with little notice, demanded immediate attention, and had significant consequences. The leaders telling such stories spoke wearily, expressing the continuing doubt that they had handled the situations well. They appeared to be on a downward spiral, looking forward only to retirement or a quiet exit to another position. As I began to reconsider whether administrative leadership was a calling I wanted to explore, I noticed that other leaders began to speak differently of the same type of events. Several spoke energetically of how both they and their institutions were better for having experienced the crises. These leaders were clearly on an upward trajectory of newfound confidence and meaning, vitally engaged in their role and with their institution. "I wouldn't wish this sort of experience on anyone, but I am a far better leader for having gone through it," one college president told me. But what made the difference in the stories these leaders had to tell? On that day, I decided that the answer to that question would determine my own leadership journey, for I wanted not only to fulfill the call on my life, but also to be fulfilled by following that call.

Exploring the difference in these leaders, between those who floundered and those who flourished, led me to the topic of resilience. The statement by the college president who became a better leader for having experienced a crisis is echoed in the research on human thriving: many psychologists believe that the heights of the human experience can only be fully known by those who have experienced the depths as well, "those who have run the gauntlet."[1] In this chapter on thriving leaders, the emphasis will be on their resilience. Rising to a challenge is the hallmark of the most effective leaders; it is their ability to emerge from those crises stronger and reinvigorated that distinguishes the leaders who make a difference in the institutions they serve.

A scan of *The Chronicle of Higher Education* provides ample evidence of the challenges facing leaders in higher education. To those questioning whether they are called to lead, the number of challenges may seem daunting. Observing the number of university leaders who stumble in crises can be discouraging as well. Yet there are numerous examples of leaders who flourish even in the midst of fire, who rise above the challenges they face. The issue is not whether there will be challenges, but how the leader responds to those challenges.

Thriving as a Leader: The Power of Perspective

"Flourishing" has emerged from the positive psychology literature as a concept that describes the experiences of human beings who are vitally engaged in their work and in significant relationships, who find meaning and fulfillment in the contributions they make—in short, those who thrive. Flourishing goes beyond effectiveness—it means not only doing a job well, but also experiencing deep satisfaction and a sense of purpose in that role. Flourishing people look beyond themselves to the welfare of others and to making the world a better place. According to Corey Keyes and Jon Haidt, authors of the book *Flourishing: Positive Psychology and the Life Well-lived,* such people rise to the challenges of life, growing and learning important life lessons from the adversity they face. Each of these features of the flourishing individual can provide university leaders with clues for thriving in their roles.

Foundational to flourishing as a leader is a positive perspective. The ability to see the big picture, to discern "what's going on here," to understand multiple viewpoints, and to see a situation and our role in it realistically is key to effective leadership and to maintaining a vital engagement in leadership over the long haul. Leadership authors Ron Heifetz and Marty Linsky call this "achieving a balcony perspective" and view it as an essential leadership skill.[2] Leaders who flourish are able to rise above the action to discern larger implications. They are also able to take the perspective of others, so they have multiple options available to them, rather than succumbing to tunnel vision when they rely only on their own experiences and emotional reactions in the heat of the moment.

Rather than an unrealistically optimistic view of the world, a positive perspective enables us to come to grips with difficult situations more readily. It is not just "feeling good about life"; rather, it is a way of perceiving events and coping with difficulties. Leaders with a positive perspective remain confident of their abilities to achieve the final outcome, even when progress is painfully slow or challenges are difficult. They tend to take the long view of events and focus on the bigger picture. They also notice the positives in others and expect good things to occur in the future.[3]

Flourishing leaders utilize this positive perspective in four key aspects of their work: how they see the situations that arise, how they see themselves, how they see others, and how they see the future. In each of these aspects, a particular strategy distinguishes the flourishing leader from those who flounder.

Strategy #1: Rise to the Challenge

Thriving leaders see the situation around them differently. They interpret crises in a way that enables them to remain hopeful, engaged, and striving toward meaningful goals. Rather than being crushed by adversity, flourishing leaders are challenged by it. They take adversity in stride and learn from it. They may struggle during a crisis, but they do not get stuck there or become defined by it. In their book *Leading for a Lifetime*, authors Warren Bennis and Robert Thomas describe this resilience as an *adaptive capacity* that enables leaders to handle challenges with integrity and grace, deriving meaning from even their worst experiences. These leaders have learned that it is when they have struggled and pushed themselves to their limits that they realize their greatest potential and strength. As psychologists have studied resilience, they note that there are certain personality characteristics that predispose some people to be more resilient than others.[4] But these pale in comparison to specific strategies that resilient people employ when facing challenges. Resilience is not an inborn trait—it is a learned response to life events, and particularly to negative events. Two specific actions of resilient leaders are that they explain negative events differently and they reframe challenges as opportunities.

Employ an Optimistic Explanatory Style

The key to resilience lies in what psychologists call "explanatory style." Explanatory style refers to the way we explain negative events in our lives. Thriving leaders have an optimistic explanatory style: they perceive negative events as situational and changeable. This perspective enables them to adapt and bounce back from adversity.

In contrast, those who attribute the adversity primarily to their own inadequacies and perceive such events as stable and global have a pessimistic style that leads to passivity. A pattern of passivity can result in feelings of depression or discouragement that lead individuals to disengage from active problem solving; rather than tackling their problems, these leaders retreat and avoid. As is often the case when problems are not addressed early, the situation then only gets worse. University of Pennsylvania psychologists Karen Reivich and Andrew Shatte call this pessimistic thinking the "number-one roadblock to resilience."[5] For example, consider the following example of one response to a tense meeting:

> As President Davis leaves a meeting with the faculty senate, he thinks, "What a disaster! I think they hate me—everything I said was criticized. I don't understand why they feel so strongly, but it seems as though everything I do and say is wrong. I can't imagine how we'll get through this year when there is such animosity!"

President Davis exhibits all the features of a negative explanatory style. He perceives the situation as being a function of his internal character ("they hate me"), global in nature ("everything I do and say is wrong"), and stable ("I can't imagine how we'll get through this year"). In contrast, listen to an alternate interpretation of the same event:

> *President Williams walked away from a meeting with the faculty senate thinking, "Wow—that was unpleasant! Clearly, there are issues that are of real concern to them. I'm glad they felt comfortable enough with me to express how strongly they felt. I'm going to do some investigating of their concerns and schedule a meeting with them again next month. Maybe if I come better prepared and spend a little more time hearing them out instead of being so quick to give my explanations, the next meeting will have a more positive tone."*

President Williams's ability to recover from the negative meeting is likely to be better because of the ability to put it in perspective. Williams acknowledged the meeting was unpleasant, but interpreted the faculty's reaction as a function of their deeply felt concerns, not solely of his own inadequacies. By also recognizing personal shortcomings and a need to prepare better next time, Williams is already setting up for more positive events in the next meeting, without assuming that the negativity will be a recurring feature of presidential-faculty senate interaction.

Reframe Negative Events

Rising to the challenges of leadership in higher education is a daily task, given that problem solving is integral to a leader's role. Perceiving inevitable challenges as learning opportunities that can strengthen one's leadership changes the internal reaction to the challenge. And it is precisely this internal reaction that often gets in the way of effective problem solving. The psychological skill of reframing can calm a personal reaction that is out of proportion to the event by helping individuals perceive an adverse event from a different perspective. For example, asking "What aspect of this situation is my fault—and what isn't?" helps leaders to adjust the internal/external dimension of their explanatory style. Similarly, asking "Is it always going to be this way, or is this a temporary setback?" addresses the stable/changeable dimension, and asking "Is this likely to influence everything I do or just this situation?" can help leaders perceive the global/situational nature of their explanation of the negative event.

Leaders with an optimistic explanatory style tend to be proactive and problem-focused, rather than reactive and avoidant. They quickly accept reality, then take the initiative, seeking out information and taking steps to ensure success; they reframe negative events to see others' perspectives and learn from the experience; they use humor to cope. When they fail, they recognize the event as a temporary setback and they look for different approaches for future success. These strategies create more positive outcomes, including greater leadership satisfaction and success.

Strategy #2: Realize Your Potential

Thriving as a leader is not only a function of how negative events and challenges are perceived, but also how leaders see themselves and their role. Flourishing leaders tend to be self-aware; they know their strengths and weaknesses. They also are likely to see their leadership role as a calling, rather than as a job that provides evidence of their significance and self-worth. Consider these two self-evaluations from university leaders:

> Dean Hernandez is proud of her leadership role as dean in the large research university. A talented engineer, she eagerly applied for the open dean's position as the next logical step in her journey to become a college president. Her significant publications and grants swayed the search committee, who overlooked the lukewarm references from colleagues. In her first year as dean, Dr. Hernandez has become discouraged and frustrated. "I don't understand why my faculty don't appreciate my leadership—I've clarified policies, provided guidelines for receiving research funds, and cleaned up the budget spreadsheets so everyone knows how much money they have left. Why did I get such a low score on my leadership evaluation? Maybe I should look for another position at a different institution."

Dean Hernandez has overlooked her limitations and has not taken the time to ascertain whether the talents she has to offer are a good fit for the position and the setting she is entering. Viewing her leadership role primarily as validation of her worth to the university, she has left behind an area where she has experienced success—her faculty researcher role—assuming she will be equally successful in her new role as dean. But without a careful examination of her strengths and weaknesses, as well as the degree to which the position and expectations are a good fit for her and energize her, success may remain elusive. In contrast:

> *Dean Romero cannot believe how fortunate he is to get paid to do what he loves. Energized on a daily basis by his work helping faculty and providing resources for his school to reach its goals, he sees his dean role as a calling that provides meaning and purpose in his life. Dr. Romero recognizes that his talents are in his ability to strategically envision a future and communicate that effectively to others, and he has used his strategic talents to delegate budget details to his associate dean, whose strength lies in her attention to detail and her comfort level with finances—areas that are not his greatest talents and that do not energize him. Together, they are a dynamic duo, both playing to their strengths to serve the higher purpose of supporting their faculty and reaching their school's collective goals.*

Dean Romero has a strong sense of self-awareness that has led him to seek out a leadership role that is a good fit for his talents and interests. He has also strategically partnered with others in those areas that are draining, where he is not as interested, or where he does not bring particular talents to bear, making success even more likely.

Realistic Self-Appraisal

Realizing your potential as a leader begins with a realistic appraisal of that potential—your strengths as well as your limitations. Marcus Buckingham, bestselling author of *Go Put Your Strengths to Work*, emphasizes that strengths are not just "what you're good at," but also what energize you and lead to fulfillment. However, it's important to not only recognize your strengths, but also those times when you tend to overplay your strengths.

Leaders who flourish in their roles have taken stock of their greatest talents, are aware of the types of environments that bring out their best, and realize the limitations that may interfere with their success. They operate from their strengths, applying them to the obstacles and challenges they face. They also know the shadow side to their strengths and know the times when they tend to overplay their strengths. Thus, rather than trying to become like someone else by following a blueprint for effective leaders, your greatest likelihood of flourishing in your leadership role occurs when you become the best version of yourself. The integrity and authenticity that arise from that approach will be not only gratifying to you as a leader, but will also elevate the trust and confidence that others place in you.

But knowing your talents is not enough. There are a multitude of examples of talented people who do not flourish in a leadership role. The talent must be accompanied by energy, knowledge, and skill. Thriving leaders are energized by the leadership process; they relish challenges, they thrive on setting and reaching goals, they shine when they are advocating for others or for their vision. That talent and energy is then multiplied by the investment of time and effort to gain the knowledge and skills to become a more effective leader. Flourishing leaders regularly seek opportunities for professional growth and leadership development, recognizing that connecting to other leaders and learning from them strengthens their skills and equips them with the tools they need when challenges arise.

Work as a Calling

When leaders view their work as a calling, a natural result is that they invest time, effort, and energy to become more effective in their roles—which increases their chances of flourishing. Across many different professions, however, people tend to be evenly divided in how they view their work role: as a job, a career, or a calling. Those who view their work as a calling are optimally engaged in and passionate about their work and perceive that it makes a meaningful contribution to the world. They spend more time in their work and derive greater enjoyment and satisfaction from it; their calling orientation leads them to view work as "wholly enriching and meaningful, a passion in its own right" and also to connect to others with whom they work, forming a strong sense of community.[6] Many university leaders, particularly in faith-based institutions, report that the major reason they are in a leadership role is because they see it as a calling. "Being a leader is not something I sought, but clearly God called me toward this role at this time," is the type of statement researchers have often heard in qualitative studies of leaders in Christian colleges.[7] These leaders understood their calling primarily in relation to how their gifts and talents fit the needs of the leadership role. Congruent with Gordon T. Smith's conceptualization of calling, they also perceived their leadership role as a journey that was taken one step at a time: what is God calling me to do today, at this moment?

Perceiving your work as a calling provides the motivation to invest energy and effort into the role; the value and meaning of the role then helps you persevere when challenges are encountered, leading to a higher likelihood of success. When you believe you are making a difference, within your institution and, beyond that, into the world, you are much more likely to try different strategies and to persist in the face of difficulties. And when you believe that God has called you to be a leader in this place at this time, that sense of purpose provides the fuel to help you rise above the difficulties. Although work is not the sole focus of life, finding meaning in your work adds considerably to your ability to flourish as a leader.

Strategy #3: Relate to Others

Thriving leaders' positive perspective applies not only to the situations that arise and how they view themselves in their leadership role; that perspective also extends to the people around them. Relationships are the most important source of satisfaction and well-being in life,[8] and both psychologists and leadership researchers agree that the emphasis leaders place on personal relationships is often an indicator of leaders' success. Martin Seligman, former president of the American Psychological Association, notes that "very little that is positive is solitary."[9] Those who find the most meaning in their role as leaders also report the strongest relationships with others at work.

Consider the following:

> *Provost Brown has carefully surrounded himself with people who share his academic vision. Meeting with his staff monthly, he reiterates the strategy he has crafted and asks for updates from each office*

regarding what they have accomplished to move the vision forward. At one such meeting, a dean mentions that his faculty have started vocalizing serious concerns about the wisdom and expense of one of the provost's pet projects. Dr. Brown's response is to ask for the names of these "resistant faculty," and after the meeting he pulls the dean aside and says furiously, "Don't you ever embarrass me in public like that again. If your faculty have issues, you need to straighten them out and then come tell me how you've resolved it. Don't ever bring it up in a meeting again!"

This provost clearly views relationships in win-lose terms: those who are with him and those who are against him. Valuing only those who agree with him, he has created his own world of yea-sayers and is then taken by surprise—and deeply embarrassed—when evidence arises that all is not well. In contrast, Provost Green has created a different relational environment:

Recognizing the importance of partnerships and multiple perspectives, Provost Green has surrounded herself with competent people who bring different gifts and strengths to the table. Her academic vision was a collaborative effort that spanned the first year in her position. She regularly asks for dissenting viewpoints; at the last staff meeting when one of her deans shared his faculty's vocal concerns to one of her projects, her response was, "Let's check this out. How about putting their concerns in writing so I can be prepared to come meet with them next week?"

These are two very different perspectives on the importance of relationships, the role of colleagues, and how to respond to conflict.

Relationships Matter

One of the myths arising from older hierarchical models of leadership is that relationships are peripheral, with the potential to interfere with the task at hand. In this model, leaders were discouraged from making friends at work or socializing with co-workers because it took the focus off the task. In contrast, newer models of transformational leadership have documented the ways in which relationships are vital to organizational health, as well as to job satisfaction and longevity. Leadership researchers Sally Helgeson and Julie Johnson have noted that "as organizations become more weblike, more dependent upon relationships and the nurturance of talent, the strategic nature of tending the social fabric becomes more apparent. . . . In a world of webs, the ability to see decisions in a larger human context becomes an essential, and profoundly strategic, advantage."[10]

Likewise, leadership theorists Heifetz and Linsky refer to positive relationships as "one of the distinguishing qualities of successful people who lead in any field."[11] Leadership simply cannot be executed alone. Thriving leaders recognize the power that relationships have in shaping their vision, in providing support during difficult times, and in making tough decisions. But relationships are not only a buffer for the challenges of leadership, they also provide joy in the journey. A Turkish proverb frames it this way: "No road is long with good company." But what kinds of relationships at work are most able to sustain a leader and lead to flourishing?

In their book *Resonant Leadership*, Richard Boyatkis and Annie McKee describe "resonant relationships" as the key. Resonance occurs when leaders are in tune with the needs of those around them. Such leaders build trust by being aware of the emotional tone in the room and consistently exhibiting a deep concern for co-workers. They are able to read others and the organizational culture accurately and bring out the best in the people around them. When making difficult decisions, these leaders stay connected to people, listening carefully and responding empathically to those most affected by their decisions. Their intentionality about connecting to the people with whom they work is the hallmark of resonance.

Such relationships are foundational to flourishing, according to psychologists who have studied the power of personal relationships.[12] They add to the daily enjoyment of life and work, they serve as a buffer during stressful times, and they enable us to bounce back more quickly from adversity. Having someone to listen to us, understand us, validate our concerns, and care what happens to us is a vital part of what makes life meaningful. In his book *Vital Friends*, bestselling author Tom Rath suggests forming your own personal "board of directors"—friends and mentors both inside and outside the work environment who can speak into your life and provide support for your leadership journey.[13]

Thriving leaders not only nurture their relationships at work, but also recognize the importance of all the significant relationships in their lives. They know that intimacy, affection, and play renew their souls and add a depth of meaning to their lives that simply cannot be found in their work. So they make time and space for their spouses, partners, children, parents, and friends. They also cultivate those relationships, using what Martin Seligman calls "actively constructive responses" to convey their enthusiastic support for the good news their loved ones share. This type of response is the single best way of strengthening a relationship—responding positively and specifically to what the other person says. For example:

> After a particularly long and difficult day at work, Chris was looking forward to a hot bath and time alone with a good book. But her husband had other ideas as she walked in the door. "Honey, I won that big contract today! A huge bonus is coming in my next paycheck!" In a former life, Chris might have responded with "That's great, sweetie," or if she was feeling particularly grouchy, the response was more likely to have been "I've had a horrible day! I'm going up to take a bath," or even "Wow—what are the tax implications of that for us?" Now that she knows how important her response is to good news, she says, "Terrific—I'm so proud of you! Tell me all about it while I'm in the tub—start at the beginning with where you were when you heard the news."

Strengthspotting

The perspective you take toward others creates a culture that defines your sphere of influence. When those around you feel heard, validated, and cared for by you, they are more willing to be active partners in a shared leadership vision. They give you the benefit of the doubt because they have learned to trust you. They are willing to go the extra mile when needed because they know you have their best interests and the mission of the institution at heart. The perspective that enables this type of culture to develop is a habit of noting the potential in yourself and others, or what psychologist Alex Linley calls "strengthspotting."[14]

As a leader, you have a fundamental choice to make about where to focus when you interact with other people: you can choose to focus on their deficits and weaknesses, or you can choose to focus on their strengths and potential. When the focus is on deficits, conversations revolve around mistakes and areas in need of improvement. When the primary focus is on strengths, conversations revolve around what has gone well and how to take that success to the next level. Psychologist David Cooperrider asserts that "merciless criticism often makes us dig in our heels in defense, or worse, makes us helpless. We don't change. We do change, however, when we discover what is best about ourselves and when we see specific ways to use our strengths more."[15]

Noticing what is going well or what others are doing right does not mean that mistakes are ignored. Rather, it creates an environment in which colleagues feel valued and are then able to hear feedback more openly, because they recognize such feedback arises out of your care for them. They also feel better equipped to respond to areas in need of improvement because they have been affirmed for specific strengths they can use to address those challenges.

This appreciative perspective creates a culture where compassion is the norm. Compassion has been described by Boyatzis and McKee as "empathy in action."[16] A culture of compassion has as its hallmark a desire to connect with others and meet their needs. Connecting with others begins with active listening. Suspending judgment and listening carefully for the meaning behind the words can enable leaders to discern "the next right thing," in the words of theologian and noted author Wayne Muller.[17] They slowly become in tune with other people and what they need in the moment, but they also create a culture in which people care about each other and act together in service of something greater than themselves.

As this culture of compassion develops within a university, staff and faculty look forward to coming to work and begin to enjoy their jobs more. As a result, students benefit—they see the institution differently, as a place that cares about people and is trying to meet students' needs. Vanderbilt University psychologist and retention researcher John Braxton and his colleagues have documented that this visible commitment to student welfare actually contributes to higher levels of student persistence to graduation.[18]

How You See Others During Conflict

Even within a culture of compassion, conflict is bound to occur, as people have different goals and values they bring to their work. But flourishing under fire is mostly a matter of perspective. Learning to take the perspective of the other person when you are in conflict is a key ingredient to not only stronger relationships, but also a better solution to the problem. In their book *Strengths-Based Leadership*, Tom Rath and Barry Conchie noted that the most effective corporate teams they studied were not afraid of conflict—and conflict did not destroy them. On the contrary, the presence of healthy debate signaled the team members' strong commitment to finding an effective solution. These teams had a common goal that they agreed was best for their organization and a perception of one another as being on the same side about what really mattered—getting results. In contrast, dysfunctional teams tended to personalize their disagreements and become territorial during conflict; as a result, conflicts ultimately fragmented the team.

Leaders thrive when they are able to take the perspective of others during a conflict—not only putting themselves in the other person's position, but also communicating an understanding of that perspective to the other person. Unfortunately, in conflict, we tend to focus on the negative behaviors of the other person and attribute those behaviors to the character of our opponents. Social psychologists refer to this human tendency as the "fundamental attribution error": interpreting our opponents' negative actions as evidence of their personality, while attributing our own misbehavior to the situation in which we find ourselves. Translated into practice, the fundamental attribution error may look like this:

> *Provost Lee is in the midst of a disagreement with Dr. Morgan, this year's chair of the faculty. Dr. Morgan has just made the statement that improving faculty salaries ought to be the top priority of the provost, as faculty morale is dangerously low and there has been no raise in the last three years. Provost Lee thinks to himself,*

"How can Dr. Morgan be such an ungrateful person, after all I've done to support her leadership?" When he responds grumpily to her by saying, "Leave it to the faculty to think only of themselves at a time like this," he views his words as a justifiable reaction to an unreasonable request.

Because our brains are wired to pick up negative cues more easily than positive ones, and we tend to interpret negative communication as evidence of people's "true character," the way we communicate during a conflict matters. In studies of high-performing teams, the number of positive statements made outweighs the negative statements almost 6 to 1.[19] Interpreting others' behavior in light of the situation, giving them the benefit of the doubt, and communicating that you understand their perspective will go a long way toward resolving the conflict and improving the entire climate of your institution.

Strategy #4: Reach Forward

Flourishing leaders tend to be future-oriented. They are able to take challenges in stride primarily because they take a long view of events. Seeing the bigger picture and having a solid vision for what they want to accomplish, they are able to put into perspective the daily difficulties they encounter. This future orientation is vital not only to their own personal health and longevity as a leader, but also to the health of their followers and the organization itself.

In national leadership studies, the single most powerful predictor of employees' engagement in their work was whether their organization's leadership made them feel enthusiastic about the future.[20] Most leaders claim that they create a vision and take initiative, yet their actions often convey a different reality. Most of a typical leader's time is spent reacting to the needs of the day. It seems to be almost a reflex action when we encounter problems— solving problems is our first priority, and we put other priorities on the back burner. But solving problems could take all of a leader's time, day in and day out. Identifying future opportunities, crafting and communicating a vision, and creating strategies that prevent future problems are far more important to a leader's health and long-term success. The bottom line: being proactive rather than reactive is the hallmark of a thriving leader.

Seeing the big picture and having a vision for the future creates a sense of energy within the leader, but effective leaders also transmit that energy to their followers. The specific way they do that is by creating hope within their institution. Hope is a key component of flourishing, for it generates energy that pulls us forward into the future and creates positive emotions that lead us to be more creative, open-minded, and resilient. Psychologist Rick Snyder conceptualizes hope in terms of GPA: Goals, Pathways, and Agency. The goals must be clear, realistic, and meaningful. If the goals cannot be self-selected, then a leader must clearly articulate the goals and provide a logical rationale for them. Pathways are the strategies, the specific actions to take, along with alternative strategies when obstacles are encountered. Agency is the "willpower," the motivation to reach the goal by investing effort and believing that the goal is attainable.[21] Numerous studies have documented that when organizational leaders have high levels of hope—and communicate that hope to their followers—the satisfaction and productivity of their followers is also likely to be high.[22] Here again we have two different leadership approaches:

> *Faculty President Simmons is preparing for the first faculty senate meeting of the new academic year. As she thinks about how to frame the agenda, she finds herself focusing on the faculty unrest that defined the previous academic year. Determined to tackle the problem head on, she crafts a statement about the source of the unrest and what behaviors will not be acceptable in this year's faculty meetings. After the meeting, she notes that faculty seemed even more disruptive than usual. "Why do all the problem faculty keep getting elected to the senate?" she wonders.*

Dr. Simmons chose to focus on problems, rather than paint a vision of the future that created hope for the faculty and pulled them toward a better future in the coming year. In contrast:

> *Faculty President Evans prepares the agenda for the first faculty senate meeting with a keen awareness of the unrest that defined the previous academic year, but has decided to frame the meeting in terms of her vision for the role of faculty. As she crafts her opening*

*remarks, she focuses on new opportunities for participatory deci-
sion making, consciously expecting the best of her faculty and the
administrators with whom she works. "It's a new beginning," she
thinks. After the meeting, she walks back to her office energized by
the willingness of the faculty to dialogue and by the creativity of
their ideas for moving forward in the coming year.*

Creating hope does not miraculously dissolve entrenched problems, but it
does create a positive climate in which people are more likely to work together
and support one another to reach their goals. A hope-building campus climate
often has a non-hierarchical organizational structure that values ideas and
strategically aligns people's talents with their job descriptions. Leaders communicate in an open and transparent manner, treat people fairly and empower
them to do their best, and create a shared vision that reminds people of the
meaning in their work.

As a leader, how you see the future is key to creating hope on your campus
and within yourself. Painting a meaningful picture of the future can sustain
both you and your university during difficult times. Belief in the importance
of the goals you have chosen and your ability to eventually achieve those goals
is what leads to the perseverance and resilience that characterize thriving
leaders. At the heart of this perspective on the future is your sense of how your
leadership role serves a larger purpose. From a spiritual viewpoint, hope ultimately rises from a belief that there is meaning and purpose to each person's
life. Seeing the future as under God's control, and viewing your role as part
of that larger plan, enables you to take the "long view" that bolsters resilience.

Conclusion

The journey of administrative leadership in higher education is full of complexities and challenges that make the road difficult to travel at times. As was so clear to me fifteen years ago when contemplating whether I was called to travel that path, the destination is insignificant compared to the ability to flourish along the way. Those leaders who thrive are able to see meaning and purpose during the journey, recognizing that even the most adverse events have shaped and strengthened their leadership. Feeling a strong sense of call, being able to keep a positive perspective during challenging times, staying vitally connected to others, and being pulled by a future that is larger than themselves—at the end of the day, these leaders know they wouldn't trade a single moment of their journey, for it has made them into the people God called them to be.

Notes to Chapter One

1. Carol D. Ryff and Burton Singer, "Flourishing under Fire," 16.

2. Heifetz, Ronald A., and Marty Linsky, *Leadership on the Line*, 53.

3. Ibid.

4. Warren G. Bennis and Robert J. Thomas, *Leading for a Lifetime*.

5. Karen Reivich and Andrew Shatte, *The Resilience Factor*.

6. Amy Wrzesniewski, Paul Rozin, and Gwen Bennett, "Working, Playing, and Eating," 189.

7. Karen A. Longman and Jolyn E. Dahlvig, "Women's Leadership Development."

8. Harry Reis and Shelly L. Gable, "Toward a Positive Psychology of Relationships."

9. Martin Seligman, *Flourish*, 20.

10. Sally Helgesen and Julie Johnson, *The Female Vision*, 84.

11. Heifetz and Linsky, 75.

12. Ibid.

13. Tom Rath, *Vital Friends: The People You Can't Afford to Live Without*.

14. Alex Linley, *Average to A+*.

15. See Seligman, *Flourish*, 72.

16. Richard E. Boyatzis and Annie McKee, *Resonant Leadership*.

17. See Wayne Muller, *A Life of Being, Having, and Doing Enough*.

18. See for example John Braxton, ed., *The Role of the Classroom in College Student Persistence*.

19. Barbara L. Fredrickson and Marcial F. Losada, "Positive Affect and the Complex Dynamics of Human Flourishing."

20. Tom Rath and Barry Conchie, *Strengths Based Leadership*.

21. C. R. Snyder, "Hope Theory: Rainbows in the Mind."

22. Fred Luthans, Carolyn M. Youssef, and Bruce Avolio, *Psychological Capital*.

FOR DISCUSSION

1. Think back over your own leadership journey. When were you most challenged and stretched in your role? How did your perspective on those challenges affect your ability to respond effectively?

2. Choose an adverse event that has occurred recently. What have you learned from it? How could you reframe the event so that it doesn't take such a large emotional toll?

3. What specific strengths do you bring to your leadership role? What areas are not your strengths—areas where you will need team members with complementary strengths? What skills do you need to acquire to move to the next level of leadership in your journey?

4. What relationships are most important in your life? How do you nourish those relationships as part of your leadership journey?

5. Replay a recent conflict you have had at work. Imagine yourself in the other person's shoes. What do you think was that individual's perspective of the issue over which you disagreed? Put that perspective into words. How does doing so change your view of the issue? Of the other person?

6. What is your vision for your span of care in your current leadership role? Paint a picture of what the future will be like in five years if your vision is realized. How will you communicate that vision to those with whom you work? What will energize them to engage that vision?

Chapter Two

LEADING FROM THE CENTER
Body and Place

MaryKate Morse

*"I've learned that people will forget what you said;
people will forget what you did;
but people will never forget how you made them feel."*

—MAYA ANGELOU, I Know Why the Caged Bird Sings

*"No matter how much knowledge you have,
there is still a limitation to what
you can do around 'this table.'"*

—African American participant
in CCCU Leadership Institute

Recently I traveled from Charlotte, North Carolina, to the dairy community of Trenholm, Virginia. I was trying to combine a business trip with a visit to relatives. I flew into Charlotte from the west coast, picked up my rental car, set my "Dennis Hopper" voiced GPS device for the journey, and started on my way. I left at five in the evening and misjudged the distance between those two places, so it was getting darker and darker as I drove. Just before dusk, I arrived in Farmville, Virginia. I had no idea I would be driving through Farmville, Virginia. I hadn't consulted a map. I had just let Mr. Hopper lead the way.

Going through Farmville, and not expecting it, especially in the mixed light and grey of evening, stirred in me intense waves of emotions and memories. I had gone to college at Longwood University in Farmville. I moved there from Heidelberg, Germany, where I left my dad and four siblings and the grandmother who did the housekeeping and made sure we didn't kill each other. I didn't know anyone when I arrived. And though I sat in classes and did well academically, it wasn't the campus I remembered now but the town.

As I drove through Main Street, I felt anew the offense of seeing young men in confederate uniforms marching through the center of town with a confederate flag, just as they did every Saturday morning at ten. I passed the street on the right, lined with buildings, where I had an ecstatic spiritual experience involving a ragged and bent-over beggar, and the wonder of it filled my soul. I shuddered as I drove past the church on the left with its impressive white columns, where the pastor got too friendly after I went to him for spiritual counsel. It was the same church where, after I had invited a black female student to Sunday service, the elders came to the college on Monday, met with her in the president's office, and asked her not to return. They were uncomfortable with her worshipping with them. Then one long block down on the same side was the African American church where I had begun worshipping the following Sunday, and where I had been welcomed like a long-lost child. I had been overwhelmed with their embrace.

It wasn't just my mind going back. My whole body remembered these forgotten things. The anger, the wonder, the confusion, the belonging, all flooded my adult sensibilities. Though the people were long gone, and the town and Longwood were not at all like they were in my college days, the place was etched on my body. Out of those experiences, many of my leadership passions—for healthy spiritual leadership, for justice, and for the marginalized—took initial form. My call was shaped by the place of Farmville, Virginia, and the person I was in that place, and I was remembering.

In this chapter, I want to focus on the intersection of body and place in leadership. Our bodies—our physical beings that house our instincts, thoughts, and feelings—are shaped by the environments—the culture, characteristics, and history—of places where we work and live. The relationship of body and place has particular import for Christian leaders, precisely because of our belief in the central role of Jesus Christ in our lives. There is an overlay of the body and place of Jesus on our bodies and places. He came in the flesh to first-century Palestine and through his death and resurrection, he made possible our new life. He lived out of his body a relationship of love and mission to those who yearned and hoped for more. People experienced his physical presence in specific places when he taught, healed, prayed, and served.

This chapter is based on the underlying premise that Christ calls us to lead like him in body and place. We have a desire to conform to the life and character of Jesus in our bodies and in the places we serve. As Christian leaders, we have Christ's indwelling presence. We have at a central place in us, "Christ in you, the hope of glory" (Col. 1:27). It's more than having a positive spirit toward our work, defined by Goldsmith (named one of the most influential business thinkers by Forbes) as a feeling starting on the inside and radiating out.[1] For us, that positive spirit comes from our investment in and calling to Jesus Christ. Christ in us is Christ with us, braided into our natures. We are partners. Leading with Christ at the center of our physical beings and at the center of our workplaces requires a particular attention to our own physical beings in our work places.

I will begin by unpacking the relationship of our bodies and places to our calls. I will then propose three types of places and physical behaviors that are vital to leading like Jesus.

Embodied Leadership: The Call to Body and Place

We are called to lead like Christ. Call constitutes the universal possibilities innate in each person. We desire to do meaningful work that contributes to God's purposes in the world. In his book *Courage and Calling*, Gordon T. Smith, president of reSource Leadership International and author of this book's foreword, distinguishes between a general call to follow Jesus and a specific call that is a person's unique vocation and contribution to God's mission.[2] An individual's specific call is reflected in the collection of his or her gifts, life experiences, and passions that get expressed in a meaningful vocation. Arthur Miller, the founder of People Management International, and Bill Hendricks, founder of the Hendricks Group, make the point that we are designed for unique contributions and not for becoming anything we want.[3]

Calls that come out of prayer, personal and communal discernment, and a desire to serve others, often result in individuals living courageously and honestly in today's complex and challenging world. Michael Steger, Natalie Pickering, Joo Yeon Shin, and Bryan J. Dik, in the *Journal of Career Assessment* wrote, "Recent scholarship indicates that persons who view their work as a calling are more satisfied with their work and their lives."[4] The leaders who are most effective in addressing the many community and global needs of our day are those who have a sense of purpose and calling.

One of the reasons that we are designed for *unique* contributions is that our calls are influenced by who we are in our bodies and by where we are in differing places. Our calls unfold in places that shape and define us. Body and place are inextricably woven together like the filaments of a spider's web. Movement in any one area affects the entire web and alerts the spider to a change. Like the spider, the human brain is constantly assessing all the incoming information and adapting the body's response to the environment. But the world is hectic, and the brain has to make sense of large volumes of information in short time periods. Without an organizing process, the brain gets overwhelmed and doesn't function rationally and clearly. Focus is necessary. A call provides focus.

Elite performers know this well. A high-caliber athlete does not want to "freeze," be distracted, or be overwhelmed by the challenges of the environment or the limitations of his or her body. Therefore, athletes want to move from *explicit learning*, the craft and knowledge associated with one's sport, to *implicit learning*, learning practiced so often, over and over, that it physically becomes second nature. The body knows the skill without conscious thought. The skill is embedded in the unconscious and in the midst of pressures, the body reenacts these skills. In the same way, the leader who senses the call of God *implicitly* in his or her body has a focus to lead like Jesus in any type of situation.

As leaders in Christian institutions, being mindful of the role place and body play in our calls will help us lead more like Christ. As the brain assesses incoming information, the more we *lead implicitly* as Christ, the more effective we will be. Colleges and universities have unique demands and challenges placed on them, ranging from responding to a rapidly changing world, to developing sustainable financial practices in a stressed economy, to paying attention to the myriad of constituents and stakeholders in the institution's mission. The constant onslaught requires an implicit response from our beings. Otherwise, the stressed, distracted, or overworked leader often begins to function from inner survival mechanisms rather than from the living presence of Christ.[5] "The call" becomes "the grind." The leader moves from "I love this" to "I can handle this."[6]

The brain as an organ of information and decision making is constantly gathering three kinds of information and assessing it: information about the environment, information about the body, and information about the connections between the two, both good and bad.[7] Our brains are always and unconsciously discerning if our bodies are safe or unsafe. Our most primal response is ensuring our safety. Our environments—place—include location and people, culture, and events. Our bodies include external features such as race and gender, and internal features such as personality and strengths. All of our bodily realities influence how we manage ourselves in various places.[8]

Call and Body

Call is influenced by one's body. A person's ethnicity impacts his or her perspective on call in different places. Ethnicity shapes a person's understanding of belonging. The dominant group shapes the collective consciousness about how things "should" work. Therefore, the non-dominant group is less likely to be heard; a person's perspective within that group is less likely to be sought out or valued. Primarily, the persons most in positions of power, with a collective force, assume that the way they see the world is the only reality. Often, they are not intentionally shutting out other possibilities; they don't know other possibilities exist; they don't even know to look.

In my opening story, the pastor of the church was a very influential and charismatic leader. He was beloved by his congregation. My experience of him revealed a dark side to his character. I don't think I would have been believed at the time if I had complained to the elders. My black student friend also experienced a dark side to this church's leadership, an assumption of the threat of the black people.

Gender, too, affects a person's calling and direction. "It's a boy," or "It's a girl" tends to be the first news heard after the birth of a child. Then the place, the cultural setting of the child's life, further structures the arch of possibilities as he or she grows. For example, in traditional cultures, females are *defined by their bodies* and by their role as nurturers, and males are *defined by their minds* and by their roles as competitors and providers.[9] These conceptual frames impact the leadership options that men and women have and recognize.[10] Women leaders and men leaders have differing challenges as to even the possibility of what they hear as a call. Women usually are encouraged, networked, and mentored less, and take fewer risks than men, not necessarily because they are risk-averse but because there is more at stake if they should fail.[11] One's male or female body often impacts one's imagination about the potential or possibility to fulfill certain roles. Therefore, women sometimes don't think of themselves as executive-level leaders as easily as men might.

Whether they are socialized into a specific understanding of gender roles or not, men's and women's experiences are influenced by their gendered bodies. The very constructions of the body, the rhythms of the body's cycles for men and women, the hormones that wash male and female brains, all bend us toward particular tendencies.[12] More testosterone compels a person to be more competitive, and more oxytocin compels a person to be more caring. All human bodies have both testosterone and oxytocin, but the amount varies from person to person. Thus these and other physical features of our gendered bodies will take in the world and interpret varying responses. Because we are shaped by the experience of our body, we bring different things to leadership.[13] Since men and women are made in the image of God, both reflect God's nature.[14] Good leadership is focused and competitive as well as encouraging and empowering of others.

Understanding the impact of body and place can contribute important perspectives on leadership challenges, especially in our call. Our bodies, which reflect gender and race, impact the world we experience and the leadership opportunities we have (or don't have) and our approach to leadership. There are other ways in which our bodies influence our perception of our call, such as physical features, physical and mental capacities, and our natural personalities. Ethnicity and gender are the most obvious.

Call and Place

Formation of our sense of self and our call is also a place phenomenon. Our identities are formed by how safe or unsafe we feel in physical environments. If a person feels safe, he or she will be more open and relaxed and more likely to grow and interact. When a person feels unsafe, he or she is more likely to withdraw and protect or react. We know who we are by where we are. This is why family homes, towns or farms, and places where we work all are part of the shaping force of our sense of self. Whenever we spend time in a place with smells and sights, touch and sounds, we are inevitably shaped. We are conformed to our world. This is not necessarily good or bad; it just is. Physical place limits and defines us, but it also gives us a place from which to move out.

The brain keeps track of the environment around it. Our sense of well-being is shaped by how safe and known we perceive ourselves to be in a physical environment. People create a mental map that is grounded between the place, their emotional well-being, and the capacity to stay rational despite the circumstances. The power of physical place is made clear by what happens when people are alone in an unfamiliar location. Persons who get lost in the woods can enter into such a state of panic that within forty-eight hours they are dead, even with clothing and resources at their disposal to survive.[15] Neuroscientists have found that the brain becomes inordinately confused when it doesn't recognize anything in the surrounding environment.[16] The body is unable to connect to anything familiar. People who are overwhelmed by this confusion may not survive.

In the same way, leaders can become disoriented when challenges overwhelm them or they are in unfamiliar territory. There can be an internal panic, and even though the body is present and engaged, the internal emotional systems may run amok. Leaders can rise to these challenges and manage their emotions only when there are *implicit responses* ingrained in their physical beings. Implicit responses are instinctive because the response has been internalized through constant repetitive practice. The response becomes automatic. When a leader moves from anger or frustration to responding authentically, like Christ, then the response is usually implicit. Or at least, the leader will backtrack and admit mistakes or ask for forgiveness. Otherwise, an angry, uptight, or reactive leader has allowed his or her environment to subvert the call from vocation to survival.

Environments add another level of complexity to the experiences of females and males in leadership. Girls who tend to have had small environmental spheres, limited to their homes and safe places, carry the impact of that world in their sense of self and their sense of possibilities. Boys, on the other hand, who are more often allowed to roam, wander free, and try new things, will tend to grow up to have a much more expansive vision of their call.[17] The freedom to be dominant in one's environment, take risks, and explore, shapes the person's imagination for the possibilities of leadership. Though a challenge, the nature of the environment does not limit a woman's capacity for leadership. Taking risks and imagining possibilities are not character traits but learned skills. Anyone limited by his or her environment might have a leadership advantage. Since power is not a privileged expectation for such people, they see and often empower those in lesser positions of influence. This action has positive economic and social implications.

Assumptions about how environments work, such as the example above, illustrate the nature of mental models. They are useful, but they can also have limitations. Because of the complexity of the world, we create mental models of an expected reality to help us respond in perceived appropriate ways. This strategy is not only natural, but necessary. However, sometimes leaders are wrong. Sometimes leaders get lost. The mental map often needs adjustment when the environment has changed, and if the leader doesn't adjust his or her mental map but persists in the path chosen, disaster usually follows for the leader and the institution. People get lost, leaders get lost, because they refuse to retrace their steps. They've constructed a new reality that is so compelling they push ahead to a point where they are unable to return. They don't go back to the fundamentals. Calls of individuals and organizations are important precisely because they remind us where we started and what we value most.

Body and Place Together

As leaders who lead in institutions with a high sense of mission and calling—such as Christian colleges and universities—an awareness of the impact of body and place on our leadership is necessary. Both body and place influence the sphere of our call and our response to the challenges we face. Next I want to suggest three types of body behaviors and spaces that will help us lead implicitly with Christ at the center: (1) the body and intimate/private space, (2) the body and social space, and (3) the body and public space.

Body and Intimate/Private Place—It's about God

As leaders called to serve in Christian institutions, our relationship with God is a fundamental aspect of our identity and our work. Search committees, boards, and constituents often care that an applicant for a position is a person of faith and a person committed to the faith values of the institution. Persons with whom leaders work expect a certain level of integrity and authenticity in the expression of their leaders' faith. Because most Christian institutions have deep historical roots in a particular religious tradition, leaders who do best are those who also have deep personal roots in God. Therefore, effective leaders find ways to nurture their faith in concrete and regular ways, and their relationship to God becomes implicit.

The first and primary commandment in the Old Testament is "I am the Lord your God . . . . You shall have no other gods before me" (Exod. 20:2–3). In the New Testament, Jesus's radical obedience put God and God's call before everything else, even to the point of death on the cross (Phil. 2:5–10). In John 5, Jesus proclaims his equality with God and his dependence on God for judgments, actions, and healings. To lead from the center as Christ led, we too must have no other gods before us and must depend on God for our judgments and actions. To live in that extreme place of dependence requires an intimate place for being with God. All our life and work comes out of that place. From that place, we learn that it's all about God.

Edward Hall, a ground-breaking anthropologist who died in 2009 at age 95, coined the term *proxemics* and wrote about the impact space has on animals and people.[18] Hall believed that communication was the core of life and that we need to have intimate and personal relationships to stabilize our bodies. He distinguished four different types of physical spaces: intimate, personal, social, and public:

1. Intimate space occurs when bodies are 0–18 inches apart, as between a husband and wife, or parent and child, or the closest of friends.
2. Personal space is 18 inches–4 feet, which occurs between good friends, such as when they are having coffee together.
3. Social space is a distance of 4–10 feet and occurs when persons are together for a common purpose, such as in meetings and on project teams.
4. Public space is the preferred personal distance of 10 feet or more from strangers, such as on a beach or in a restaurant.[19]

In this section, our focus is on intimate and personal space—particularly in the spiritual context of intimacy with God. This close proximity suggests safety and honesty. The body in this distance with others tends to be authentic. With these distances, if there is frustration or anger, the body instinctively moves apart, and the reverse is true if there is affection. The more intimate a person is to someone else, the more physical contact is desired.[20]

The result of such intimacy is transformative. The psychologists who authored *A General Theory of Love* came to the same conclusion, writing, "Who we are and who we become depends, in part, on whom we love."[21] The development of a loving relationship only happens when real time and space are designated for interactions. Intimate and personal space depends on proximity and privacy. Therefore, to become like Christ and to grow in Christlikeness demands time and space dedicated to that purpose.

Jesus himself regularly went off to pray alone or with a small group of devoted followers. After those times of prayer, he came back energized for next steps, he discerned decisions, he refocused, and he was affirmed and comforted. Jesus told his disciples to abide in his loving and redemptive presence (John 15:1–11). Such primal trust can only happen when our bodies have a place for regular personal and intimate attentiveness to Christ.

Reflective space, both physical and linear, is needed daily and weekly. Many find benefit in taking thirty minutes to an hour each day for prayer, reflection, and study. Weekly space, the day each week we are called to Sabbath-keeping, may seem an extraordinarily strange command alongside those such as "do not murder and steal" and "do not create graven images."[22] Yet since the rhythm of creation and daily life from sun-up to sun-down is intimate space with God, Sabbath-keeping prepares the leader to embody Christ in a thoughtful, nonreactive way. Furthermore, since we are shaped by place, physical space is as important as time. The creation of a sacred space that quickly draws a leader into God's presence can help establish the value of intimate space: "To survive, you need a sanctuary where you can reflect on the previous day's journey, renew your emotional resources, and recalibrate your moral compass."[23]

I don't know of any other behavior that has a more stabilizing, Christ-in-us effect than non-legalistic daily time for reflection, study, and prayer and observing a weekly Sabbath. Rest is directly connected to the well-being of our bodies. The busy leader has a busy body and, more often than not, a stressed body. Our cognitive capacities, and thus how we think and interpret the world around us, are directly related to how rested our bodies might be. Under stress, the body releases cortisol to help the body handle extreme moments of pressure and danger with a clarity that allows for the possibility of survival. However, the constant release of cortisol eventually has the opposite effect and begins to impair cognitive function, though most times, the person doesn't recognize the shift. Such a person sees less, hears less, and makes poorer decisions than when he or she is rested. Eventually malformed perceptions create new realities for a leader and lead to tragic mistakes, often the type that hurt others.[24]

In *Leadership Ethics*, Terry Price, professor of Leadership and Philosophy at the University of Richmond, makes the point that leaders at the top are more likely to make colossal moral mistakes because their brain rewires to exclude important reality-checking information.[25] Because they see themselves as unique, they don't need to follow the standards that guide others. They believe that somehow they will escape the fate that others might expect. Therefore, they begin to make small immoral decisions that lead to larger mistakes. For leaders to thrive, they must first have regular immersion in times and places dedicated to communion with Christ precisely so they do not wander away from reality-checking their call and character. Sacred space replaces hectic space.

Body and Social Place—It's About Others

The next critical space where body and place shape a leader's call and identity is social space. Edward Hall, as stated earlier, described this distance as four to ten feet. Social space consists of those settings where a group of individuals are interacting with each other around a common purpose or are engaged together in a common event. The closer the physical space, the more sensory data is picked up by the body, which means more opportunities for an emotional exchange and thus for a relationship. Leadership author Sally Helgesen has written, "Identity is inseparable from relationship."[26] The embodiment of a leader's character and call are experienced more clearly in social settings, especially when individuals are seated around a table or are in a small group setting. When Jesus allowed the sinful woman in Simon's house to touch him in social space, he communicated volumes about the people he valued, the people he came to serve. Leaders typically talk a lot, but how a leader functions in social space communicates more than the leader's words.

I recall attending a small retreat at which an internationally known, charismatic leader presented. When he was not up front speaking, he was on his Blackberry and reading books on his Kindle. He would leave the room often and was not available to engage the attendees. In contrast, I recently attended another small retreat that trained leaders from all over the world. The attendees were from countries including Latvia, India, Russia, Philippines, Nigeria, Kenya, and Mexico. The training was designed to create spiritual mentoring communities to invest in and sustain the next generation of catalytic Christian leaders. The four to six trainers all held doctorates and had served in significant leadership environments nationally and internationally. The trainers were not introduced beyond their first and last names. When they were not presenting, they were participating with the attendees.

On the fourth day, a woman from Kenya said, "I don't get who you people are. Who are you?" She could not comprehend how persons of social status and achievement would assume positions of identification with the attendees. The message of the trainers' presence was one of interest, partnership, and value. She was confused that they sat next to the attendees and spent time with them, even giving up their free time to listen and pray with participants. She commented, "What has changed me most is the experience of these important leaders taking time for me. I can do this for others in my country." These busy persons of influence embodied Christ-centered leadership that was relational and other-centered.[27] The first retreat leader was not present; the second retreat leaders were. When a leader is physically present in social space, the capacity for influencing others is greatly enhanced.

Meals are especially important social space opportunities. Jesus ate with sinners. He took time to engage with persons the culture had labeled as outsiders. Leaders who take time to eat socially with their staff can expect to see and hear more than they ever would from a report. As Helgesen observes, "Eating and drinking with others cements an elemental bond and implies a basic trust. . . . I could not help but note how often vital exchanges occurred in informal but comfortable communal spaces that defined the true image people had of the organization."[28] When a person of less role influence has a meal with someone of more—especially when the leader spends the time listening, asking questions and simply getting to know the other person—the experience has great potential to build mutual trust.

There is a physical "wholeness" observed in community, not just by a handshake or smile, but by the gift of focused time and a relaxed and attentive body, which communicates a message of value to the recipient. This whole physicality is dynamic, not fixed and stylized. Who a leader is behind closed doors in a meeting or in small gatherings is a more accurate portrayal of how that leader lives out his or her call than a mission statement written on a website. Therefore, in small social spaces, the effective leader brings a body that is rested, attentive, and focused on serving others and the institution.

Body and Public Place—It's About the Mission

The final place where a leader's call is embodied is in public space. Hall describes public space as occurring when the preferred distance is ten or more feet. Public settings include large events where the leader is expected to speak or represent the institution. Public space is powerful in institutional life. In the fall of 2008, our university experienced an ugly racial incident when four students hung a cardboard cutout of then-presidential candidate Barack Obama from a campus tree. Within a few hours, our campus was inundated with reporters and camera vans, and the story made international headlines.

One of our highest values at George Fox University is racial reconciliation, and we had worked with focus to create an ethnically diverse campus. By the time of the incident, we had managed to attract a student body that was 25 percent people of color. The "prank" hurt many students on our campus, particularly our African American students; it also shamed our university. The president, Robin Baker, gathered the local community for a public statement to the press, the students affected, and to us. The resolute public presence and words of our president clearly and eloquently renounced the act and affirmed our mission. He met over and over in public venues with local African American leaders to listen and learn and to affirm our commitment to diversity. Because of his heartfelt public response, our humiliation led to a determination to work harder to have a safe and diverse campus.

Though the public arena for a leader is extremely important, especially in times of crisis and change, it has limits to how authentically a leader is known. The authentic inner self is primarily known in more personal relational settings. This is obvious with the many stories of major public figures who surprise us with moral failure. Communicating powerfully is a gift, but it does not guarantee integrity. Face-to-face encounters are more authentic expressions of Christlike leadership. Therefore, embodying one's call in a public place is helped greatly by walking around and engaging the random people one might meet. Public space can be turned into social and personal space simply by walking from the stage to an office space or table in the eating area. Jesus did a lot of ministry in public space, yet he was unique as a rabbi in that he traveled. Most rabbis would establish themselves in a specific location, but Jesus was itinerant.

In earlier years, I had a dean who had a habit of walking around and outside the seminary visiting faculty, staff, and the various persons who served seminary students. He would go downstairs and check in with Sheila, our beloved admissions counselor, and ask her how things were going and how she was doing. He would drop in on faculty and share his thinking and wondered what each one thought. He would connect regularly with the provost, outside of required meetings, simply to touch base and visit. For busy leaders, casual walking around visits can seem like a luxury. I argue that it is a necessity.

Tom Peters popularized "management by walking around" in the 1980s. Walking around became important in that decade because leaders felt that they were becoming more and more isolated from their employees, customers, and constituents. It was found to be an extremely effective leadership practice. Peters called the practice the "technology of the obvious." By walking around and engaging a wide variety of persons impacted by the company, a leader would get a more accurate picture of the actual state of affairs.[29]

This practice is even more important in our technology-rich environment where emails are the common means for getting things done. Technology probably saves hundreds of work hours. However, Christian institutions are faith-based organizations that should model the mission of the institution by being the presence, the "face," of it to others. Administrators who walk around and talk to admissions counselors, financial advisors, groundskeepers, cafeteria workers, administrative assistants, students, and faculty embody the caring and purposeful mission of the institution. Vital exchanges that occur in informal public spaces are meaningful for the leader as well as for those benefiting from the leader's time.

Resistance to "walking around" in public space often comes down to two concerns—not having enough time and wanting to avoid the trap of "blame and complain." The best way to manage time is to tame it. Walking around does not need to take much time. If a leader were to allow for informal fifteen-minute conversations two or three times a week, it would make a considerable difference in the long run.

To minimize getting caught in those inevitable "blame and complain" conversations, leaders can begin conversations with a focus on the other person's family and interests, and then ask what is meaningful and what is challenging with their work. Some things leaders will hear do need to be fixed. Some people will need encouragement. Sometimes things can be redirected. Most of the time, though, people feel respected when a leader listens to them.

When my dean walked around, using public space for personal encounters, the students, faculty, and staff experienced his energy, his love of the seminary, his pastoral touch. In these types of conversations, the leader embodies the mission and values of the institution.

Embodied Leadership—Tying it Together

Thriving in uncertain times is often defined more by outward success, but for Christian believers it is also defined by a deep conviction that Christ is the source and the reason for why we do what we do. We are *Christian* administrators and leaders. We have a holy calling. We are engaged in a holy vocation. We lead from the center of Christ in us.

This type of leadership is more than following Jesus' teachings. It is a life lived out of an inner conviction of the indwelling presence of Christ. Therefore, ours is a uniquely embodied leadership, and even more so when our work is in institutions that are shaped by faith convictions. We must live out our callings in specific physical ways and in specific places. Jesus came in the flesh to physically express the nature of God and God's work in the world. By routinizing our physical behaviors in physical spaces, we can lead more *implicitly* like Jesus. These behaviors are central to effective leadership.

Notes to Chapter Two

1. Marshall Goldsmith, *Mojo*.

2. Gordon T. Smith, *Courage and Calling*.

3. Arthur Miller, Jr., and Bill Hendricks, *The Power of Uniqueness*.

4. Michael F. Steger, Natalie Pickering, Joo Yeon Shin, and Bryan J. Dik, "Calling in Work: Secular or Sacred?" 82.

5. Donald Norfolk, *The Stress Factor*; Ulf Lundberg and Cary Cooper, *The Science of Occupational Health*.

6. Wayne Muller, *A Life of Being, Doing, and Having Enough*.

7. Laurence Gonzales, *Deep Survival: Who Lives, Who Dies, and Why*, 32.

8. MaryKate Morse, *Making Room for Leadership*.

9. The field of gender studies disagrees on whether gender differences are primarily nature or nurture. Books that support physical differences include Anne Moir and David Jessel, *Brain Sex*; Deborah Blum, *Sex on the Brain;* David Barash and Judith Lipton, *Gender Gap;* and Bryan Sykes, *Adam's Curse*.

10. Heather A. McKay, "Gendering the Body."

11. Anna Fels, "Do Women Lack Ambition?"; Lois Frankel, *Nice Girls Don't Get the Corner Office*; Scott Jaschik, "Too Nice to Land a Job"; Alice H. Eagly and Linda L. Carli, *Women and the Labyrinth of Leadership*.

12. Mary Stewart Van Leeuwen, *Gender & Grace*; Michael Gurien, *The Wonder of Boys*; Michael Gurien, *The Wonder of Girls*.

13. Judy B. Rosener, "Ways Women Lead"; Sally Helgesen, *The Female Advantage;* Loren Cunningham and David Joel Hamilton, eds. *Why Not Women?*; Sue Freeman, Susan Bourque, and Christine Shelton, eds, *Women on Power*; Sally Helgesen and Julie Johnson, *The Female Vision*.

14. Kristina LaCelle-Peterson, *Liberating Tradition*.

15. Gonzales, *Deep Survival*, 51.

16. Joseph LeDoux, *The Emotional Brain*; Joseph LeDoux, *The Synaptic Self*.

17. Rachel Sebba, "Girls and Boys and the Physical Environment"; Norma Carr-Ruffino, *The Promotable Woman*; Catherine Herr Van Norstrand, "Words, Space, and Sexism"; Herminia Ibarra and Otilia Obodaru, "Women and the Vision Thing."

18. Edward T. Hall, *The Hidden Dimension*.

19. Ibid.

20. Persons can also use proximity for aggressive and self-serving purposes such as how an abuser or narcissistic leader might move in close to assert authority. However, the instinct on the part of the one "attacked" will be to move back. If he or she cannot move back physically, the instinct will be to move back internally and to close off.

21. Thomas Lewis, Fari Amini, and Richard Lannon, *A General Theory of Love*, 144.

22. Many books have been written on this commandment, including *Sabbath* by Wayne Muller, who served as a senior scholar at the Fetzer Institute.

23. Ronald A. Heifetz and Marty Linsky, "Managing Yourself: A Survival Guide for Leaders."

24. Andrew Campbell, Jo Whitehead, and Sydney Finkelstein, "Why Good Leaders Make Bad Decisions."

25. Terry Price, *Leadership Ethics*.

26. Sally Helgesen, *The Web of Inclusion*, 16.

27. Walter Wright, *Relational Leadership*.

28. Helgesen, *Web of Inclusion*, 256–57.

29. See Olivier Serratt, "Managing by Walking Around."

For Discussion

1. How have your ethnicity, gender, or other physical features impacted your understanding of your call?

2. How have the places of your upbringing and your current setting shaped your understanding of your call?

3. How does your calling intersect with the mission of the organization you serve?

4. What would you describe as the key character qualities and leadership behaviors of Jesus, and which ones have you incorporated into your leadership style?

5. How have you nourished "Christ at the center" of your life? Where, when, and how do you create intimate/private space to reflect, study, and be with God on a daily and weekly basis? How might you enhance this space and time?

6. Ask trusted others how they experience you personally in social space. How might you enhance your presence in social space? Which behaviors would increase people's perception of your attentiveness and interest in others and in the purpose of the meeting?

7. Have you experienced the effectiveness of leading by walking around? If so, think again about its impact and make a specific commitment to implement the practice in your life. If not, try it for two weeks and keep brief notes about what you experience. Then evaluate its effectiveness.

Chapter Three

HONORING GIFTEDNESS
A Strengths Approach to Leadership

Deborah J. White

"The place God calls you to is the place where your deep gladness and the world's deep hunger meet."

—FREDERICK BUECHNER, Wishful Thinking

"Today I understand vocation quite differently—not as a goal to be achieved but as a gift to be received."

—PARKER PALMER, Let Your Life Speak

A number of years ago, I was able to spend part of a summer visiting several cathedrals from New York City and Washington, DC, to London and Stockholm. As I took the tours and listened to the stories of how these architectural wonders came to be, I was amazed by the enormity of the mission, the expansiveness of the dream, and the astonishing amount of human, physical, and financial resources that it took to bring these structures into reality. I was profoundly impressed with the commitment of the builders: the time, the patience, the love that must have fueled this great devotion. I was also deeply moved by the incredible beauty of these places of worship. The *whole* structure was obviously a masterpiece of design, a profound work of art, but this was also true of each intricate detail.

At each cathedral, I kept noticing a repeated phrase that appeared on plaques, printed materials, and was frequently etched in stone on the walls and floors in various locations throughout the structure. The words simply said, "to the glory of God." This phrase gave meaning and inspiration to the many people who dedicated themselves and their artistic abilities to the greater cause. So many people had devoted their lives to creating a place for worship, refining every detail of design, building a structure to honor and reverence the majesty of God, giving grace to things both great and small, from the gigantic columns and enormously high ceilings, to the tiniest details in a wood carving, or the select color of a very small piece of stained glass. All done "to the glory of God."

After one of these cathedral visits, I attended a leadership conference at Eastern University in St. David's, Pennsylvania. At the opening session, the director asked us to take our Bibles and find a quiet place to read Isaiah, chapter 43, and listen to what God was saying to us. When I got to the words, "whom I created for my glory, whom I formed and made," the words practically jumped off the page. I was taken back to those cathedral walls where I had noted the words etched in stone, "to the glory of God." A magnificent structure of art for God's glory—yes, I got that. But _me_ a work of art for God's glory? I had not at all contemplated God as the supreme artist, creating _me_, a work of art, and the fact that _I_ was created for God's glory.

Immediately following this leadership conference, I visited the National Cathedral in Washington, D.C. Standing inside that magnificent building, I was overwhelmed with the same impressions. The cathedral was awe-inspiring. I noticed with new awareness that most meaningful phrase, "to the glory of God." Part of this cathedral tour occurred outside so that we could view the exterior architecture, the gardens, the gargoyles, the arches. As I strolled down the adjacent sidewalk, I encountered a group of teenagers walking in front of me who were also on the tour. While the tour guide was pointing out interesting features and sharing many cathedral facts, I was amazed to find that the teens' attention was drawn to the cars parked along the side of the street to their right. As this cathedral tour was happening, they pointed, compared, and admired various kinds of _cars_, and kicked gravel along the sidewalk to entertain each other. I held myself back from yelling, "There's a CATHEDRAL on your left, people! Don't you realize what you're overlooking? Don't you have a clue as to the value and beauty of what is here beside you?" I was appalled at their obtuse attitudes and the missed opportunity. I ended the tour with the mindset of an indignant and self-righteous college professor.

Later that evening as I reflected on that scene, I had to confess that daily I walk by God's creation without a pause, without any awe or appreciation, without the time to even notice the Creator's handiwork. My attention is often diverted to the mundane, to the things that matter to me and my world, to the things that I value, like those "cars" parked along my street and the gravel on my sidewalk.

As I continued to draw insight from that experience, Ephesians 2:10 became a guiding scripture: "For we are God's workmanship, created in Christ Jesus to do good works, which God prepared in advance for us to do." The word "workmanship" is the Greek word, *poiema*, the source of the English word, "poem." That word can also be translated "masterpiece" or "work of art." In other words, we are formed with masterful intention, with beauty and thoughtful design to accomplish God's purposes. Leadership from this perspective values each person, recognizing that we each bring our unique gifts and talents, our strengths, to the work that God has called us to do.

As leaders we may shy away from this high view of ourselves as God's works of art, because we want to avoid pride or any hint of arrogance. But this biblical truth does not leave God out of the picture. God is the designer. As Madeleine L'Engle writes, "our acceptance of ourselves as created by God, and loved by God, no matter how far we have fallen from God's image in us, . . . is not a self-satisfied, self-indulgent acceptance, but a humble, holy, and wondrous one."[1] The created is appropriately in awe of the Creator; the leader humbly recognizes and accepts the gifts of leadership.

In addition to accepting and developing my own gifts, I also need to recognize and value the unique design that is present in those I lead. When leaders fail to see the unique gifts of those who are part of our staffs or leadership teams, we are guilty of walking through a priceless art gallery with no time or attention given to the masterpieces on display. In doing so, we are missing the opportunity to truly appreciate the beauty and genius of the works of art that are right in front of us.

Strengths-based Leadership

Dr. Donald O. Clifton, researcher and developer of the *Clifton StrengthsFinder* assessment, invested much of his adult life in studying individual talent patterns across a wide array of professions. He began by asking the simple question, "What would happen if we studied what is right with people?" The strengths philosophy that emerged from his decades of research has been summarized as follows: "Individuals gain more when they build on their talents, than when they make comparable efforts to improve their areas of weakness."[2] In other words, the highest potential for reaching personal and professional effectiveness, in ourselves and in others, will occur around those areas of natural talent. "Each person's greatest room for growth is in the areas of his or her greatest strength."[3]

It is so tempting to begin our personal leadership development by comparing ourselves to other effective leaders, wishing we had their gifts and abilities, perhaps even trying to emulate who they are and how they lead. Granted, there is much to be learned from carefully observing "the best of the best" in all areas of life. But attempting to simply copy others is not an authentic approach to developing our own leadership style. Rather than attempting to function like leaders we admire, or practicing a "top ten" list of characteristics of effective leaders, our time will be best spent in understanding the talents that each of us brings to our leadership role and finding ways to strengthen and build on those. Instead of expecting all leaders to follow one cookie-cutter approach to success, a strengths-based approach encourages us to become the individuals God created us to be in order to do the leadership work that God has called us to do.

Leaders also face the temptation to look within and focus on areas of inadequacy. If we spend our leadership development efforts trying to fix our inadequacies, we will be left with little time and energy to grow the gifts and abilities that we do possess. Individual leadership development is not about well-roundedness; it's about identifying personal talents and focusing on growth. In other words, "If you spend your life trying to be good at everything, you will never be great at anything."[4] As Peter Drucker once said, "One should waste as little effort as possible on improving areas of low competence. It takes far more energy to improve from incompetence to mediocrity than it takes to improve from first rate performance to excellence."[5]

To best focus on what we do well as leaders, we need a way to identify our unique gifts and talents. It's not just about what we are good at doing, or what leads to our moments of success. Individuals can be good at many things and competent in many arenas. In seeking to recognize your gifts, consider all that you do. What brings you energy? What is so self-reinforcing that it leads you to invest greater time and effort? Such self-analysis is not about focusing on competency; it's more about discovering what brings fulfillment and deep satisfaction, what feeds personal intrinsic motivation. In *Cure for the Common Life*, Max Lucado calls it finding your "sweet spot."[6]

Although you may be aware of your abilities and effectiveness as a leader, several online instruments are available that provide a specific strengths vocabulary for your self-assessment: Values in Action (VIA) Classification of Strengths and Virtues by Christopher Peterson and Martin Seligman, StandOut by Buckingham, Realise2 by Linley, and the Clifton StrengthsFinder from Gallup, Inc.[7] The VIA Classification of Strengths is a free assessment that identifies a person's "five most notable strengths" from a list of twenty-four strengths organized under six overarching virtues (wisdom/knowledge, courage, humanity, justice, temperance, and transcendence). These virtues are derived from human traits that are valued across cultures. StandOut is an assessment that reveals a person's top two strengths roles from a list of nine (advisor, pioneer, connector, creator, equalizer, influencer, stimulator, provider, and teacher). These roles are predominantly related to the world of work and the behaviors that are prevalent in the workplace. The assessment is available by purchasing the book *StandOut*. A British contribution to strengths assessment is the Realise2 program, which is purchased online. This assessment looks at sixty strengths across the dimensions of energy, performance, and use. These dimensions are explored across the four categories of realized strengths, unrealized strengths, learned behaviors, and weaknesses. The Clifton StrengthsFinder is an assessment that is available for purchase online or through codes provided in texts such as *StrengthsQuest* and *StrengthsFinder 2.0*. It examines the presence of talent within thirty-four themes. Individuals receive a profile of their top five signature themes.

Clifton believed that individual strength emerges when talent is multiplied by an investment of effort in acquiring knowledge, developing skill, and then having experience in using that talent to maximize its potential. You may recognize that many of your own leadership strengths have emerged over time as your experiences have allowed you to build on your natural talents.[8]

After years of interviewing and analyzing the talents of effective leaders, Clifton concluded, "A leader needs to know his strengths as a carpenter knows his tools, or as a physician knows the instruments at her disposal. What great leaders have in common is that each truly knows his or her strengths—and can call on the right strength at the right time. This explains why there is no definitive list of characteristics that describes all leaders."[9]

Leaders' Differing Strengths

So what do great leaders do differently? Everything! Their effectiveness comes from their competence and their authenticity. As researcher Jim Collins has noted in his book *Good to Great*, they are not trying to lead like someone they admire; they are simply bringing their own gifts to their leadership role. To demonstrate this point, I will describe (using pseudonyms) four leaders in higher education who I've come to know through conversations with them about their Clifton StrengthsFinder top five signature themes.

Cynthia, a vice president for academic affairs, leads from strategic and contextual strengths. As a strategic leader, she begins every day with a plan. She can visualize outcomes and generate possibilities. She is also an avid learner and resource gatherer, operating with a wealth of information as she develops plans to move the faculty and curriculum forward. Cynthia will tell you that the contextual approach is at the core of her leadership. She functions effectively in the present because she values the lessons learned in the past. Having been at her university for over thirty years, she knows the institutional story, understands its mission, and has helped to shape its culture. Her strategic leadership flows out of this contextual framework.

Greg, a senior vice president, brings a unique set of strengths to his leadership role. He is frequently asked to find ways to make things happen and he is very good at doing that by arranging all of the details necessary for success. He is commended for his loyalty to his staff, to the institution, and specifically to the president. People are drawn to him because of the self-confidence he exudes. He speaks with authority and cultivates trust. He is passionate about the university and its mission. In his words, he is "all in." His beliefs guide his passions. This is clearly reflected in his approach to leading.

Mary, a provost at a faith-based university, leads by making things happen, influencing people, and building relationships. She leads with a strong sense of responsibility, and because of this, she is known for her utter dependability and her tireless work ethic. She also leads with a smile. Her optimism and encouragement of others are contagious aspects of her leadership. Even in the midst of an institutional crisis, Mary led with grace as she brought a sense of calm to the chaos; she led with hope as she brought her energy and enthusiasm to a seemingly overwhelming task. In her leadership role, she is a person of influence who is known for her strong powers of persuasion and the ability to make things happen. This has enabled her to attract a strong faculty and quality administrative personnel during her years of service.

Michael, a vice president for student life, is first of all a relational leader. His role requires frequent interaction with staff, faculty, and students in a variety of settings. With the ability to respond appropriately to the various groups, he is able to develop genuine, authentic relationships across the campus. His world is full of decisions large and small, so he is called upon to think strategically, and then to lead others to act on those decisions. Michael states that the strength at the center of his success is the ability to adapt. He is actually energized by the need to respond to the unexpected, to constantly multi-task, to adjust personnel assignments, venue usage, and event details. He believes that his strengths match the demands of his leadership role.

The effectiveness of these four very capable leaders comes not from their similarities, but from their uniqueness. They lead from who they are. They honor God's design and live out their giftedness in these leadership roles in very different ways.

Finding Your Strengths

Even without a specific strengths assessment, there are clues to your leadership talents. Clifton identified these through his years of interviewing the "best of the best" across many career fields. To become more aware of your own talents, ask yourself these questions:

- What am I naturally drawn to?
- What comes easily to me?
- In what activities does time seem to fly by?
- When do I have those glimpses of excellence where I think, "How did I do that?"
- When do I experience satisfaction that causes me to ask, "When can I do that again?"

Your answers to these questions will reveal some of your best leadership talents.[10]

Sometimes our gifts for leadership seem so ordinary, even underwhelming, that we ignore them or give them little value. When a strengths assessment tells you that you like to gather all of the relevant facts or that you care about including people in the decision-making process, you may downplay the significance of those talents. It can be very enlightening to allow those you lead to provide feedback for you on your areas of talent. People who work with you or know you well may be able to see and affirm your talents at work in ways you don't see. Many of these talents are so natural that we simply take them for granted, assuming that other people act, think, or relate in this way. With a strengths vocabulary in mind, however, you may find a new recognition, a conscious competence, that emerges as you become more aware of your talents in your daily thoughts and actions.

As a strengths-focused leader, what do you do with your areas of weakness? First of all, it's important to acknowledge them, because they really can't be ignored. We are not good at everything. None of us brings all the talents necessary for successful leading. Second, understand what a weakness is. Leadership weaknesses are not all the things you cannot do. Perhaps you are not great at conflict resolution. In some fields of employment, that would be a definite weakness. However, if your leadership role does not require you to resolve conflict on a regular basis, then that lack of talent would not be considered a weakness for your leadership. Weakness is defined as "any lack of knowledge, skill or talent that negatively affects your performance or that of others."[11] Knowledge can be learned and skill can be developed to compensate for lack of natural talent in some areas. However, if there is an essential area of leadership that does not flow naturally in your work, you may find that the effort necessary to be successful in that area is simply energy-draining, being both mentally and emotionally exhausting. If the energy demand is too high, and the mental and emotional efforts are overwhelming, then you may decide that that particular leadership role is not a good fit for your talents.

When you are operating from areas of talent, you are energized and deeply satisfied. Marcus Buckingham, in *Go Put Your Strengths to Work*, suggests an exercise called "Love it/Loathe it," in which you examine your work responsibilities and determine the balance between these two categories.[12] When your talents are a good fit for your leadership role, the greater portion of your work week will fall into the "love it" category. This sense of loving what the workday holds is what you hope for as you seek a leadership role that honors your giftedness.

In the book *Let Your Life Speak*, Parker Palmer recognizes the importance of fit when he states, "Despite the American myth, I cannot be or do whatever I desire . . . . There are some roles and relationships in which we thrive and others in which we wither and die."[13] In honoring your giftedness for leadership, it's important to find the right fit for the talents that you possess. Good leaders can wither and die when they find themselves in a role or in relationships where their talents are not recognized, valued, or encouraged to grow. Good leaders can also wither and die when they find themselves in roles that require talent, knowledge, and skills that are beyond their capacities. In honoring our giftedness, it is equally important to be fully aware of our inadequacies as well as our talents.

If a true area of weakness is having a negative impact on your leadership effectiveness, it must be addressed. First look to your areas of strength to determine if there are ways to compensate. For example, a leader who is not particularly gifted in conversation with strangers, but finds that behavior very necessary on certain occasions, may lean on his strengths as a learner or resource gatherer to approach the situation with curiosity rather than dread.

A second approach would be to find a complementary colleague who excels in areas that don't come easily. Learn to delegate to others those areas that are not your strengths. This strategy could actually allow others the opportunity to thrive in their areas of strength and would ultimately encourage the efficiency and effectiveness of the leadership team. I had the opportunity to experience this when I served as a director of a career center. My talents lie in learning, gathering resources, generating ideas, and taking time to reflect deeply on all of these aspects. Knowing that I could be slow to develop strategies or act on my ideas, I hired a uniquely talented assistant director, who brought strength in those areas. As soon as I had an idea, she was developing strategy and preparing a timetable for action. We were very effective partners, and the career center flourished under this configuration of leadership talents.

Successful leaders do not need to do everything well. They do need to understand their talents and the talents of others, so that they build a team that can function well together and bring out the best in each other. This approach recognizes that weakness is present in all of us and compensates for it through the talents of others.

As leaders, we must also realize that some of our talents can be overused or misapplied to the point that they have a negative impact on our effectiveness or create the opportunity for a misunderstanding of our leadership style. For example, a strong strategic leader may rapidly sort out all possibilities and come to quick conclusions with great confidence, leaving others to second-guess those decisions because they were not part of the process. Team members may feel left out of or even dismissed from the process and wish their opinions and ideas had been considered. A gifted communicator may dominate the discussion because thinking out loud and speaking for the group comes so naturally. A leader with high standards of excellence may never be satisfied with the end result, leaving those who have worked very hard on a project feeling like they can never do enough to please. Since the leader is operating out of an area of talent, he or she may be totally unaware that these "shadow sides" even exist.

A strengths-based leader needs to be aware of the potential for the dual nature that resides within each signature theme. Our talents are there to be used in productive and beneficial ways, but each area of strength also has the capacity to get out of balance. The hard-working achiever can quickly become the overachiever and experience burnout, while expecting the same drive from others. The inclusionary leader can keep enlarging the circle until efficiency suffers. The person with a strong vision of the future can be so "out there" that the realities of the present are not even on the radar screen.

Honoring giftedness as a team means that the diverse contributions of its members are appreciated. A strengths-focused team leader will realize that everyone is not equally good at everything. Assignments and roles will be thoughtfully distributed, and team members will be valued and celebrated for their unique contributions. This strengths awareness within a leadership team can encourage honest individual assessment and frank conversation, allowing each person to identify individual tendencies and giving members of the team the opportunity to express concern when they perceive talent being misused or overdone.

There are many ways to honor giftedness and engage employees through their strengths. An initial conversation about a person's fit with a given job description is a good place to begin. By matching talent, knowledge, and skills to the expectations of the job (or team assignment), the leader gains valuable insight. Then the incorporation of a strengths perspective into the existing professional development program with conversations occurring at three-month, six-month, or twelve-month intervals can continue to connect strengths to performance. For example, faculty at one college were asked on the annual review, "In what ways do you utilize your signature themes [from the Clifton StrengthsFinder] to fulfill your faculty responsibilities?" At another university, faculty members were asked to set performance goals for the next year that would encourage growth connected to their signature themes. Another university brought strengths into the professional development of Residential Life staff by beginning the annual review on this positive note: "Identify your primary contribution in the past year, and state how that contribution is consistent with your talent/strengths."

Other questions to encourage strengths engagement with your staff include:

- What is your favorite part of your job?
- At work, what is it that you do best?
- At work, how often do you get to do what you do best?
- Describe one of your best days in the past month? How did any of your talents contribute to the satisfaction you felt on that day?

- Do you get to bring your talents to work each day?
- Have you had opportunities to learn and grow within your areas of talent?

There is the potential for these strengths-focused conversations to lead to a refinement or a reassignment of job or team responsibilities, living out Jim Collins's directive to get the right people in the right seats on the bus.[14] For example, two employees in a university business office were allowed to switch roles within the office after they were introduced to their talent profile. This strengths identification helped them understand why they were always wishing they could do the other person's job. One worked on financial reports at a private desk, the other was assigned to the front window to assist students with their payments and financial questions. Neither was happy in her role. After a discussion of strengths, they were able to explain themselves and their attitudes toward their jobs in a positive way. Their strengths-based manager allowed them to adjust their job descriptions and switch roles, giving both employees the opportunity to bring themselves to work with full engagement. This resulted in improved productivity and employee retention.

These strengths conversations can change the tone of a performance review from a weakness-fixing mindset into a more positive and hopeful dialogue. Problems and weak spots cannot be ignored, but the professional development is done through a strengths lens, viewing the person as one with talents to offer and gifts to be honed and developed. When employees are encouraged to live out their strengths in the context of their work, they are given the opportunity to experience satisfaction and fulfillment through their ability to bring their authentic selves to work.[15]

Strengths and Calling

Areas of talent provide clues to how God has designed each person. In *Let Your Life Speak,* Palmer provides this advice related to exploring one's vocation: "Before you tell your life what you intend to do with it, listen for what it intends to do with you."[16]

Knowing who we are and what we have to offer is the biggest step toward discovering our best fit and effectiveness in leadership. Through a strengths lens, we can start seeing ourselves and others in terms of who we really are, rather than in terms of who we are not. We can begin to understand, respect, and value the way that we have been designed by a loving Creator. We can understand our styles, motivations, shadows, and weaknesses. We can stay true to who we are.[17] And we can offer to others this understanding and the possibility of greater integrity. As strengths-based leaders, we can create environments where our own natural abilities, and those of our co-workers, are acknowledged and given the opportunity to flourish. This strengths climate encourages authenticity, positive energy, and a good fit of talents to tasks that, in turn, encourage active engagement and high productivity for each person involved.

John Ortberg, in *The Me I Want to Be*, explains the idea in this way:

> God himself works with strength, freedom, and joy. When you discover your strengths, you are learning an indispensible part of what it means to be made in the image of God. When you help other people discover their strengths, you are helping the image of God to be restored in another human being. You are part of the work of redemption—the liberating of work from the curse. You are doing the work of the Spirit.[18]

Similarly, Gordon T. Smith, writing in *Courage and Calling*, says it takes courage to be true to yourself and to your gifts:

> The essential and mature act is simple: come to a full realization of who you are and what you have been gifted to do, and embrace it eagerly. Do it. Be true to who you are. Be true to your call, true to how God has made you. Your call is not a superior call or a more sacred call; it is merely *your* call.[19]

So what would happen to your leadership style and effectiveness if you focused on what is *right* with you as a leader and *right* with those with whom you work most closely? If you believe that your gifts and talents were given by God so that you can fulfill God's purposes, then working to understand your individual strengths and how those connect to your effectiveness as a leader and team member, as well as working to understand the strengths of those around you, will be critical to your team's success.

As you examine your giftedness for leadership, here are some questions to consider:

- How has God designed me?
- What gifts do I bring to the leadership role?
- How do my talents fit the job description?
- How can I leverage what I do well within this leadership role?
- Do I often find myself fulfilled and energized or empty and drained?
- Do I have the opportunity to do what I do best on a daily basis?
- Do I have opportunities to learn and grow into the person God designed me to be?

In addition to recognizing, appreciating, and utilizing the talents that are present in each team member, a strengths-focused team leader may also encourage the team to periodically discuss the answers to these questions:

- What are our strengths as a team?
- What do we need from each other in order to be successful?
- What are the best ways for us to accomplish our tasks?
- How do we communicate with each other?
- How do we make decisions?
- How do we resolve conflict?
- What motivates us as members of this team?
- What are our potential blind spots and barriers?

Conclusion

My call to strengths-based leadership emerged from my experiences touring cathedrals one summer. The magnificent cathedral built by human hands "for the glory of God" serves as a reminder that each human being is lovingly designed for God's glory as well. Each of us honors the Creator when we live and lead according to our giftedness and when we honor the giftedness of others. The beauty and genius of God's design is on display in us and in those who are part of our worlds. A beautiful campus with wonderful buildings is important, but wherever we find ourselves, we are leading in the midst of a glorious art display, not because of the natural or physical surroundings, but because of the *people* who are there.

Notes to Chapter Three

1. Madeleine L'Engle, *A Stone for a Pillow: Journeys with Jacob*, 89.

2. Donald O. Clifton and James K. Harter, "Investing in Strengths," 112.

3. Marcus Buckingham and Donald O. Clifton, *Now, Discover your Strengths*, 8.

4. Tom Rath and Barry Conchie, *Strengths Based Leadership*, 7.

5. Peter F. Drucker, *Classic Drucker*, 6.

6. Max Lucado, *Cure for the Common Life*.

7. Christopher Peterson and Martin E. P. Seligman, *Character Strengths and Virtues;* Marcus Buckingham, *StandOut*; Alex Linley, Janet Willars, and Robert Biswas-Diener, *The Strengths Book*; Donald O. Clifton, Edward "Chip" Anderson, and Laurie A. Schreiner, *StrengthQuest*.

8. Donald O. Clifton, Edward "Chip" Anderson, and Laurie A. Schreiner, *StrengthQuest*, 97.

9. Quoted in Rath and Conchie, *Strengths Based Leadership*, 13.

10. Buckingham and Clifton, *Now, Discover Your Strengths*, 71–75.

11. Clifton, Anderson, and Schreiner, *StrengthsQuest*, 76.

12. Marcus Buckingham, *Go Put Your Strengths to Work*, 100.

13. Parker Palmer, *Let Your Life Speak*, 44.

14. Jim Collins, *Good to Great*.

15. Marcus Buckingham and Curt Coffman, *First, Break all the Rules*.

16. Palmer, *Let Your Life Speak*.

17. Rath and Conchie, *Strengths Based Leadership*, 93.

18. John Ortberg, *The Me I Want to Be*, 220.

19. Gordon T. Smith, *Courage and Calling*, 52.

For Discussion

1. What are your unique leadership strengths?

2. In what ways do you recognize and honor giftedness in yourself and in others?

3. How have your gifts been developed through your leadership experience?

4. Discuss the tension that exists between honoring giftedness and acknowledging weakness.

5. What is the connection between your strengths and your sense of calling?

6. If you took a tour of the "art gallery" on display when your team convenes, what gifts would you appreciate?

PART II

The Social Intelligence of Thriving Leaders

Chapter Four

TELL ME A STORY
Using an Old Tool to Sustain Culture, Embrace Change, and Envision a Bold Future

Patricia S. Anderson

"The ability to create and tell certain kinds of dramatic stories is not only a useful tool, but an essential prerequisite to being a first-class winning leader."

—NOEL M. TICHY, The Leadership Engine

I looked into the faces of my audience. As I had been taught, look to the left side. Blank faces. Right side. Blank faces. Middle. Blank faces. I had prepared my charts and data tables to show the faculty the changes that had occurred in the past several years. I had used a multiple regression formula to make statistical predictions about important outcomes. "This is not working," I thought. I needed to break the gulf of silence. I summarized the main points and had the table groups consider two proposals. As the faculty embarked with lively discussion, I listened to them! Sitting at one table after another, I heard stories of students who faced educational challenges and were succeeding at our university. The faculty told stories that trumped my charts and graphs that day.

As I have moved through various leadership roles, I have been struck by the impact that stories can have on those listening. Speakers who use a story skillfully illustrate the point and help the audience become part of the story in a way that allows everyone to "feel" the experience and easily grasp the main points. Stories, much more than PowerPoint bullets or graphs, prompt discussion from the listeners. Perhaps more importantly, the stories are what listeners remember.

Over time, I have learned that a story can bring a connection between the storyteller and the listener. Yet while great gulfs of misunderstanding can be closed with the choice of a compelling personal story, stories can also be used to poor effect. Some presenters tell story after story without a conclusion; others, after telling a powerful story, merely make a summary statement such as "take a risk" or "let's move forward on this project." Still others use stories as jokes or anecdotes to elicit a laugh that has nothing to do with a presentation's purpose. Over the years as I have listened intentionally for the role of stories in public presentations, I have assessed their potential power for organizational leaders.

As I have reflected, I have been reminded that the history of story is as old as humankind. Anthropologists infer characteristics of an entire culture from markings on cave walls. Worldwide, storytelling provides the glue from generation to generation. In our own culture, children's stories provide ample warning to avoid wolves, witches, and gremlins. Many of us listen to preachers who revel in retelling the stories of the Bible. More recently, business, political, and educational leaders are learning that the right story can build trust, frame the big issues that face an organization, reinforce values, or promote a compelling vision. Clearly, while my tables and graphs might be persuasive to a point, the well-crafted story serves to better sustain the hearts of my listeners.

To say that my ears in recent years have been more attuned to story is an understatement. I have looked eagerly for stories and narrative shared by leaders. In teaching a graduate class on leadership, I embedded leadership stories in assignments using the work of Annette Simmons, author of *The Story Factor*.[1] Students wrote four stories as a small part of their assignments and responded to the stories of each other. The enthusiastic response of the students to this assignment cemented my conviction that good storytelling should be an indispensable tool of today's leaders.

Storytelling Has a Valuable Role

The power of storytelling lies in its ability to connect the teller's story to the audience—physically, emotionally, and intellectually. Through story, the historic duality of heart and head merges. When used in any organizational context, the many chasms between leader and followers or between and among functional teams can be effectively bridged.

An increasing number of books, journal articles, blogs, and websites describe the effectiveness of story as a communication tool for leaders and their organizations. In one example, *Leading Minds: An Anatomy of Leadership*, author Howard Gardner maintained that storytelling is a core skill of leadership. He summarized, "In addition to communicating stories, leaders *embody* those stories . . . [and] convey these stories by the kinds of lives they themselves lead."[2] Leadership scholar Noel Tichy similarly has noted: ". . . the ultimate hallmark of world-class champion leaders . . . is the ability to weave all the other elements together into vibrant stories that lead their organizations into the future."[3]

The expanding literature on storytelling results from its successful application by leaders who recognize the ever-present challenges in gaining follower engagement and support. Stories have the ability to draw the listeners into the past and can play an important role as part of the organizational story going forward. Obstacles that have seemed to be beyond resolution can be reduced to solvable steps. Leaders who gain the support and involvement of their community members have a powerful advantage in identifying those necessary steps to move forward.

Beyond followers, a storyteller may use this craft as a tool in presentations to many groups—from professional associations, to community groups, and in other settings where inspiration and motivation are essential to the outcome. A story is an account of events that are connected and intentionally told to offer insight, understanding, inspiration, and engagement. In short, stories help make your ideas "stick."[4] Randolph Barker and Kim Gower, writing in the *Journal of Business Communication*, declare, "The strengths of storytelling as a communication method, recognizing all humans as storytellers with the ability to send and receive messages that establish a value-laden reality, establishes common ground among all participants and provides a faster method of establishing a social relationship."[5]

For those in leadership, it is especially important to note that effective stories involve a reporting of a history that is essentially true, whether or not they are always factual. Obviously, trust is lost if a story implicitly told as fact can be confirmed as inaccurate. Yet sometimes, tellers combine elements of true stories or claim a hypothetical anecdote to illustrate a truth that the audience needs to hear. For example, I have often told a story about monkeys to those who came to my office to give me their problem to solve. The visual image in the story, which may be familiar to some readers, involves a proverbial "monkey" that is about to be transferred to me for resolution. If I were to allow that, however, my office would soon fill with monkeys that are hungry, jumping from bookcase to bookcase, distracting me and future visitors, and leaving their banana peels and other refuse for me to clean up. The monkey anecdote tells a truth: taking on problems that belong to others leads to chaos.

Beyond illustrative anecdotes, we find truth in vision stories, which look toward the future. While not narratives of something that has "really happened," these are stories of truth, assuming that the story describes realistic possibilities. These stories, however, must be plausible in that the elements of the story align with the needs, interests, and potential of the audience. One of the most well-known vision stories was told by Martin Luther King, Jr., who reminded his audience of the current condition of his people. He called on his audience not to wallow in despair but to embrace the dream of equality as proclaimed in the Declaration of Independence. King's "I Have a Dream" speech represents a compelling truth story.

A story may also report a series of misfortunes that led to a positive or a negative outcome. The positive outcome encourages the audience to maintain hope and faith in the face of trial or uncertainty. Negative outcomes remind listeners to be cautious or to avoid similar situations. A story stimulates the emotions by changing the mood of the presentation, drawing in the listeners with a description of obstacles and a sense of urgency in needing to overcome barriers. A danger for leaders is ignoring the difficult stories where real problems reside. Screenwriting coach Robert McKee advises, "... executives sweep the dirty laundry, the difficulties, the antagonists, and the struggles under the carpet. They prefer to present a rosy—and boring—picture to the world. But as a storyteller, you want to position the problems in the foreground and then show how you've overcome them."[6]

In *The Secret Language of Leadership*, Stephen Denning argues that change is seldom sustained by reason alone—through facts and figures and arguments. Stories, however, appeal to the heart as well as the mind. Denning poses a three-step process that a story must reflect in order to get at the heart of change—a frequent story for leaders. First, a story must indicate why the change is needed as seen through the eyes of one who will be affected by the change. Significantly, the story should feature community involvement, rather than portraying organizational problems as being resolved by a removed outside party. Second, the story should tell how a desired change will be implemented to achieve a better future state—again, preferably with all participating. Third, the story must include why the change will work to achieve personal and institutional goals.[7] These elements suggest ways in which leaders can cultivate positive emotions in their constituents that will help the organization avoid complacency and gain the energy needed to move forward.

Story Elements

The simplest premise for a story is describing a situation or a person who is either a protagonist or antagonist. Such stories contain a problem or predicament, action, a turning point, and resolution. Initially, the story has a *beginning* that sets up the coming events. What is happening, where, and who are the individuals involved? Then the story has a *body*, in which something happens to change or challenge the balance described in the beginning. The developing stressors are described and expanded. The story's inherent interest must be such that the listener is drawn in. In the *climax*, the conflict reaches a crisis point, forcing change in the characters or situations. Finally, there is a *resolution*, where those involved reach a new balance. Something is learned. Values are reset or reinforced.

Storytellers should be cautious about setting aside any of these elements of effective storytelling—the beginning, the body, the climax, and the resolution. The listener needs to wonder, "Will the difficulties be overcome?" It is not the beginning nor the ending but the process that pulls the listener in. Listeners will be facing "real-life" experiences that vary in intensity—financial dangers, tension among personnel, threats to student well-being. Living vicariously through crises and resolutions in stories prepares people to respond effectively to situations in which they must make practical decisions.

Story Archetypes for Higher Education Leaders

Various organizations provide varying cultures and contexts for effective storytelling. Annette Simmons describes four story archetypes that organizations tend to employ most often. These include the introduction of the new leader (the "Who I Am" story); reinforcing the values and norms of the community (the "Who We Are" story); dealing with change (the "Challenge" story); and confirming a bright future (the "Vision" story).[8]

Table 4.1—Four Story Archetypes for Leaders

Story Type	Purpose	Characteristics
Who I Am	To gain trust To invite listeners to know you To establish your credentials to influence To be authentic To share life lessons	Identifies strengths, core values, or vulnerabilities Provides colorful details of context Reveals characteristics of overcoming, resilience, focus, achievement, or hope
Who We Are	To remind listeners of shared history, values, commitments To engage communities for service and sacrifice To reinforce teamwork To establish work as significant	Focuses on transformed lives from history and from the present (particularly, those of faculty and students)
Challenge	To see the need for and specify the details of change To take action To gain engagement and support throughout the institution	Discusses multiple risks and opportunities Remembers past successes in the face of great challenges Addresses the "What's in it for me?" question for students, faculty, community Models change for listeners
Future	To support a bright future To mitigate current challenges through future opportunities To engage and energize key stakeholders	Provides minimal details Offers significant new direction Envisions clear outcomes Stays positive and exciting Invites group imagination

Who I Am

The "Who I Am" story is typically addressed to a new audience to demonstrate who you are, describe your background, and offer a personal human interest story.[9] The audience responds with trust to storytellers who exhibit authenticity through such stories. Common themes include overcoming obstacles, facing fears, escaping boredom, telling truth when no one would know otherwise, or finishing strong—all these infuse the storyteller with realism and contributing to trust-building between teller and listeners.

Leaders can present "Who I Am" stories to elicit faith in past successes and proposed goals. In *The Story Factor*, Simmons writes: "Story is the path to creating faith. Telling a meaningful story means inspiring your listeners— co-workers, leaders, subordinates, family, or a bunch of strangers—to reach the same conclusions you have reached and decide *for themselves* to believe what you say and do what you want them to do."[10] Such advice by a seasoned story maker helps leaders to identify elements of an engaging story. A "Who I Am" story has to be much more than a recitation of the facts of the speaker's life to date; rather, it shares some choice aspects of the personal and professional journey that have led to this new place of service. These turning points, struggles, or decisions provide the drama for the story. Individual stories sustain hope and strengthen confidence in the teller and among listeners.

Leaders must be in touch with their own stories—stories that have many elements that are sifted and crafted over a lifetime of experience. Howard Gardner notes, "The true impact of a leader depends on the story that he or she relates or *embodies* . . . ."[11] An unintended consequence of reworking one's story is the opportunity to reinvent oneself. Author Gail Sheehy writes, "Psychologists have found that the way people tell their stories becomes so habitual that they finally become recipes for structuring experience itself, for laying down routes and finally for guiding their lives."[12] By making thoughtful choices about which stories to tell and how to tell them, leaders can chart new courses for themselves and their listeners.

Every organization has multiple opportunities each year to hear "Who I Am" stories, partly in listening to the aspirations of various applicants for job openings requiring leadership skills. Often, during critical junctures in any organization, it is helpful to hear a "Who I Am" story from the leader as a means of overcoming division or distrust among elements of the organization. The leader may use a "Who I Am" story to rebuild trust and support. The following examples provided by two university presidents illustrate the power of "Who I Am" stories.

Who I Am—Story 1

My grandparents had lost their Indiana farm during the Great Depression and had moved to the city of Lafayette. My parents literally abandoned me one winter night and my grandparents took me in to live with them. My grandmother was a real saint and prayer warrior. She was one of the most generous and giving persons I have ever known. She promised to introduce me to my real father "Jesus" when I was old enough to make that decision to follow Him. She raised me at her knee and instilled the values that have served me well to this day. My grandparents were poor, financially speaking, but gave me spiritual direction that was priceless.

I developed a thirst for higher education because of two or three high school teachers. I excelled in their classes because they believed in me and challenged me to my utmost. But college seemed out of reach financially. My grandparents were unable to give me a dime to go to college. I did not receive any scholarships or financial aid to go to college. I started working in construction and hoped to pay my college bills from my earnings.

On the last Sunday night before I would leave for college, my church family presented me with a gift. It was an old cigar box wrapped with white paper and had the words printed in black ink: HELPS TO HIGHER EDUCATION. It contained $34.43. But rather than the amount, it represented the faith and confidence of my local church family. On many occasions I would drive back to my hometown. When I would leave the church on Sunday night to return to school, in my car I might find food, clothing, and even an envelope containing cash with a note saying they were praying for me. That support sustained me when I had doubts about continuing in college.

My hard work in the summers did provide for most of my expenses even though I had to drop out twice for a semester to earn and save enough in order to return to school. I finished college and more, as you know.

Thus as a university president, I kept that box in a prominent place in my executive desk. I might fill it with pictures and stories about my students. But it was always a reminder to remember the generosity of support that I received and a personal challenge for me to help enable every one of my students to succeed wherever I could do so personally or professionally.[13]

Who I Am—Story 2

I came to leadership reluctantly. In fact, I have never thought of myself as a "leader." Having said that, for the past nine years, I have found myself in various positions of leadership, first as provost and now as a college president. I've had to learn about leadership as I go. My comments, then, are very much lessons of the road.

First, the call to leadership is often closely linked to particular communities and particular tasks. It does not just come to people who think of themselves as leaders, or to those who have taken classes in "leadership training." It behooves each of us to be prepared for moments when the needs of our communities invite us to consider stepping into leadership roles for particular seasons. Leadership is never about us, or at least it is never only about us. It is about being available when our communities' needs intersect with our own journeys of preparation to meet those needs. God may well call some people to be leaders and to think of themselves as such. But the Scriptures remind us that the call to leadership is just as often a surprise to those being called . . . .

I tend to think that the Lord calls us not to "leadership" as a lifetime call, but to faithfulness in particular moments as part of the larger work of Divine Artisanship in which he works on us, even as he calls us to good works.[14]

Who We Are

"Who We Are" stories serve important purposes when a leader seeks to develop a partnership with those they lead. Since community culture sustains higher education institutions to a large extent, leaders can draw on their shared histories to remind the audience of past sacrifice, vision, perseverance, and hope. The stories drawn from institutional history often establish uniqueness, generally through past sacrifice. "We are unique and therefore significant," these stories emphasize. Elements of this story archetype explain the origins, reinforce norms, and define a community identity that is different from all others.

"Who We Are" stories are told by institutional leaders who draw on historical values of the institution in order to encourage the audience as heirs to a common history. By identifying with this uniqueness, individual community members bond with the institution, its history, and with each other. This story identifies past and present leaders, students, and others as central characters. A story of this type easily generates and narrates the values inherent in an institutional metaphor (e.g., being a "flagship") or brand (e.g., "To be Known").

In a higher education context, "Who We Are" stories also tell about the "product"—particularly, the university's impact on the lives of students. Students enter with an abundance of motivation for higher education. Each institution focuses on changing lives through various intellectual, social, physical, and spiritual experiences. In many ways, students enter a college as "I" and inextricably become part of the "We."

Who We Are—Story 1

Our school was founded over a hundred years ago. Three outstanding women, Mary Hill, Ruth Smith, and Bertha Dixon, established the Training School for Christian Workers in 1899 for the purpose of providing education and support for those called to the Great Commission—going into the world to teach people eternal truths. Students sacrificed as they worked in jobs at the school while taking classes. Missionaries regularly returned to the School to share their experiences of privation, loss, and success from their mission posts around the globe.

During the first several years, forty to fifty students a year attended the School. Soon, many students, and teachers Hill and Dixon, responded to the call to foreign missions in China. Dixon returned from China after her two small children died. Hill remained for over thirty-five years. Smith was called to Guatemala and served there for forty-one years, giving her all to the passion for the mission she so embraced.

The call of the founders of our university to sacrificial service around the world is as fresh today as it was in 1899. While we have grown to a university of ten thousand, our core commitments include our personal call to prepare to serve sacrificially throughout the world."[15]

Who We Are—Story 2

At 7 a.m. on Tuesday morning, a university employee discovered a life-sized cardboard cutout of Barack Obama attached by fishing line to a tree. A sign which read "Act Six reject"[16] was taped to the cardboard cutout. The employee immediately removed the display.

When I discovered this I was very outraged and disheartened. I have spent my professional life trying to teach people why it is essential to understand others. Further, I state boldly to our world that those of us who love Jesus will lead the community in our efforts to serve and love others. This act causes some to question our commitment. Whoever put that cardboard piece up yesterday was wrong and I want you to know that I condemn it in the strongest terms.

In the past, our University has had problems recruiting people of diverse backgrounds to our campus. Like many suburban campuses we have drawn primarily white students to live and study here. We've tried many things to increase our enrollment from individuals from diverse communities but without much success. Several years ago, we entered into a partnership to recruit student leaders from the city to join our community. My vision was to bring students here to help us see new perspectives—to create a richer dialogue in our classrooms and in our student life programs to enrich the life of our community.

The good news is that it has worked. For the first time in our history, 25 percent of our entering class this year came from diverse backgrounds. We are becoming the place I believe God has called us to be. This change will not come without challenges, like yesterday's; but we will work through them together.

Behind me today are the Act Six students and some of the people who support the mission and calling of Jesus here. I want you to understand that I love all of you. You are my brothers and sisters in Christ. What you see up here today is a reflection of what the Kingdom of God will look like in heaven. John in the Book of Revelation described heaven this way: "After this I looked, and there was a great multitude that no one could count, from every nation, from all tribes and peoples and languages, standing before the throne and before the Lamb . . ." We want to be a part of this Kingdom.

I want you to do something for me today, tomorrow, and for the rest of the term. Live to show everyone in our community that the person who displayed the cardboard cutout was absolutely wrong in their thinking, and that we find that display unacceptable. We love people here. We care about justice and equality and we seek after peace. We value everyone created in the image of God because we live by the words and model the actions of Jesus. "Now, go and do likewise."[17]

Leading through Challenge

Whether any higher education institution has ever had periods of idyllic or halcyon days is doubtful; colleges and universities are multi-layered, culturally and traditionally tied, and risk averse. They are proud organizations made up of faculty, administrative leaders, professional student services staff, support staff, fundraising staff, athletic complexes, and more. Each group has unique callings, and all must intersect seamlessly to function well as a whole. The external realities facing any campus include the unpredictability of public and private funding, political and accrediting requirements, and alumni and businesses that benefit and are benefited by the university.

The challenges facing a university or college can be very obvious (as when a tornado strikes your campus) or more subtle (as when the bottom line seems to move upward or downward without clear explanations of underlying causes). Even when a leader understands the dynamics of what change is needed, the community must be encouraged to move from the known to the unknown. Leaders have to present realities that are unsustainable and articulate reasonable goals in which everyone has a stake—whether those include finding housing for displaced students or cutting budgets to establish a stable financial foundation.

Challenge—Story 1

You know it's not going to end well when your boss starts a conversation with, "This is the hardest thing I've ever had to do."

My wife and I had two young kids, a mortgage we couldn't afford, and an idyllic life in the house of our dreams. I had recently left a well-paying job that took me away from home at a rate that had become destructive to our family life and accepted an administrative position at a well-known college.

And then it ended. The program I managed was cut back and my job eliminated. I was angry, terrified, and embarrassed, thinking others would assume I was fired for incompetence. This was the worst moment of my life. And though

I didn't know it at the time, it was also one of the best moments because I was about to learn some profound lessons.

Angry and frustrated, I called a well-connected mentor and friend at another university and unloaded. I hoped she would offer me a job. Instead, she told me to get over it and hung up. Moving on is easier said than done.

Nights were the worst. I'd sleep for several hours and then toss and turn until morning. Sometimes I'd sit in the dark living room thinking about how unfair everything was. I'd pray and cry. When Saint John of the Cross wrote of "the dark night of the soul," he wasn't exaggerating.

I was at the end of my rope. Desperate, I prayed at 2:30 one morning: "Lord, I can't do this anymore. I can't get past my anger at the college for what has happened. I can't wish away my fear. This burden is too heavy for me to carry. I can't seem to let it go; you will have to take it away."

I relaxed, and a sense of peace like I'd never experienced before literally swept over me. The next thing I knew, it was 8:00 a.m. I had not slept that late in years. From that point on, I could sleep again. Though it didn't change my circumstances, I learned I had to let go of everything—anger, fear, frustration—before I could experience God's healing touch. The former was a conscious, rational choice; the latter was the powerful work of God.[18]

Challenge—Story 2

Okeyo was eager to attend this Christ-centered college in the U.S. and was off to an exciting start. Then he noticed a marked change in his health. He reported that he seemed cold and had difficulty walking up a flight of stairs.

He made it through the first semester, stopping in to the health center many times. In the beginning of his second semester, a friend found him struggling for air and burning hot. He was rushed to the emergency room. His breathing was labored and painful as he experienced septic shock and cardiac arrest. The medical people did what they could to stabilize him but he needed to be flown to the Cleveland clinic. He survived the flight, but initial surgery to repair the mitral valve leakage was unsuccessful as the heart ruptured, requiring heart massage while a second surgery was performed.

A Cleveland alum physician and several students came to Cleveland to support their friend. The alum knew that if Okeyo's situation didn't improve, doctors would recommend custodial treatment. His friends helped the doctors recognize that there was improvement even though Okeyo's brain did not comprehend the English commands of the doctors. Once an interpreter was brought in, it was clear that Okeyo was doing better.

Okeyo recalls that this period was a significant point in his life. He recalls that "it was spiritual. It did not occur to me to ask God, 'Why?' during these days. But I did ask God, 'Will I live?' I remember the answer clearly and it was, yes."

Back at college, Okeyo had to take speech therapy as well as relearn walking, talking, eating, and waiting. Again, alumni and others responded with getting Okeyo to his many appointments.

In early November, Okeyo started coughing and the increased heart rate meant something bad was happening. The heart patch was coming off. Another trip to the Cleveland Clinic and repair was in order. But soon, the symptoms of heart failure returned and staff and alumni jumped in to transport Okeyo to the University of Michigan where it was hoped that he would be admitted as a special case. They found mold on one of his valves and his left ventricle failing and another surgery ensued. Alum and others knowledgeable of the situation provided housing and support as Okeyo tried to heal from this fourth surgery.

Six weeks later as Okeyo returned to the college, he learned that the patch was again coming loose, so back to the University of Michigan for surgery number five.

On long-term antibiotics, Okeyo returned to classes but found himself without energy and feeling depressed. Concerned, the associate chaplain drove Okeyo back to the University of Michigan, where it was determined that a heart transplant was the only option. But now there were visa problems and health insurance challenges due to his long absences from school. Dedicated college staff members and doctors at the University of Michigan negotiated the many hurdles. Now, they had to wait for a heart.

"My breathing was difficult, and I was put on nitric oxide," Okeyo said. "My heart was literally tearing apart as the sutured mitral value was pulling out of place." Then, everything went black. When he awoke, his doctor came in and told him a heart had been found and his survival was a miracle.

It is not lost on Okeyo that the college's seal contains the picture of a heart in a hand. He repeated the words of the college motto—"My heart I offer"—and concluded, "I take this as God's sign that I was called to be here. This is His call to me."[19]

The Vision Story

The final type of story is one that describes a positive future for the university, mitigating current challenges or problems. For example, the current demographics of the United States will force every institution of higher education to rethink its targeted student populations. Few will be able to draw on the same demographic of the past decades. Similarly, many institutions are finding that they cannot continue to increase the discount rate offered to students in order to bolster enrollments without diminishing the bottom line. The future scenario must be powerful enough to allow the audience to envision possibilities of reaching that future.

Since the future is not guaranteed, stories used to describe the future are not static. Yet a future story can still be described as a truth story, for it reflects current reality, including values and mission, and extends these boldly into a future replete with opportunities. The vision story is intended to engage every listener as a planner, implementer, or minimally as a cheerleader, for the steps that must be taken collectively to achieve the positive future.

Vision—Story 1

I had the opportunity to attend the Harvard Management Institute for Higher Education Executives in the summer of 2000. One of the most popular speakers to this group was a well-known Harvard professor.

Always a storyteller, our speaker told this brief story before proceeding to others. I remember what a great storyteller he was. There was not even a rustle of paper as 150 people listened. Here is what he shared:

In the days when students were assigned to an advising professor, a student came to our speaker with the information that he would be leaving Harvard. When asked why he would leave, the student responded simply, recalling an incident that made the critical difference. He told our speaker that he was waiting with a group of students for his professor to arrive and open the door so that classes could commence. The professor finally arrived, well past the starting time of the class, and upon noting that the door was locked proceeded to call maintenance to open the door.

Several minutes later, the maintenance person arrived, and the faculty member began to berate him in very strong language. Things like "stupid," "lazy," "incompetent" were the words that could be repeated. The student said that once all students were settled in the classroom, the professor continued to grouse about the incompetent maintenance staff. Then he began his lecture on "moral leadership."

The student confidently told our speaker: "I think I can find better examples of moral leadership at another institution of higher education."

The details of this story may be a bit fuzzy to me some years later, but the message has always been crystal clear. Our behavior has to fit our lives and our teaching. The "do as I say," rather than "do as I do" model has never worked very well for anyone, least of all for teachers. The second message is harder. We must constantly be self-reflective and self-regulating so that when we are tired, busy with other things, or angry with another, we can avoid slipping into dangerous territory and risk the loss of confidence by those important to us.

Do you suppose there are many who know of similar stories? While we know of the young man's Harvard experience, we do not know what happened to him. We can be inspired, however, by his decision to seek a consonant life of purpose and integrity. That is my desire for all of us as we lead this year and beyond. May God grant it![20]

Vision—Story 2

In contrast to Stephen Carter's book, The Culture of Disbelief, *our college has, in contrast, a culture of belief. One of the geniuses of this college lies in the capaciousness of its motto: "Culture for Service." This motto has been wide enough to contain all of the liberating arts and sciences, and emphasis on the Jesus-way of peacemaking, and care for our neighbors here and around the world.*

When I was trying to decide whether to accept the call for candidacy for this position, I read an article about one of our recent graduates, Alicia Showalter Reynolds, in the Baltimore Sun. *Alicia had been abducted March 2 and had not been heard of since. Let me share an excerpt:*

Mrs. Reynolds, a doctoral candidate in pharmacology at the Johns Hopkins School of Medicine, was described as being a devout Mennonite whose love for the education she received at Goshen College in Indiana led her to aspire to become a college professor.

"She had some women that were influential in her life that were very good science professors, but she said there weren't enough women," said Amy Clemens, a pediatric cancer nurse at Hopkins Hospital who had befriended Mrs. Reynolds at Goshen. "She said she wanted to be a good role model for women in science." . . . At Hopkins, Mrs. Reynolds was trying to devise a vaccine to ward off schistosomiasis, a tropical parasite disease afflicting 250 million people each year.

These words describe for me what "Culture for Service" means in practice. It is rooted in love, it seeks justice, it is intellectual and spiritual work of the highest order. The spirit of Alice Showalter Reynolds will never die. And where better to keep that spirit alive than at her alma mater?[21]

Tips for Storytellers

We live in a story-filled world. For all who want to introduce stories in their calling as leaders, the following suggestions can aid in preparing to include clear, succinct, well-positioned stories in their presentations.

- **Listen for stories**

  Stories are all around us. Some inspire and motivate, while others fall flat. Listen to the stories told by others in daily conversations. A story is told because the storyteller believes it has human interest and an important point to make. Listen for stories that contain memorable gems and have the potential to sharpen the effectiveness of your communication. The lives of leaders, drawn from history, literature, or contemporary society—as well as members of your own workplace—provide a wealth of material. For example, Steve Jobs shaped his commencement address to the Stanford class of 2005 around three stories, telling of his dropping out of college, being fired by

Apple, and facing a life-threatening cancer.[22] Each story held the audience and reinforced his point, a single life lesson—find the things you love.

- **Write out the story**

  As you think about the story you will tell, writing the story will help to organize the beginning, body, climax, and ending (the resolution). Your story should have a thesis and should draw in your listeners—taking the time to craft the details and shape of your narrative will give it greater effect.

- **Review your story**

  Read your written story aloud to yourself. Ask yourself whether there is a good flow. Will the audience be able to visualize the story in their minds? Ask whether there are descriptive words that can paint a clearer picture in the listener's mind. In speaking the story out loud, you may remember new details that add depth to the story. Finally, ask whether the story energizes you; if not, it likely will not energize listeners!

- **Try it out on others**

  Try your story out on another colleague or family member. Ask for feedback, including whether the purpose or point you wanted to make is clear. Ask whether the story provides a visual picture of what is going on in the story. Feedback should include whether the story is the right length for your presentation. Finally, ask whether the story relates or rings true for the listener—does it address the question of "what is in this for me?" You may want to rework the story based on the feedback you receive. Trying a story out with someone else and making appropriate revisions can give you confidence that the final story is right for your presentation. Practicing on others will also help because great storytelling is performance. The more you do it, the easier and better your storytelling becomes.

- **Do it now**

  Before you move on, create your own "Who I Am" story. Think about your experiences in life where you were challenged, overcame a great obstacle, did something foolish, or accomplished a goal that was beyond your expectations. What were the shaping experiences or moments? Relate these elements in your personal story. Identify the purpose or point of your story that you want your listeners to walk away with. Follow the tips above. Enjoy the experience.

From Practice to Primetime

As you sharpen your own stories, you will want to look for opportunities within your organization to practice. Practice is essential for the emerging storyteller to become a great storyteller. This practice could be in a newly forming team or in one where you are currently a member, perhaps its leader. Teams usually meet to gain consensus in recurring business, to address challenges, to reinforce team expectations, or to envision the future. Team meetings are an ideal place to inaugurate your personal or collected stories—stories that create an environment for overcoming obstacles, sharing values, building customer satisfaction, and achieving organizational objectives.

When you share your stories with others, they may also then look for stories that likewise share and reinforce the purposes of your organization. Those in higher education will find that stories about students and employees are a great repertoire that can serve institutional purposes. Practice in telling stories will bring truths and values that will become part of your organizational culture. The challenge is to take the risk of being authentic in your storytelling, revealing humanity as you lead.

This chapter's final story demonstrates how one higher education leader used the power of storytelling to begin a new senior administrative role. This is what she shared with colleagues in a leadership institute:

> *Greetings to you all! . . . The president at my university introduced me to the faculty and staff in a special meeting Monday afternoon as the new provost. I have been warmly received and am excited about the opportunity. As you can imagine, I have been on a whirlwind ever since. I literally moved into my office Monday night and started meetings on Tuesday—it's been nonstop since.*

I was asked to speak at this meeting Monday and use what we have been learning on "stories" and vocational calling from our time together to tell a little bit of my story. I started out by telling them that if I were in their shoes, they would be wondering, "who I am," "how I got there" and "where do we go from here."...I told them two short stories to give them an idea of who I am and one story on my calling ... the question of "where do we go from here?" will come later.[23]

This leader was able to leverage the shape and content of leadership stories to establish a connection with the university community, also communicating a vision for the university's future. My hope is that you, too, will be able to use storytelling as a practical asset in your work as a leader. The challenges of leadership in the decades ahead require powerful communication tools. One of the best of these is storytelling.

Notes to Chapter Four

1. Annette Simmons, *The Story Factor: Inspiration, Influence, and Persuasion Through the Art of Storytelling*. Simmons identifies six story types, of which four are used in this chapter.

2. Howard Gardner, *Leading Minds: An Anatomy of Leadership,*9–10, 42–57. See also Stephen Denning, *The Leader's Guide to Storytelling,* 9, and Peter Senge, *The Fifth Discipline: The Art and Practice of the Learning Organization,* 10–11.

3. Noel M. Tichy with Eli Cohen, *The Leadership Engine,* 173.

4. Amy Sample-Ward, "Telling Stories."

5. Randolph T. Barker and Kim Gower, "Strategic Application of Storytelling in Organizations," 302.

6. Robert McKee, "Storytelling That Moves People," 53.

7. Stephen Denning, *The Secret Language of Leadership,* 36.

8. Simmons, *The Story Factor,* 8–26.

9. Ibid., 8–12.

10. Ibid., 3.

11. Gardner, *Leading Minds,* 10. Emphasis added.

12. Gail Sheehy, *New Passages,* 169.

13. Richard Felix report to the Board of Trustees at Azusa Pacific University, Spring 2000.

14. Shirley A. Mullin, "Leadership."

15. Author's memory of a foundational story at one institution.

16. Act Six was a program to increase institutional diversity at this university.

17. George Fox University, University Response to Campus Incident, Presidential Response, September 24, 2010, available online at http://www.georgefox.edu/featured_stories/campus_incident_students.html.

18. D. Merrill Ewert, "Fired: Seven Lessons of Unemployment." Used with permission. As indicated in this article's subtitle, the author shares seven lessons he learned from his period of unemployment; "letting it go" is the first of those.

19. Story summarized from Mike Van Denend's "Heart in Hand."

20. Author's notes, Harvard University, Institute of Executive Management, July 2000.

21. Shirley Hershey Showalter, Presidential Inaugural Address; the *Baltimore Sun* article is by David Folkenflik.

22. Steve Jobs, Commencement Address, Stanford University, June 14, 2005.

23. Mary Jones, email July 16, 2008, to author and others.

For Discussion

1. What are the significant stories from your organization's history that best reflect its values?

2. Can you retell at least two stories that reflect your organization's mission and vision? If not, identify key individuals you will meet with to gather information in order to learn these stories.

3. Do you believe that stories recounting hard work and achievement are more powerful to audiences than those recounting adversity and overcoming? What makes the difference?

4. There are undoubtedly some organizational or personal stories that are not ready for "prime time" in your organization. Identify some of these with your colleagues and discuss what makes a story ready for telling.

5. Rewrite your personal introductory "Who I Am" story, sharing your values, including how you faced and overcame adversity.

6. Start your collection of stories by recalling a story about:

    a. A student overcoming a significant challenge.

    b. Teamwork run amok and survival.

    c. A leadership mistake and success.

    d. A personal challenge overcome.

    e. A decision that made "all the difference."

    f. An institutional misstep that was overcome.

7. What story best reflects your personal overcoming of adversity? What were the key themes that still guide your life?

Chapter Five

THE DIFFERENCE
TRUST MAKES

Shirley V. Hoogstra

"The trust level is the thermometer of individual and group health."

—JACK GIBB, Trust: A New View of Personal and Organizational Development

"With integrity and transparency, you create trust."

—RONALD J. NYDAM, professor of pastoral care, Calvin Theological Seminary

I lead a group of senior leaders who meet every other week.[1] One meeting is a two-hour discussion about policy and programs; the other is a one-hour "round table" gathering. The purpose of the round table is simply to share—each member has six uninterrupted minutes to convey what is happening in our areas of responsibility and to talk about what's on our minds professionally or personally so we can pray as a group.[2] Our director of career development, who has training as a counselor/therapist, suggested this discipline of uninterrupted sharing and listening, and I think most of us look forward more to this meeting than any other.

At a recent round table, our director of campus safety—who looks as protective as his job title sounds, a firearm snug on his belt—started the discussion. He was eager to thank his colleagues in the counseling center and residence life for offering a helpful training session on the college's new mental health policy.[3] He felt that the training had been an example of effective collaboration, where his team came away knowing they were part of a supportive network of professionals who genuinely cared about them.

"Our new policy is an example of innovative thinking," he told us. "I am proud to have such capable colleagues to work with."

That simple but sincere affirmation set the tone for the next fifty-four minutes. It was a reflection of what happens when a senior leadership team is marked by trust.

Trust is the single most important key to effective leadership, but it can be difficult to define, let alone build. Modeled well, it is distinguished when individual members respect each other personally and professionally. They collaborate with their fellow directors and deans to make the larger organization better. They give honest feedback to each other, usually privately, but also in the group setting because they know they can without risking the team relationships. When they are frustrated with each other, they follow up and try to determine why the communication stream is blocked or ideas are misunderstood. When there is trust, the team moves on after mistakes are made or members have been unintentionally overlooked. A colleague's absence from a strategic meeting need not be interpreted as a lack of commitment or a professional snub. In fact, such imperfection is generally received with charity, because the team members have high trust and they seek to practice trustworthy behavior—that is, consistent, principled actions that guide them each working day.

The individual competencies and personalities of the team contribute to a sense of individual and collective flourishing. The team's commitment to high trust is non-negotiable, and consistent efforts to engage in trustworthy behavior contribute to this flourishing. Obviously, it is not difficult to know and believe that trusting teams are better than cynical teams, or that loving teams are better than fearful teams. Nonetheless, creating such teams, empowering them, and participating in them, is no easy task. Such teams require deep commitment, perseverance, and prayer, but they are critical for an institution's impact on the world.

The famous phrase "You know it when you see it" is true about trust. I've experienced trust between people and within groups and organizations, as have most leaders. Psychologist Jack Gibb, an early writer on organizational trust, has noted:

Trust enhances the flow of mind-body-spirit processes. Energy is created and mobilized. All the creative processes of a person or system are heightened. Feeling and thinking are both more focused and energized. People act in more direct and effective ways. Consciousness is awakened. When trust is high enough, persons and social systems transcend apparent limits—discovering new and awesome abilities of which they were previously unaware.[4]

Yet Gibb also notes the converse—that is, what happens when fear defines a system rather than trust:

When fear levels are high, relative to trust, individuals and social processes are impaired. The life forces are mobilized defensively. Consciousness is restricted. Perceptivity is reduced. Perspectives are narrowed. Feelings and emotions become disruptive and disabling. Thinking, problem solving, and action become unfocused, displaced, and dysfunctional. The processes of the mind-body become segmented and discordant. When fear levels are high enough, individuals and social systems become immobilized, psychotic, or disruptive.[5]

One need only consider the fear-based society, vividly portrayed in Eric Metaxas's biography of Dietrich Bonhoeffer in Hitler's Germany,[6] to understand this.

Fear-based systems can occur on a smaller scale in institutions or organizations. Especially in an academic environment where ideas should be freely explored and opinions expressed, fear can unfortunately be fueled when peers or administrators treat a colleague rudely, when fewer resources are distributed to particular departments, or when the process of promotion or tenure is made difficult through ostracizing or marginalizing a person. A culture of fear can undermine the fulfillment of an organization's mission. Therefore, the leadership of any organization must make building and sustaining trust a priority and an essential characteristic of organizational culture. Even when mistrust is observable, a culture can be changed over time with wise leadership.

For the Other:
Building Trust with and between Colleagues

Trust is built when we want the best for our colleagues, when we are *for* them regardless of what they have done or can do for us in the future. Being *for* another assumes community is valued and nurtured, which too often runs counter to the individualism within much of higher education. A classic joke among provosts and deans reinforces this: "When faculty members take a survey to measure institutional climate, how do they respond to the statement, 'Your boss treats you with respect'? By filling in the circle 'not applicable.'"

Individualism, then, is frequently seen as an inherent by-product of the faculty member's very job: a professor teaches in an independent classroom; does independent scholarship; attends and presents independent work at conferences rarely attended by institutional colleagues. But when we seek to understand each other and the roles we play, we are a step closer to establishing trust and learning what it means to be *for* the other, promoting authentic community rather than individualism. Yet, when we do not acknowledge the formal and necessary structural arrangements and responsibilities that exist in all institutions, we impede the ability to have empathy and tolerance for either our administrators or our faculty members.

Being *for* the other is helped not only when we understand roles but when we value the responsibilities of the other. It is a commitment to truly knowing each other. A telling example of this surfaced when Jenell Williams Paris, an admired faculty member and author, visited my institution to lecture on her recent book. She had previously attended a leadership development institute at which I was one of the facilitators.[7] As we were talking, she told me that her time at the leadership institute had been an excellent learning experience in two important ways: First, it helped her to see her vocational call was not to administrative leadership, but to the classroom and scholarship. Second, she realized as an anthropologist that being at the leadership institute had been a cross-cultural experience for her as a faculty member. Previously, she had not clearly understood the language, responsibilities, needs, and perspectives of administrators. After the institute, she acted differently toward the administrators at her own college; she was more empathetic, more attuned to how she could collaborate with them. She began to see the importance of an institutional identity that could be complementary to her life as a scholar and a "member of the guild." What she described was her ability to be *for* the other, *for* her administrative leadership.

Being *for* the other is also important to administrative leaders who genuinely value the work of faculty. One senior administrator learned this first-hand when she decided to team-teach an intensive January term course with an experienced faculty member. The class met for four hours straight each day for a month. The administrator had other responsibilities, but no ongoing scholarship or publication expectations. The first week was exhilarating, the team-teaching enjoyable. Organizing the syllabus had been intellectually captivating, and the students were engaged.

By the end of the second week, there was some fatigue. The third week became more difficult. Four hours was a lot of time to fill each day, and the students weren't always participating. Papers assigned and handed in for grading seemed less of a good idea. Staying on top of the reading and adjusting the syllabus as the class progressed took considerably more effort than anticipated. By the end of the four weeks, the administrator described the experience as "really hard work," even though it was a team-taught class.

When staff and administrators minimize the strenuous nature of excellent, up-to-date, research-informed teaching, they undercut trust and are not *for* the other in the hard work of teaching. When a quip is heard that faculty only work three days a week and leave by 3:00 p.m., that flippant remark damages trust. Likewise, when faculty mumble, "What do administrators do all day, anyway?" trust again is undercut. By understanding and extending a charitable mindset to those who do different but important work, trust is built.

Another element that defines the concept of being *for* the other is what I call "having your back." Equally crucial in higher education, *having your back* implies some behavior that has a risk-taking edge, a possible element of danger—one that might negatively affect the reputation of the scholar, administrator, or institution. These are harder calls, requiring humble discernment. Author and psychologist Henry Cloud describes how "having another's back" is essential in organizations that want to be known for establishing high-trust environments. Cloud distinguishes the interconnection between high trust and leadership that "looks out for your interest as well as his or her own interest." Cloud also notes that although some colleagues might not lie or steal and might keep their word, they rarely think of what is best for those around them, over and above what is good for them. This self-involvement is why we all decide to get some things in writing.[8]

In contrast, when both faculty and administrators feel that others support them, they can let down their guard; this usually occurs because both sides are trusting that the other will be looking out for their interests. When this happens, Cloud asserts, organizations are more productive because "people get open, creative, take risks, learn from each other and deliver fruits in whatever their endeavor to a much more leveraged degree than if they were in the protection mode."[9] The high trust is mutually beneficial, with individuals able to say, "I am going to go to bat for you, and I know I can count on you to do the same."

Faculty expect that their hard efforts at scholarship will be supported by the administration, who will also be proud of their work, promote it, and defend it. As professors trust the administrative leadership, they begin to view their scholarship as both a contribution to their field and to the larger organization's reputation, as well as their own. Administrators also want to be the kind of people who support the work of the academy—and faculty are the heart of the academy. Administrators may not be called to a specific research agenda, but they have legitimate responsibilities as keepers and spokespersons of the institution's mission and identity to their communities and trustees. Faculty members cover their administrators' backs by keeping them informed about cutting-edge, or perhaps controversial, scholarship. This dance between academic freedom and institutional support is delicate, but vital to long-term institutional thriving.

The Secrets of Trust

Confidentiality is another aspect that builds trust within teams and organizations. Countless scenarios require facts or ideas to be held tightly in a group. Perhaps some information is time sensitive; though it will become public later, it is now in the planning stages and needs to be kept confidential. Perhaps there are federal regulations that limit dissemination of the information. Perhaps a leader needs advice about a troubling situation and seeks the wise counsel of another.

Yet, when we share confidential information with a colleague either about our shared work or our own lives, it can feel risky. Will that person be able to hold the material without leaking it to someone else? If information is power, will the person entrusted with confidential information be tempted to abuse that power? Secretary of State Hillary Clinton pointed out such a tension when she noted (in response to the WikiLeaks news), "In almost every profession—whether it's law or journalism, finance or medicine or academia or running a small business—people rely on confidential communications to do their jobs. We count on the space of trust that confidentiality provides. When someone breaches that trust, we are all worse off for it."[10]

So, keeping confidence is a practice that improves with practice; doing so also builds an individual's reputation for integrity. In some ways, confidence seems like a small, certainly singular, action in trust building. Yet, keeping the confidence of another is foundational for building other trust qualities in an organization. Trustworthy behavior in one individual can inspire others to be the same, thereby contributing to culture change.

Providing regular, professional feedback loops that are confidential, honest, and supportive builds trust between colleagues and within an organization. Such trust is evident when I co-host a PBS program called *Inner Compass*, produced at Calvin College.[11] The co-hosts, sound specialists, engineers, researchers, producers, and director are a close working team. We have high trust that allows us to work nimbly on getting the "shoots" prepared, recorded, edited, and ready for national broadcast. This agility is crucial, since the nature of interviewing is dynamic and challenging. Guests might be experienced and know how to give succinct answers, but the opposite might also be the case. The topics our program covers can be deeply philosophical or depend on compelling narrative. The producers want the show to be great—which requires giving immediate corrective feedback to the co-hosts. Because co-hosts perform, often with thousands of people enjoying and critiquing each show, producers must provide feedback succinctly and clearly. They have honed the art of good feedback, based on support, confidentiality, and evidence, and they offer it regularly, with each communication bettering our overall performance.

Our main producer also takes pains to listen well to any observations I have about the particular show we are discussing. She brings a unique humility to such exchanges, with the goal of delivering the best possible programming. This kind of mutuality invites the listener—including co-hosts like me—to take a non-defensive posture.

In a similar way, a good annual review process can serve to build institutional trust. A good performance review process, done well and with confidentiality, requires significant preparation on the part of the evaluator. For instance, I consider my employees' self-evaluation carefully, marking notes on work performance that has been exemplary. I try to identify the unique contributions of each colleague, and craft the language in a way that is accurate and honoring of the colleague's hard work. If there are areas of performance needing improvement, I offer examples and suggestions. And I typically consult only with the director of human resources to ensure that my language and suggestions meet with the best practices of the profession. I check to see if there are any professional development resources to assist the employee in improving, maintaining confidentiality throughout the process.

In other words, members of an organization are honored when supervisors spend the time and effort to fairly and confidentially evaluate them with a constructive and developmental plan. The supervisor can convey gratitude for the individual's contribution to the larger mission and, if necessary, address troubling behavior before it causes professional damage. The yearly evaluation can thus be a time to affirm direct reports, reinforce trust, and coach individuals in the development of their skills and gifts.

We have all experienced employees who are no longer seen as positive contributors to the organization, disrupting a culture's trust. Perhaps the opinion is justified, but the employee may also have lacked developmental feedback—"No one ever told me." Whether true or false, a person who is let go and feels blindsided can negatively affect the trust and morale for the other members of the organization. Likewise, an employee who has consistent unproductive behavior that is not addressed also negatively affects trust.

The Fun of Trust

While misperceptions and the breaking of confidentiality can be detrimental to an organization's trust, playfulness alongside work can build—or repair—it. Retreats with teams are not a waste of time because they foster relationships of a broader nature. I am a latecomer to the belief that retreats add real value to organizational success. In fact, they function like an investment in the future—for that inevitable day when trust is tested.

In one corporate board setting, I realized how helpful the investment of time was when some business on our agenda required restructuring. As we confronted necessary changes, we did so as a team, buoyed by common experience from previous positive retreat experiences. We knew each other well because we had each invested in time away to talk about what mattered to us. We had put some muscle on the skeleton of a group of board members. The trust account was high.

Cultivating a spirit of gratitude within the organization also serves to bolster trust. A prior mentor of mine and one of Connecticut's fierce trial lawyers, Howard A. Jacobs, often advised me to "never miss an opportunity to celebrate."[12] His perspective was profoundly wise, shaping my leadership to include regular celebrations of small and large "wins."

Each time an organization celebrates, it conveys that we don't take people and their efforts for granted. Far too often, faith-based institutions expect people to give their all without complaining because they "work unto the Lord." Celebrations and acknowledgments of the real contributions made add to the joy of a job well done, together.

Such was the case after our student life division, along with faculty colleges, designed and implemented a new first-year seminar initiative. The course was launched and met with both "glows and grows." The division had completed an enormous assignment with creativity, collaboration, and optimism. To celebrate the year of planning and the successful inauguration of the course, the student life professionals and faculty involved all went to a local BBQ restaurant for wings, meatballs, and karaoke, a small expense to reward a hard-working team of people. By celebrating with a fun evening, we built morale and trust for later challenges and harder assignments. My mentor was right.

Trust That Serves Students

Certainly, as is true for the administration, faculty, and staff who run universities, being *for* young people—having their backs, honoring confidentiality, and celebrating with them—builds crucial trust for student retention and alumni success. But building trust with tomorrow's scholars, servants, and leaders sometimes demands a different approach than doing so with adults further along in their careers.

While leadership sets the tone in an institution, modeling it for students requires a teachable spirit. We simply don't know, or have to know, everything. Consequently, we can value and show gratitude to others who have more expertise. And when a leader shows the grace to defer to others, those around often extend grace back to that leader, and to each other. If we share a Christian faith, we have been recipients of the abundant grace of a loving God. Mirroring God's grace to ourselves and to those with whom we work softens our shared environment.

Creating an environment that has grace as its soil allows the community to handle mistakes carefully. Nothing eats at the trusting environment more than reacting with assumptions when a mistake is made. Obviously, mistakes will happen in an institution's life as well as in an individual's life, and when they do, we are often at our lowest, most vulnerable point. We rarely need others to remind us of our imperfections.

As the senior student affairs officer, I am responsible for enforcing the university's rules and carrying out the institution's initiatives—thankfully, with a group of trusted fellow professionals. But I have always believed that the "buck stops" with the senior person, a tension tested the year my son was a junior at the college.

By all accounts, Dave was a hard working, thoughtful student who loved his mother and respected authorities. Yet there was also a problem in the college's off-campus housing practices. It was a broken system, and we had an unfortunate institutional practice of avoiding fixing it. The college's culture often disregarded the zoning ordinances of our city, which required that "no more than four unrelated people [live in] a house within city limits." Ignoring the rule saved students money, allowed them to live with the friends they wanted, and brought landlords higher rent, three significant motivators. The city did not have the enforcement power to address all the many out-of-compliance student houses. With so many colleges and universities in the city, a disregard of the zoning ordinance was widespread.

My son wanted to live with his four best friends, together making five, a housing arrangement that was out of compliance with the zoning ordinance. We respectfully talked about it in the summer as a mom and her son. I advised him that the arrangement was problematic but allowed him to make the final call. He knew that my role as vice president for student life brought added scrutiny for him in any situation.

With the economic downturn, housing values fell, as did the ability to sell real estate quickly. Neighbors in some city sections increased their awareness and surveillance of overcrowded student housing because it was potentially affecting resale value and, in some instances, quality of life. Off-campus, overcrowded student housing was easily identified because of cars, noise, and sometimes party behavior out of character with the rest of the block.

The situation grew to crisis proportions. Nearby neighbor associations complained to the college, saying we had acted too slowly. At the beginning of the school year, neighbors adjacent to our campus organized with the local authorities to serve students with eviction notices, and to serve landlords with zoning violations notices, as was their right. The college had to act and think quickly about how to care for students in a housing crisis, how to respond with integrity to a present problem, and how to move into the future with integrity.

My dean and I called a meeting with students. They were angry and believed the college had caused the evictions. We explained that we had not given the police student addresses, but we did believe it was within the city's prerogative to enforce the zoning ordinance and that the students should seek other housing. I did not mention my own son's living situation at the meeting, and he did not live in a neighborhood that was going to activate evictions. But another young man confronted me after the meeting, asking how I could tell other students to comply when my own son's living arrangement was not in compliance. He was right. This was a very teachable moment for me, and for my son.

I wrestled with my own response. I believed that a young man, even if a son, was allowed to make independent decisions and take whatever consequences followed. I also believed I made a mistake in not disclosing my personal situation. My son, watching this unfold, came to me immediately with the news that he was going to move out of his house in order to live in compliance with the ordinance. Within twelve hours, a group of other students, who had heard that Dave was moving out, called and invited him to live with them. I also decided that I needed to own my mistake to all of the upper class students. I wrote an email to these two thousand students, telling them of my mistake and asking them to forgive my shortcoming.

Interestingly, many students expressed appreciation. They responded by extending grace to me and also to my son. Clearing the air further allowed me to model what other parents, and even board members and faculty landlords were realizing—that we had made a mistake, but we were able to make the situation right.

As a result, we did the following: I asked my deans to organize student meetings to do some case-based problem solving. I was a participant, not a leader, in those meetings, giving me a better platform to listen. I asked another dean to organize a neighborhood association meeting, and the police were invited to share their perspective. We formed an internal task force in the division to develop a plan that encompassed the feasibility of promoting and enforcing housing ordinance compliance for off-campus students. We came to an agreement to enforce the requirement for students to live with no more than four unrelated persons. We agreed upon the next steps, developing a communication plan in which the deans would talk to student groups and I would talk with the student life committee, the board of trustees, and the mayor of the city.

We presented our case for change to all involved and asked for their participation and endorsement. The results went beyond our best expectations. Students reported that some landlords lowered the rent when the students no longer would collude with them to disregard zoning rules; students rented duplexes; and students complied with the law, enjoying the benefits of no overcrowding. The neighbors stopped complaining and respected the college. Students appreciated the clarity and the call to living respectfully and responsibly.

This outcome was successful because stakeholders were included, the solution was supported by those involved, and there was a good communication plan. The bottom line, though, was that trust was built through a series of actions: college officials helped students who lost their housing and involved students in problem solving; college officials also were transparent about the options and showed a teachable spirit. Each step served our students with a sense of integrity and trust, which is an important goal, after all, of Christian higher education.

Building Lasting Trust

Certainly, there are a number of other ways to help students understand the value of trust. We must spend time praying for and challenging them to move beyond fears and insecurities to bonds of commitment and dedication. We must model for them how to extend and receive grace. We must provide for them opportunities that stretch them—and us—in new ways. That might mean attending a political event together or sitting with them at a hospital when a tragedy occurs. It could be as simple as attending a basketball game or as significant as mentoring a young couple as they consider ministry in a developing country.

The point is that no amount of intellectual assent about trust in leadership replaces the simple power of presence. Time spent with students and with colleagues, whether faculty, staff, or administrators, has more capacity to build trust than a thousand chapters in a hundred texts.

But trust does not magically appear in our lives and colleges. It is cultivated in our trust in God; that is our center point from which all other trust is built, and it grows from our nourishment by the fruit of the Spirit.[13] Such development requires good self-care that nurtures essential attributes of a healthy and reflective life: taking regular Sabbaths and vacations, having an accountability group, spending time away from electronic media and pressing obligations, giving intentional space for God. For me, practicing habits of faith communally—perhaps regular chapel attendance on campus —strengthens my connection to the source of trustworthy behavior and faithfulness, Jesus Christ.

That trust becomes our rock, during the most tragic times on campuses and during the most joyous. Without trust, an institution's capacity for greatness and fulfilling its mission is stunted. With trust, people thrive, the mission lives, and God is glorified.

Notes to Chapter Five

1. The student life senior leadership team is comprised of eight professionals who lead teams in these areas: the counseling center, health services, campus safety, campus ministries, residence life, living learning communities, career development and internships, international students, student activities and weekend programming, service learning, multicultural students, orientation, and student leadership programs.

2. We have found out how hard it is to truly listen to each other without interrupting, even if saying words of support or asking questions for deeper understanding. The affirming comments and questions are well-intentioned, but the goal is for the speaker to be able to create and direct the time for his or her purposes. It is only six minutes—kept with two small three-minute egg timers that we flip over—and yet the activity is harder than you might think and more rewarding than you might imagine when done well.

3. More and more students who have mental health challenges are succeeding in college with the help of medication and counseling. This is a national trend. There are times when someone's medication is not working or someone is in crisis prior to the onset of good treatment. During the day, professional counseling staff are always ready to respond to the crisis. But at night, residence life staff and campus safety officers desired more support as they responded to suicidal or violent situations. Three leaders (in counseling, campus safety, and residence life) met and devised a plan with our local mental health hospital to provide access to a 24/7 crisis hotline. The new protocol outlined the process and procedures for managing the crisis and getting the student safe and effective care at the local hospital or mental health treatment center.

4. Jack Gibb, *Trust: A New View of Personal and Organizational Development*, 16.

5. Ibid.

6. Eric Metaxas, *Bonhoeffer*.

7. The Council for Christian Colleges & Universities has sponsored bi-annual Leadership Development Institutes (LDIs) equipping men, women, and persons of color for senior leadership. The CCCU Women's Leadership Development Institute (WLDI) has been offered on eight occasions between 1998 and 2012. Statistics from 1998 to 2008 indicate that 105 women identified by their campuses as emerging leaders have participated in the year-long leadership development program launched at the Institute; 55 women participated over the same period in a parallel series of mixed Leadership Development Institutes involving both men and women.

    The impact of these LDIs and WLDIs on participants has been measurable and catalytic to their advancement within the CCCU. A then-and-now assessment of the women who participated between 1998 and 2008 revealed that over 50 percent of the female participants had moved into more advanced positions on their campus or elsewhere. Advancements by women attending the LDI include 3 provosts, 5 vice presidents, 8 deans, 3 directors, and 6 faculty rank advancements. The WLDI advancements include 2 presidents, 7 provosts, 11 vice presidents, 14 deans, 9 directors, and 11 faculty rank advancements.

8. Henry Cloud, *Integrity*, 76–80.

9. Ibid.

10. A *PanArmenian* article, "Clinton: disclosure classified information an attack on international community," summarizes Hillary Clinton's condemnation of the illegal disclosure of classified information in November of 2010.

11. Inner Compass aims to capture refreshingly candid conversations with articulate people who have thought broadly and deeply about issues that matter. The show doesn't tell you what to think, but just helps you nourish and exercise your own conscience as you listen to how others have tuned theirs. The show has a dedicated producer who is thoughtful and a risk-taker. She must be, to book guests and steer shows to the questions of life that can be messy. She is not afraid of conflict but sees the growth that can take place when the truth is discussed or unpacked in meaningful ways, both on the show and in her relationships. The show's website is available at http://www.calvin.edu/innercompass/.

12. Howard A. Jacobs was born in New Haven in 1924. He received a BA from the University of Michigan in 1945 and graduated with distinction from its law school in 1947. Howard served as president of the Connecticut Trial Lawyers Association in 1961–62. For more than fifty years, he was heavily involved in criminal defense, personal injury, and domestic relations litigation. He represented thousands of clients and tried hundreds of civil, domestic, and criminal cases. He tried cases in the federal courts in Connecticut, New York, and Hawaii, has argued appeals before the Connecticut Supreme Court and the federal courts of appeals in New York and California, and has submitted cases to the United States Supreme Court. Howard is included in the Best Lawyers in America in connection with personal injury litigation and family law.

    He was really tough. And always prepared. And was so *for* me as a new young lawyer. He wanted me to be the best. My Calvinist background was improved by watching his attitude toward work and play. He worked hard (and therefore, I worked hard), and he played well (and I learned to play better). When we worked on a New York City case, he taught me three things: be prepared; schedule the depositions for 4 p.m.; and, at the same time, get a reservation at a fabulous NYC restaurant. Celebrate the day's wins. I made the most of the time to pick his brain on trial strategy and to hear the "war stories" of trials won and lost. He took the time to teach the younger lawyers in the firm—and I was a beneficiary.

13. Being a trustworthy person and being an institution that is trustworthy will almost always have the marks of someone or something that is marked by the fruit of the Spirit as found in Galatians 5:22–23: "But the fruit of the Spirit is love, joy, peace, forbearance, kindness, goodness, faithfulness, gentleness and self-control." When the Spirit infuses us or forms us, the ability to be charitable toward another, grateful for another's unique contributions, confidential for the other's sake, hard-working, and truth-telling with grace is possible—maybe even probable.

For Discussion

1. Discuss the level of trust in your department or, in the words of Patrick Lencioni, your "first team"—that team that has and deserves your loyalty and best efforts. What's the temperature? Can people speak freely and embrace new ideas? Does your department suffer from silence or cynicism— a chilling effect in a team?

2. Every environment will have "temperature" or trust fluctuations. Can you identify best practices that have built trust in your environment? What threatens trust in your environment?

3. What are the obstacles, if any, for building new levels of trust?

4. What simple steps could you take to value another person in your department or on your team?

5. What could you do to show that you are *for* the other in your team or departmental relationships?

6. How could you personally do or be something that contributes to moving your team or institution to a higher level of trust?

7. Take these questions to the next rung of your institution.

Chapter Six

ORCHESTRATING A LIFE OF INFLUENCE

DEANA L. PORTERFIELD

"So much of leadership is music from the heart."

—MAX DE PREE, Leadership Jazz

My arms raised, I looked across the orchestra, took a deep breath, and motioned for the violins to begin. Standing in front of my peers, a sense of awe swept over me as choir and orchestra came together in song. How would I influence and move a 120-member group to transform the piece of music in front of me so those listening would be transported in a moment? Keeping time was my first goal, and with the motion of one hand and the nod of my head, I used measured strokes and movements to interpret the meaning of the song. With another movement, the vocalist joined, and quickly we were in rhythm together, and I was leading. The beats of music connected with the beating of my heart, and, as the song progressed, I found myself anticipating the next measure.

To my left was a trusted friend and fellow student who studied music with me at the university. We had sat together in class and heard the same techniques on how to lead and direct a choir and orchestra. At one point in the beginning of the piece, he looked up and caught my eye. He signaled the need for an altera-tion in my conducting. Trusting his cue, I adjusted my tempo. This moment of influence and trust swirled together as conductor and musicians moved to create a moment of worship.

Turning the final page of the score, I felt the eyes of the choir and orchestra members fixed on me, anticipating how I would shape the final notes. To understand this moment, I think back to the classroom, where the dean of the school of music taught us that all music should be created anew each time it is performed. This philosophy underscores the belief that we approach each interaction with different perspectives and experiences, shaping each moment into new and exciting possibilities. With the members of the choir and orchestra anticipating my next direction, I looked at another colleague at the piano and took a deep breath, signaling a slowing in the music. As my body moved to reflect the change, the movement of the pianist followed, and together with the first chair violin, we slowed the song and held the last note in a moment of awe.

As a lover of music from an early age, I decided when I entered college to major in music education. As I moved through my four years of undergraduate work, I received multiple opportunities to lead—conducting the choir and orchestra, leading a small singing group, and holding an administrative leadership position in the choir and orchestra. Each position prepared me for the senior leadership position I hold today. The excitement of music and the opportunity to influence the sound, tempo, and interpretation created in me a strong sense of meaning and purpose. I could not truly interpret the music for others unless I fully embraced the music from deep within myself.

After graduating, I accepted an admissions position at a university, and within a few years, I became responsible for leading a group of people. The push and pull between conductor and musicians became my metaphor of leadership, showing how influence can change both me and the organization. Allowing members of the team to speak into my life demonstrates how individuals bring their best work to, commit to the direction of, and embrace the values of an organization. It is possible to lead while going through the motions, but true influential leadership comes from the passions of the heart. Using this premise, this chapter considers how to become a person of influence as an individual contributor and member within an organization. It is influence that shapes the road ahead and brings new life into our daily work.

Everyone knows a person of influence. In organizations, you find individuals influencing people and decisions regardless of their roles or positions, and creating opportunities for others to shape the environment around them. At every level, men and women can affect culture, climate, process, and direction. Some do so unintentionally, while others strategically move throughout the organization making an impact. Moving organizations forward requires leaders who bring a sense of authentic influence to create value.[1] This contribution propels individuals to move from a focus of producing results to embodying a larger purpose.[2] The more we understand influence, the greater the opportunity individuals have to create positive growth in their organizations. This influence creates transformation within both the organization and the individuals themselves, bringing the music of their hearts into the outside world.

What Is Influence?

If you have worked with anyone directly, you have attempted or witnessed influence. Influence is defined in varying ways, including how an individual has an effect on another person, or the ability to shape the direction of someone or something. Each person within an organization, whether aware of it or not, has an effect on others. Influence can be in how someone responds to your statement visually—causing you to change direction—or how your words move another individual to change. Even the slightest adjustment in direction due to another's response or action reveals influence. In their book, *Primal Leadership*, Daniel Goleman, Richard E. Boyatzis, and Annie McKee point out that leaders "adept in influence are persuasive and engaging."[3] So how do leaders create opportunities to strengthen their skills as persuasive and engaging individuals?

No matter in what formal position or role, anyone can develop influencing skills and affect the future of an organization. This impact is not altered by an individual's years of service, credentials, or organizational resume. In *Making Room for Leadership*, MaryKate Morse writes, "A leader helps give form and direction, but everyone regardless of gender, age, or amount of experience, has the right and responsibility to be part of the influencing process."[4] Influence doesn't have parameters; each person brings ideas, opinions, and the ability to see from a different perspective.

There have been multiple experiences where I have had the right to influence process and chose to wait until another colleague took the lead. Over the years, I have learned to be aware of such opportunities, to influence the decisions being made. One such opportunity happened early in my career, when I learned of an opportunity for staff to participate in a short-term mission program over the spring break. The department I worked in sent teams just south of the California border to Mexico and set up camp at three locations in the Mexicali Valley. These "Barnabas" teams made trips to encourage the short-term student missionaries participating, traveling to various outreach locations throughout the week. In addition to encouragement, the Barnabas teams were responsible for connecting with over five thousand junior high and high school student missionaries, hoping to recruit them to the university.

From the moment I heard about the program, I was convinced I needed to be a leader of one of the Barnabas teams. I went to speak with the director of the department and asked if I could serve in a leadership role. I will never forget his response to my inquiry: "Deana, women are not allowed to lead or be a part of Barnabas teams." I stood in his office dumbfounded. How could that be? I was as qualified to lead one of the groups as anyone else in the office, but because I was a female I couldn't participate? I left his office and stewed on the issue for a few days. There was no reason why a woman could not lead one of the teams, so I decided to take a risk and try again.

Later in the week, I asked if I could meet with the director and gave an overabundance of reasons why I was as qualified as any man in the office to lead a team. I learned quickly the decision had come from a higher level within the university and in order for me to participate, I had to meet face-to-face with the dean over our area. I can still picture the moment as I walked up the stairs to his office, along with my direct supervisor. Though my supervisor was supportive of my position, I felt a sense of uncertainty going into the meeting. We sat down in the floral-patterned wingback chairs, and my heart began to beat faster. The dean shared the history of the program and wanted me to understand why there had been no women on the teams in the past.

After he finished, I sat up straight on the edge of the chair and began to share why I believed I was capable of not only being on a team, but of leading one. Although I can't remember everything I communicated in the moment, I remember a slight smile across the dean's face as I made my case. After I was done, he thanked me for coming, and I left the office. A few days later, the director asked to see me and shared the good news that I could lead a team that year. He said that I had done a good job of convincing the dean to let me go, and that he had never seen anyone speak so passionately.

This story provides an example of having influence, no matter what role you hold. As an entry-level staff member, I did not believe I had much influence. Yet, as opportunities and perceived injustices came my way, I decided I needed to do something. At the time, my primary desire was to lead the trip; I did not view the requisite conversation as monumental. However, looking back, I can see how that small act of challenging the norm created an opportunity for influence, changing the future of the program beyond my own experience.

What Do I Need to Know in Order to Influence?

To be a person of influence, it is important to know yourself and what it is you are called to contribute. This means understanding who you are and what you bring to the organization. If your contribution is strategic in nature, your responsibility is to bring considered ideas forward in your interactions. If your ability to influence change is evident in your decision making, make yourself available to participate in discussions where decisions are being made. This does not mean you can't contribute to other conversations; it means finding the sweet spot of what you do well and embracing it within the organization. Knowing who you are is critical to how you influence, and how you influence is directly tied to the organizational relationships in which you engage.

Relationships are critical components of influence and have an impact on leadership development. In her work on leaders, Sharon K. Gibson found informal relationships critical to career transitions.[5] As with many aspects of organizational life, relationships are foundational to the future development and movement of individuals within organizations. The relationships we form over our careers are pivotal and provide the foundation to the non-negotiables of influence.

To be a person of influence, you need to grasp five of those non-negotiables:

1. Understand your organizational culture.
2. Understand what matters to your organization.
3. Deliver what you are asked to deliver.

4. Be someone others can trust.
5. Be a truth teller.

1. Understand Your Organizational Culture

Each organization has its own personality culture, and it's important to understand that culture. Culture drives decisions, hiring, processes, and relationships. In reality, any understanding of a culture is influenced by our own experiences and perceptions and may not truly reflect the organization's dynamics and cultural norms. One way to determine the culture in your organization is to use a tool for diagnosing the traditions and organizational norms for doing work. An example can be found in Kim S. Cameron's and Robert E. Quinn's book, *Diagnosing and Changing Organizational Culture*.[6] Their "Organizational Culture Profile" tool helps assess the culture of your organization and can assist in understanding how influence might be accepted and understood. All tools are limited in some way, and it takes time to get to know the culture. Spend time building relationships and review the values of the organization before jumping into conversations and decisions.

2. Understand What Matters to Your Organization

To be a person of influence, you need to understand what matters organizationally. Each person you work with brings a different set of strengths and gifts to the organization. Understand what your supervisor needs from you. No matter how much time and energy you put into a project or assignment, if it is not of value to those you work with and for, you have wasted valuable personal and organizational resources. Evaluate your passions in light of the organizational priorities to better understand the needs and direction of the organization. Going against organizational priorities or deviating from shared values can be detrimental to your influence.

3. Deliver What You Are Asked to Deliver

To be a person of influence, you have to deliver on your goals and work. Each of us has goals and responsibilities within the organization and is expected to meet or exceed those goals. You build credibility when you deliver on your promises and commitments. This credibility is foundational to your ability to influence within the organization. Take care of your responsibilities and be the best at what you do, and you will have a path into influence. It is difficult to appreciate the individual who cannot take care of his or her own responsibilities.

4. Be Someone Others Can Trust

All of us have been in conversations and meetings where confidential information has been shared or entrusted to us. The expectation from those interactions, even if not stated, is that each member will hold the content in confidence. Individuals who hold information in confidence, regardless of how critical or non-critical that material may be, are deemed trustworthy of more information. Learning to hold information, or truthfully state your inability to share information, is critical to influence. If you cannot be trusted, access to information will soon become limited, and you will find yourself excluded from interaction with key stakeholders.

5. Be a Truth Teller

It sounds so simple, yet many up-and-coming leaders find themselves in moments of inability to speak the truth, fearing they will lose credibility or position. One of the most valuable tools leaders can have is people who will speak truth into their leadership. I recall an example that took place during a lunch with my vice president. We were sitting facing each other at a small table in a casual restaurant frequented by others from our institution. I had a list of what I perceived to be important topics for our lunch meeting. After we ordered, I began to move through my list. At one point, I looked across the table and realized the vice president's eyes were glazed over and he was not listening. In that moment I asked, "You aren't listening to me, are you?" To which he replied, "No, I was listening to the conversation behind me." Now you can view this story in multiple ways, but to me, that small moment was foundational for our working relationship. Had he said he was listening to me, I would have viewed him as not being truthful. But he didn't; instead, he told me the truth and gained my respect.

What about day-to-day opportunities to speak the truth to those in authority over you? Have you ever been in a meeting where the person in authority didn't seem to fully catch what the group was saying? These situations happen every day, and we have choices about how we will respond. Will you let the situation go and hope someone else addresses it, or take initiative and attempt to influence constructively? In reality, there is risk in this form of influence. The key is how you choose to approach others. Ensuring that your intent is not self-motivated, asking questions, and being prepared to listen to responses are important components of speaking the truth.

I can think of multiple situations when the most senior colleagues in the room have summarized a topic too quickly and moved to the next agenda item. In a typical example, the room went quiet and the group became hesitant and reserved. Someone asked to go back to the previous discussion, suggesting that additional conversation was still needed. Around the room, others began to nod in agreement. Too often, though, after a slight pause, the senior member would respond, "We are done with that conversation" and look at the facilitator; then the meeting would continue. These moments have sometimes left knots in my stomach as I have had to decide whether to have a later conversation with that individual, attempting to influence future meetings. In my experience, these conversations are hard, but everyone benefits in the end.

It is in these private conversations that some of the greatest influence takes place. You have to be prepared for the possibility of a strong negative response, but after the initial reaction, most leaders are thankful to receive honest feedback, especially if given with a supportive spirit. Every day, we have the opportunity to speak truth into situations and circumstances. In difficult moments, when others shy away from conflict, speak the truth and your ability to influence will grow.

Qualities of a Person of Influence

Research performed by the Gallup organization on the needs of followers and strengths of individuals, partnered with work on authentic leadership and defining leadership moments, identifies specific qualities of effective leaders. The research and insight from these books reveals particular qualities that can be linked to being a person of influence. Table 1 shows a list of specific qualities attributed to people of influence who have the ability to engage others. These qualities were adapted and brought together from work done by Rath and Conchie, Buckingham and Clifton, Avolio and Luthans, and Bennis and Thomas, demonstrating key qualities in not only a person of influence, but in all leaders.[7] Reflect on this list for a minute. Which of these qualities do you value or look for in an influential leader? Are there any particular qualities you see in leaders you respect? Are there any qualities you already have or want to further develop in yourself?

Table 6.1—Qualities of Influential People

Trustworthiness	Stability	Hopefulness	Confidence
	Optimism	Resilience	
Adaptibility	Motivation	Engagement	Self-Awareness

My own desire to work for and with individuals reflecting these qualities makes all the difference in my success and passion for the direction of the university where I serve. Each of these terms identifies traits desired within any organization. Regardless of your contribution or role, leaders who model trustworthiness, stability, hopefulness, confidence, adaptability, optimism, resilience, self-awareness, motivation, and engagement are highly sought after and leave a legacy at their organizations.

Deciding to Be a Person of Influence

It has never been my intention to seek influence, but through strong relationships and key behaviors, influence takes place. As a matter of fact, I have been told and reminded that my influence is stronger than I am aware. Somehow, between the reality of what is and what might be, rests a place of pure intent and passion for the future of the organization. Everything we say has an impact. Additionally, how we interact and what we say and do have an impact. Your impact can be negligible or significant, as when making a statement that changes the direction of a decision. The first step in deciding to be a person of influence is recognizing that your words and actions can make a difference.

After recognizing that your words and actions contribute to being a person of influence, the second step is intentionality of interactions. Imagine you are walking down the hallway in the administration building and pass by the president, who stops and asks your thoughts regarding a situation. In that moment, you have influence and how you choose to use that moment matters. Often, I see others immediately share what they want to see improved or changed within the institution. Stopping to understand what questions the president asked could provide a true moment of influence. Be ready—influence happens at the most unexpected moments.

Looking back, I can see how my influence has shaped my university. This influence looks different for different people; for me, it comes through conversations and brainstorming ideas with others. Whether traveling on a trip when conversation blossoms into possibilities of change and organizational movement, or setting up a leadership retreat in a way that encourages morale and sets the team on a new course of leadership, each interaction holds opportunities for influence.

Make a Conscious Decision to Be a Person of Influence

To be a person of influence, you have to be mindful and aware of your interactions. As stated earlier, every interaction provides an opportunity of influence. Too often, individuals wait for approval, asking if something is acceptable before acting. Where and when appropriate, make the decision or take action. Recently, after a leadership retreat, it was determined that the group needed to modify the format of our regular senior leadership meetings. Taking what was said at the meetings and wanting to implement and make constructive changes, I completely changed the look and format of the agenda. As the facilitator of the meeting, this technically fell within my area of responsibility. Since the president was traveling, I took initiative and made the changes. While distributing the new agenda and attachments before

146

the meeting, I stated my three objectives and goals in changing the meeting format and asked for feedback and insight. Walking into the meeting, I knew my influence needed to focus on moving more of the meeting time to allow for strategic conversations. Driving agendas, preparing topics, and facilitating conversations are all part of influencing organizational life.

Surround Yourself with Those Who Have a Different Perspective

One of the best ways to influence your organization is to understand diverse perspectives and find value in difference. In *Now, Discover your Strengths,* Marcus Buckingham and Donald O. Clifton talk about the value of differences and the contribution that an awareness of strengths can bring to our daily lives and organizations.[8] To fully understand and embrace the challenge of varying perspectives, it is important to know and recognize what you bring to the organization and how your leadership impacts the work you do. Once you understand your role, begin to identify those who think differently than you do. The power of understanding differences allows opportunity for you to understand why your opinion isn't about being right or chosen. Instead, it's about perspective and valuing diversity. Understanding difference impacts your ability to influence and the contribution you can make to those above and around you in the organization.

Network and Build Relationships

Relationships matter. As stated earlier, being mindful of all interactions is critical to influence. However, without honest and trusting relationships, influence is halted. At times, influence is misused within organizations, tearing at the fabric of trust, causing the larger organization to question the credibility and intuition of organizational leadership. You can have influence at any level of the organization as you build strong relationships.

Understand Yourself and Become Self-aware

How do you gain entry into influence? First, by bringing your authentic self to each interaction. Also, avoid "unloading" when given the opportunity to speak into a situation or problem. Instead, focus less on your personal agendas and see your role as advancing the mission and vision of the organization. Don't take it personally when your ideas or thoughts are not acted upon; celebrate the decisions and activities of the organization. Follow through on your promises, get your job done, be available when needed, bring energy to the conversation, and value the role of the top executive or leader.

Seek Feedback from Trusted Colleagues and Mentors

What does it mean to be in a trusting relationship? It means you have the freedom to speak the truth. It means holding conversations in confidence and speaking candidly when aware of conflicting actions. Early in my career, I remember a challenge I was having with another department within the organization. My frustration level increased each time we had an interaction, and we could not seem to find a balanced agreement supporting both departments' priorities. After one particular meeting, I engaged a trusted colleague in a dialogue about my frustrations. During the conversation, this colleague pointed out a different perspective and challenged me to consider how my posture, tone, and words influenced the conversation in a negative direction. Though it is difficult to hear challenging feedback, I was extremely grateful for his willingness to speak into my journey, thus influencing how I interacted with others.

Trusted mentors, colleagues, and key relationships are critical to your success as a leader. Even more importantly, individuals who speak truth into your leadership provide a resource for development and accountability. Never underestimate the power of a trusted mentor or colleague who can provide perspective and insight into your leadership and development. This is not easily done because no one wants to be challenged to think differently; however, to be a person of influence, it is important to understand how you are perceived and to adjust behavior as necessary.

Develop New Strategies for Influence

Many strategies exist for developing influence, but the journey to your influence can only be forged by you. This means finding ways to connect organizationally through committee work, informational interviews with those you want to get to know, and conversations with people in various leadership roles

148

regarding your desires. Often these meetings can create connections you were unaware of previously. Other strategies might include developing professional relationships outside of your organization and creating opportunities you can bring back and implement on your campus. Regardless of the avenue, it is important to be proactive and find opportunities to create connections.

Connect with the Organization's History and Cultural Behaviors

Each organization has established tribal stories, unspoken rules, values, and expected behaviors. Understanding how the organization works before you step out and criticize process or decisions is imperative. An illustration of this principle emerged when I assumed a higher level of responsibility about ten years into my career. Though I was not involved in the details of the area prior to supervision, I had formed an opinion of how the department worked. My assumptions created an intense reaction as I went in to "change" what I perceived to be broken. Even within the same organization, smaller cultural differences existed between departments. I quickly learned that my assumptions had a negative impact on my ability to influence the changes within the area and gain buy-in within the team. The relational foundation needed developing, and I needed to slow down my process, taking time to more fully understand the situation from all perspectives

Identify Ways to Connect with the Top of the Organization

Influence is not scheduled, is not an agenda item, and at times you may not be aware that you are actually engaged in it. It can take place on a walk between meetings, over a meal, in a non-related meeting, or during other interactions. Individuals decide what they are going to share in a conversation and what they want to communicate. You can influence an opinion, you can influence an idea, and you can influence how someone does his or her job. All of these and more demonstrate how it is possible to live a life of influence daily.

More intentional ways of connecting require honest conversations with those in more senior leadership. Volunteer for committees or task-force work, or offer to represent your area on a broader institutional project or initiative. There are many ways to connect within the organization. Be aware that with added connection comes greater expectation and opportunity to demonstrate your ability to follow through and get the job done. Still, take care to maintain your current role and relationships to avoid negatively impacting your current job responsibilities.

Keep Self out of It

To understand influence, remember that each interaction is a moment of influence, with people exchanging ideas and creating opportunities to bring those ideas to life. Directly or indirectly, words and actions make statements you may or may not intend to make. Being a person of influence means understanding who you are, what you bring, and what the organization needs.

Not long after I accepted a new leadership position, a colleague came into my office, sat down across from me, and with his arm rested across the back of the chair, stated "I told the president you shouldn't be the chief of staff." My defenses went up immediately. I clasped my hands together, and leaned forward. "And what did he say to that?" I asked. "He said you are the only one who tells him the truth." For a moment, I was shaken by the arrogance and boldness of the person sitting in front of me. Ultimately, though, the incident affirmed my credibility within the leadership team. I realized that my response to that interaction not only confirmed the strength of my relationship, it also demonstrated a lack of influence in my colleague. He had hoped to exert influence *after* the president had made a decision, and he criticized that decision without trying to understand the reasons behind it. I could have gotten caught up in the details of the situation—stuck on the fact that this colleague went to the president with doubts of my ability to fulfill the role—but I recognized that the issue was less about me and more about the person sitting across the office. Effective leaders learn to keep themselves—their personal defenses and reactions—out of situations that can derail and change focus. They focus not on being defensive but on making a difference.

Pure influence comes naturally and is not forced. It does not seek personal gain. Misuse of influence can create division, separation, and negative impact on an organization. Ego and pride need to be held in check. Unmanaged self can alter intention and expectations of influence and lead to frustration, misdirection, and self-promoting. Don't underestimate the power of your words and the influence your actions already have. You are influencing someone today—make that influence matter.

Putting It All Together

Influence is critical to leadership and organizational dynamics. The challenge comes with how individuals choose to use that influence. Each section of this chapter is designed to provide tools and insights into how leaders might practice and be aware of their influence. Seeing influence as an intentional way of working within an organization allows for greater insight and connection with those you relate to every day. How you live out influence on a daily basis will depend upon your willingness to see organizational life differently. You have the ability to influence those around you in constructive ways—will you step up to the challenge?

Lead with Influence

My first experience with the new Los Angeles Philharmonic conductor, Gusavo Dudamel, occurred while I was sitting in the audience at the Hollywood Bowl on a beautiful warm summer evening. My family received four tickets earlier in the day and decided this would be an opportunity for our youngest daughter to experience the energy of the venue and excellence of this world-class orchestra. I had previously visited as a performer, singing in a choir on the stage. It had been years since enjoying the gift of music at the Bowl, and excitement over the evening ahead came over me as we walked up the hill and entered the amphitheater.

We took our seats halfway up the amphitheater and waited for the concert to begin. I noticed two large screens hanging to the left and right of the stage. I didn't remember these from my previous visits and thought they were from another event. Entering from the left, the conductor walked onto the stage and acknowledged the crowd. I noticed his white tuxedo and full curly black hair. The orchestra tuned and he began to conduct. Immediately, the screens on each side of the stage came to life. To my surprise, the cameras were positioned in the midst of the orchestra, facing the conductor and projecting his image for us to watch. Each move he made was flamboyant; his hair bounced as he conducted. The audience seemed enthralled by his performance. It was my first time to experience the L.A. Philharmonic in such a personal and relational way.

As I observed the new conductor, I also noticed the orchestra members and audience. A level of energy and excitement rose from within the orchestra. Members were smiling, leaning forward, and enjoying the experience. At the same time, the crowd was engaged and anticipating the next sound from the orchestra, the next visual effect of the conductor. The style was unconventional yet refreshing. Gusavo Dudamel had influenced the L.A. Philharmonic and community so powerfully that the event producers changed their presentation style to showcase his influence.

When leaders and members of communities embrace influence, beautiful results like those at the Hollywood Bowl occur. By letting go of traditional constraints and conducting styles, Gusavo Dudamel began to influence the orchestra and ultimately the audience. Being a person of influence requires letting go of personal constraints and embracing the opportunity to make a difference. Organizations need people who will make a difference. Being a person of influence means offering your best, no matter your position or role.

Notes to Chapter Six

1. Kevin Cashman, *Leadership from the Inside Out.*

2. Ibid.

3. Daniel Goleman, Richard E. Boyatzis, and Annie McKee, *Primal Leadership*, 256.

4. MaryKate Morse, *Making Room for Leadership*, 33.

5. Sharon K. Gibson, "The Developmental Relationships of Women Leaders in Career Transitions."

6. Kim S. Cameron and Robert E. Quinn, *Diagnosing and Changing Organizational Culture.*

7. Tom Rath and Barry Conchie, *Strengths Based Leadership*; Marcus Buckingham and Donald Clifton, *Now, Discover Your Strengths*; B. J. Avolio and Fred Luthans, *The High Impact Leader;* Warren G. Bennis and Robert J. Thomas, *Leading for a Lifetime.*

8. Marcus Buckingham and Donald O. Clifton, *Now, Discover your Strengths.*

For Discussion

1. Are opportunities for influence created within your organization?

   a. If so, are they evident at every level of the organization?

   b. If not, what changes might be implemented to provide opportunities for individuals and teams within the organization to contribute and share more openly?

2. How can you as a leader and/or leadership team encourage and promote opportunities of influence within your organization?

3. What barriers currently exist within the organization that keep you and/ or your leadership team from encouraging the influence of others?

4. Referencing the list of specific qualities attributed to a person of influence and the ability to engage others (Table 6.1), reflect on the following questions:

   a. Are there any of these qualities you don't value or look for in an influential leader?

   b. Are there any qualities you see in leaders you respect?

   c. Are there any qualities you already have or want to develop?

5. What opportunities for influence currently exist within your organization?

6. What steps will you take to become a person of influence within your organization?

Chapter Seven

INSIDE FACULTY CULTURE

Carolyn E. Dirksen

*The central factor of an academic environment is that it contains
what was trendy some years back to call "knowledge workers."
These are people with highly specialized expertise, who are not
usually susceptible to being managed in the traditional sense of the
word. Their attitude toward administrators is often one of disdain:
a commonly heard quip asserts that an academic who takes on an
administrative role loses twenty I.Q. points.*

—C. K. GUNSALUS, The College Administrator's Survival Guide

It was a big day for the faculty, and people crowded into the room with a
keen sense of anticipation. For two years, a faculty/administrative committee
had been working on a new formula that would reduce workloads by one
course per semester, and—almost as important to the faculty—calculate the
impact of the number of advisees, the number of preparations, class size, and
committee responsibilities. The tightly knit committee, with representation
from each department, had taken the project on as a cause, working out the
details in department meetings, faculty hearings, and grueling hours around
the table considering alternatives and scenarios. We had argued and debated
and compromised, but our final meeting had almost been a party when we saw
all our hard work come together in a package that we believed would lighten
the load of the faculty, distribute the out-of-class work more evenly, and pass
the scrutiny of the president and board.

Roland, a faculty member, had been a key member of the committee, and his analytic gifts allowed him to dig into our proposals and figure out, better than we dreamers could, what the downsides might be. His insight was invaluable because it allowed us to fix things and anticipate faculty concerns as we developed the proposal. Although he wasn't always the most positive person on the committee, we listened to him because his critiques took us down the right path. In that final meeting, as the committee unanimously adopted the carefully crafted proposal, we were a united body, proud of our work, and ready to bring our final product to the faculty for a vote. The president had signaled that he would accept the proposal if the faculty voted positively, so we came into the meeting with a sense of elation and accomplishment.

The entire faculty had seen the proposal at every stage of its development, so there was no dramatic unveiling, and as I—the vice president for academic affairs—worked through the various layers of the presentation, there were very few questions, and the faculty conveyed a general sense of approval. It was time to take the vote. It was moved and seconded, and when I asked for discussion—expecting none, since the proposal had been discussed *ad nauseum*—Roland raised his hand.

"I don't think this will work. How can we quantify the relationship between serving on a committee and doing a course preparation? And we all know that preparing for some courses requires more work than preparing for others. There should be more weight for lab science courses because they take more time." I couldn't believe my ears. We had hashed out this question during the first months of the committee's work and had arrived at the conclusion that even a rough approximation of how committee work impacts workload was better than no consideration at all. We had also opted for a more streamlined model rather than one that was sensitive to every possible nuance, because we wanted something that was actually possible to implement.

Everyone on the faculty knew Roland was on the committee, so his comments at this point made it seem that we had swept his concerns under the rug in our rush to get something passed. Then, of course, there was the red herring of his saying that his courses required more work than courses in other disciplines, which sparked a controversy between the music faculty and the humanities faculty, who also believe their courses require careful and time-consuming preparation. And we were off. Lost in the debate over whether it is harder to teach a private cello lesson or a microbiology lab was the fact that—however anything was calculated—we would all teach three hours less per semester if we could just bring this to a vote. In the end, the committee prevailed, and the faculty adopted the proposal, but it was not the jubilant success we had all been anticipating. As soon as we were adjourned, the committee—sans Roland—rushed me at the podium to express their dismay that Roland had sabotaged the meeting.

Virtually every academic administrator can tell a similar story—a story about a faculty member who behaved unexpectedly, in ways that are hard to interpret. Such individualistic behavior is why people feel we academic administrators are "herding cats" and why the pages of the *Chronicle of Higher Education* are constantly filled with hair-raising stories of conflict between faculty and administration.

So what is going on with the faculty? We administrators sometimes believe we are working hard to create the best teaching/learning environment our resources will allow while faculty are so self- or discipline-centered, so autonomous, and so anti-administration that they engage in conscientious efforts to thwart our plans. In stark contrast, in *The Fall of the Faculty*, Benjamin Ginsberg states the faculty viewpoint that governance of the university has been taken over by "deanlets," administrators, and staffers without adequate academic experience who are threatening the core values of research and teaching.[1] In many institutions, the battle lines are drawn, but a better understanding of faculty culture can help any administrator navigate these sometimes troubled waters. In this chapter, I would like to suggest an alternate way of understanding the faculty that might also prompt different ways of working with them for the greater good of our institutions. Assuming this will be read by administrators, my focus will be on the demystifying faculty culture. According to Lee Bolman and Joan V. Gallos in *Reframing Academic Leadership*, "Effective academic leaders know how their stakeholders think and what they care about so that campus agendas, resource allocations, and process can respond to those concerns."[2] This chapter is intended to be a guide to how faculty think and what they care about, to aid administrators in responding to faculty concerns and in preventing the kind of institutional warfare we sometimes read about.

To understand faculty culture, it is important to remember how faculty are socialized into their disciplines, to recognize the unique strengths they bring to their positions, and to understand the alternative hierarchies to which they respond. The ideas in this chapter are meant to help bridge the communication gap between a healthy and engaged faculty and the rest of the institution. Although each faculty has its own ethos, individual faculty members run the gamut from those who bring energy and wisdom to the support of the institutional mission to those who are disengaged and resistant to the mission. While all faculties are different, these observations seek some common ground.

Academic Socialization

For a better understanding of faculty culture, it is important to remind ourselves of who faculty are and how they are trained. Most faculty have been headed toward academic life since childhood. They have been created to do this specific kind of work, and it is their nature and their calling. There is something about the romance of learning that draws them, against the pull of their peers, into the deeper challenges of the intellectual life. There is a spark that makes them ask for more explanation and takes them back to the text or the experiment to eke out one more bit of information.

As undergraduates, they begin to be acculturated into the mysteries of their disciplines. They learn a new vocabulary and acquire new frames through which to view the world, new perspectives and procedures. This socialization is crucial and life-changing. It is hard to determine whether students select their majors based on their personality types or whether their socialization into the major imprints their personalities. However it happens, they learn to think in certain ways based on the deep assumptions and methods of their field, and this imprinting comes at a developmental stage that may well shape their perceptions for life.

While being deeply and profoundly socialized, faculty are also being taught to probe, to question, and to push back. Of all the things we teach our undergraduates, one skill that we all value highly is the ability to think critically rather than taking what is presented at face value. What begins as a thirst for knowledge and curiosity about the world is shaped into a way of thinking and writing by the discipline, and enhanced by the tools for critical evaluation. Students who are successful in acquiring these skills as undergraduates proceed to graduate school where the work continues at a deeper level—they gain more knowledge, more discipline-centered assumptions and skills, and more opportunities for critical thought.

Including time as undergraduates, many faculty members have spent eight to twelve years in the intense culture of their disciplines, completing doctorates that are bestowed only on those who have mastered the particular way of thinking, researching, and writing that is characteristic of their field. They are in love with learning, so in love with it that they have been willing to devote themselves to it in ways that have required extreme concentration and even deprivation. All the time they were pursuing higher education, they were *not* doing the things their non-academic peers were doing—getting an entry-level job, buying a house, and starting a retirement account.

By the time they become faculty, they have been taught to analyze and evaluate, to question and push back, and to bring something new out of a flood of seemingly disparate information. They know their disciplines; they think like members of their guild; they produce new ideas; and their love of learning is so apparent that it attracts young scholars to the path of higher education. Their rigor and energy is why we hire them and why we value them so highly as contributors to our institutions.

Disciplines create their own subcultures, and Bolman and Gallos describe the complex and dynamic relationships across campuses as "vibrant ecosystems that house a variety of different species or groups, each with its own specific characteristics, capabilities, interests, needs and lifestyles."[3] Working successfully with faculty requires the ability to see and negotiate the blurred and dynamic boundaries in this complex ecosystem.

Understanding Roland

So let's go back to Roland. Why would Roland, after two years of work, seemingly attempt to bring down his own committee project in front of the faculty? One interpretation is that he was against the proposal from the beginning, that he never bought in, and he planned all along to use his committee membership as leverage to make sure it never passed. I worked hard with Roland,

and I know that that is not the case. He was actively engaged in and committed to the work of the committee, and he wanted us to succeed. He was not a dissident or a saboteur. But Roland has been trained as a scientist. He lives in a world of data and facts and formulas. The world of compromise and "close enough" is completely out of his realm.

As we worked through the committee process, I naively assumed that Roland was being persuaded each time we compromised detail for efficiency and each time we agreed to lump disparate things together in the hope of making some progress on the distribution of work. I was looking at the goal— the hoped-for outcome of a lighter, more widely shared workload. Roland, like a true scientist, was looking at the details of the process. He was amiably willing to go along with the committee as we worked through the issues, but when he thought deeply about the whole package as it was presented to the faculty, his tentative truce with our methods disintegrated.

Because he bought in to the work of the committee so thoroughly that he didn't want us to fail, he was willing to stop the process even as we reached our grand finale to point out the flaws in our corporate reasoning. To expect him to do otherwise was to expect him to be someone other than who he is. Roland simply couldn't be the careful, well-trained scientist in his classes, *and* the canny campus politician on the committee. He couldn't stop being analytical and critical, even though he had agreed to the proposal. We choose faculty for their perspectives and their disciplinary skills. As administrators, we can't assume that they will think or perform differently when we need their political support. Our focus as administrators is on the task we need to complete, and we want to move efficiently toward that end. Faculty are not socialized to be efficient; they are socialized to be thorough, questioning, and reflective. When these "styles" collide, administrators should recognize that faculty are not being obstinate. They are demonstrating the very skills we value in their primary roles as teachers and researchers.

Discipline Loyalty

A wall-to-wall revision of our general education core several years ago provided me with another experience in unraveling the complexities of faculty culture and led me to a deeper understanding of their discipline loyalty. After thirty years with the same general education requirements, we all agreed to take everything off the table and build a new core from scratch. We started by soliciting a list of outcome goals that we want all our graduates to achieve. Once the faculty had determined the final list, the Core Revision Task Force organized the goals into related categories. Each category was assigned to a multi-disciplinary work group, which was then given the total number of credit hours they could "spend" achieving their goals. So far, so good.

The next step was for each work group to present course titles and descriptions indicating how their proposed courses would lead students to the intended outcomes. That was when things got complicated. While the faculty had been happy to work on the goals and the general categories, and while it seemed clear from the very beginning that many existing courses would be cut or drastically revised, it was at this point that faculty realized that *their* courses could be cut or revised. To add insult to injury, their courses might be revised by people not in their discipline.

Some non-academic administrators, sympathetically looking over my shoulder during this process, shared their views that faculty reticence sprang from fear of change, a need to control, and a desire to avoid the work of preparing to teach a new course. Admittedly, all of those factors probably played a role with some faculty. But as I lived in their debates and private conversations over the next few months, I realized that the faculty's determination to keep their old courses flowed from a stronger, deeper source than obstinacy or comfort with the status quo. They really did believe that, without a thorough introduction to their specific discipline, students would miss the most crucial aspect of their undergraduate education. The biologists were passionate about biology; the sociologists were passionate about sociology, and the English teachers feared for the future of students without two semesters of literature. The historians wanted twelve credits of history; the political scientists wanted at least one course in political systems. For months, there was general chaos in the work groups, and the lives of the Core Revision Task Force members were miserable because they were caught between the need for change and the faculty's strong resistance to any discipline-specific sacrifices.

As any good academic leadership book will tell you, any change in the academic sector is not a top-down process. It is a mammoth political maneuver that requires endless discussions, conversations, and deals, and that is how this complex task was eventually accomplished. In that jungle of interacting ecosystems, Bolman and Gallos argue, "goals and decisions arise from a continual process of bargaining among coalition members."[4] In our case, in addition to the political dimension of forming an adequate coalition to bring about this significant change, an interpersonal dimension was also at work. Through all our conversations, discussions, and debates, the Core Revision Task Force came to a new and deeper understanding of the discipline commitments of all our peers. We all had a discipline we loved and would fight for. We all believed that our single specialization was the most crucial to a meaningful education, so we did our best to hear that perspective in the arguments of our peers. We worked hard to convey to each discipline's faculty that we respected their position and understood that it came from their deepest desire to give our students the education they deserved. In short, we worked hard at building trust.

We also worked hard in those conversations to present the advantages of changing the core. We listened to specific objections raised by some faculty, and we presented again and again the positive ground we could gain. During these endless discussions, my best strategy was to go to the people with the strongest reservations and most persuasive voices and hear them out. As we sat together over coffee or over a desk piled high with student papers, we were always able to find common ground—our shared intense desire for our students to yearn for knowledge the way we do. I never left the room after one of those conversations without a greater understanding of my colleagues or without a sense of their appreciation for having a chance to express their concerns. That stronger interpersonal framework greatly increased the chances of cooperation and success.

These conversations were not mere political gambits; they were real opportunities to hear where the flaws lay in our plans and real opportunities to improve the proposal. We value the faculty because they are intelligent and insightful, and we need to take the time to hear their perspectives on our ideas for change. Faculty don't always have to "win," but they do want to be heard. As Bolman and Gallos point out, academic change requires patience, persistence, and process.[5] It isn't something that can be rushed. While academic change may seem glacial, solutions that lack these three "p's" are seldom long-lasting.

In the end of our core revision process, after all the credit hours had been distributed and all the syllabi had been developed, the whole massive proposal came before the faculty. After all the work and debates and hearings and conversations, I wasn't confident that it would pass. Because of the proposal's complexity, the faculty decided that it couldn't be amended from the floor, so the vote was simple—adopt the new core, or keep what we had. After some spirited debate, the vote was taken, and the new core passed with a substantial majority. Now, many years later, the "new core" is alive and well. Over time, it was enthusiastically embraced by the discipline faculty, and what didn't work has been changed so that we have a dynamic, meaningful center to our educational enterprise.

By leading the Core Revision Task Force and chairing the Faculty Workload Committee early in my tenure as chief academic officer, I learned a lot about working with faculty that I hadn't learned in my years as an English teacher, a department chair, or as dean of the College of Arts and Sciences. As our circle of influence and responsibility widens from the narrow perspective of our own discipline, the dialects of academic life that we encounter become less and less mutually intelligible. Appreciating the faculty's perspective and disciplinary language provides academic administrators with a clearer understanding of what underlies their actions.

Faculty Views of Hierarchy

One last bit of insight into faculty culture has helped me frame their actions and reactions in more positive ways. Most faculty tend to view the academic hierarchy in ways not shared by non-academic colleagues or even by academic administrators. Faculty have their "chain of command"—the chair, dean, and academic vice president—but a leadership position in the chain *per se* does not grant status or authority. Administrators on any level, even formerly valued colleagues, must earn the faculty's trust and confidence. As Bolman and Gallos point out, "[Authority] works only to the degree that subordinates accept it and choose to cooperate with it. Tenure, academic governance structures and the collegial culture of the academy magnify those basic limits to authority—and academic leaders are at risk if they overrely on it."[6]

While Ginsberg's *The Fall of the Faculty* takes a polemic position made obvious in its subtitle (*The Rise of the All-Administrative University and Why It Matters*), many faculty members believe that their institutions have too many administrators and that the work of those administrators detracts from the faculty's perceived right of governance. They are not convinced that administrators have any authority or that they are helpful in working toward the central mission of the institution. To be successful with faculty, administrators must understand that their authority is earned through hard work in building relationships and trust; it is not given along with the title and nameplate. Most of this is foreign territory to non-academic administrators who come from a more hierarchical culture in which real authority comes with positions. As one of my colleagues, a retired Air Force colonel, told me, "When I was in a position of responsibility like yours, I wore my authority on the shoulders of my uniform, and no one dared question it. You have to negotiate it anew every day."

In addition to the "management hierarchy" of chairs and deans, academic administrators who come from classroom ranks respect the hierarchy of academic rank and tenure. However, this hierarchy may also have less influence with faculty than administrators imagine. While tenure status definitely does affect the role a faculty member is willing to play in faculty politics, rank may not be as crucial a factor. Although moving up the ranks is generally valued by faculty and is a source of prestige, in some institutions, holding a higher rank doesn't necessarily give a faculty member more influence among departmental colleagues. Administrators may attempt to heighten their own authority by courting the higher-ranking faculty as allies, but these individuals may not be the power players in the invisible world of departmental politics.

At least two other hierarchies do play a role in faculty culture. Faculty often grant status and authority on the basis of discipline accomplishments—publications, positions in key organizations, and general scholarly respect, which may or may not correspond with academic rank. On student-centered campuses like ours, student acclaim is also a key factor in faculty status and influence. Because administrators and faculty may well determine status differently, when administrators attempt to find meaningful support for proposals among those we perceive as faculty leaders, we sometimes make treaties with the wrong chiefs and are then baffled when the support we counted on isn't there.

The Importance of Process and the "Speed of Trust"

Of the three p's identified by Bolman and Gallos—patience, persistence, and process—process carries the most weight with faculty and deserves separate consideration. As the authors point out, "Faculty will often assent, albeit grudgingly, to things they don't particularly like, so long as they feel the process was legitimate."[7] A recent example from my institution will illustrate this concept. For many years, we have had a recycling program managed by the director of the physical plant. An outside company comes to campus and picks up recyclable items at no charge and sells them to the recycling center. At some point, the company told the physical plant director that this arrangement was no longer profitable because the volume was too low, and they were going to discontinue services. The director tried several means of appeasing them to no avail, and after six months, they abruptly stopped picking up the recycle bins and dropped our contract. So, the director of the physical plant sent workers around to recover the blue recycle cans from all the offices. When the faculty asked where they were going, the workers told them that we would no longer be recycling.

A huge uproar ensued. Many faculty care deeply about recycling and consider it part of their faith commitment to care for creation, and they led the charge. However, even people who didn't recycle joined the fracas because a significant institutional decision was made without faculty input or discussion. No process was followed. The director of the physical plant was following a hierarchical model: He is responsible for recycling; the company we were using dropped us, so he collected the recycle bins until he could find another company. His method was quick and efficient, and I'm sure it didn't cross his mind to consult with the faculty on a matter that was completely under his authority. The faculty's perspective was quite different. Since recycling is an ethical and even spiritual issue for them, they felt that something essential had been taken away without notice or consultation.

Quite expectedly, we don't have any written guidelines in our constitution or handbook for dealing with the termination of recycling, but the faculty called for a process just the same. An ad hoc faculty committee was quickly formed to present the faculty's objections and offer solutions, and a process was developed on the spot. The faculty wanted to be informed and consulted because recycling matters to them. While I don't believe the faculty would accept a real termination of recycling even if a process they recognized had been followed, what appeared to them to be a total lack of process created a firestorm.

While the patience, persistence, and process model of academic governance make change slow and complicated, there is a factor that can speed things up—the element of trust. Shirley Hoogstra, earlier in this volume, has discussed at length the importance of and strategies for building trust. In addition, Stephen Covey's book *The Speed of Trust* demonstrates how trust cuts out the need for a huge bureaucracy of checks and balances, which points to the role of trust in accelerating academic processes.[8] As it turns out, the faculty at my institution, despite their rapid and heated response to the recycling debacle, actually do trust the director of the physical plant. He has been sensitive to their issues—ensuring well-maintained classrooms, accessibility for students with special needs, a pleasant campus environment—so they believe that he will respond positively to their concerns about recycling. It seems that he also trusts the faculty. Within hours of hearing their concerns, he returned the blue bins and assigned a crew from his staff to manage the recycling until he could find another company to do it. Within days, the faculty committee had met with him, and a long-term solution was quickly designed.

Mission at the Center

While it is essential to the health and flourishing of the community for administrators to value the faculty and to understand how they think and where they are coming from, it is also essential that we keep institutional mission at the center of our discussions. No assumed faculty prerogative is more important than the core mission of our institutions. Faculty are socialized to be members of their guild, and they reason and work according to that socialization. However, faculty are also members of a community with the shared goal of teaching students to be responsible Christians in a complex world. Just as faculty were socialized into their disciplines, we must be intentional about socializing them into culture and norms of our institutions.

One of my most treasured responsibilities as chief academic officer is the orientation of new faculty. The department chairs and I carefully select a mentor for each new person, and I engage the mentors in a workshop on "Mentoring for Mission," using Caroline Simon's book by that title. Administrative colleagues and I acquaint new faculty with the written rules, and the mentors acquaint them with the "invisible" rules. New faculty meet twice a month for their first year, learning about our institutional culture and expectations, and I ask them to read portions of *Joining the Mission* by Susan VanZanten. In the summer, I lead them in a two-day Core Values Retreat, where we once again discuss our mission, our institutional values, our theological heritage, the integration of faith and learning, and their role in sustaining this unique enterprise. By the end of their first year, faculty clearly understand our expectations and our vision. Like every institution, we have our distinct culture, and faculty can make an informed decision about whether the life of our community is right for them.

Tying It Together

Of course, there is no perfect formula for working with a body as diverse and individual as faculty, so the following are merely common-sense principles.

In discussions with faculty, come to the table with the assumption that all participants are people of goodwill.

Faculty have a distinct perspective based on years of training in their discipline, but they are responsible, caring members of the campus community. When they are consulted and taken seriously, they are amazing team players, willing to work with their faculty peers to reach consensus.

Take time to seek faculty input.

Faculty are intelligent and well-trained, and every proposal can be strengthened by their insightful suggestions. Even if their revisions don't make the final draft, their wisdom and thoughtfulness will enlighten the process.

Remember that process matters.

Whatever the outcome, the faculty cares deeply about the means you used to get to the end. Academic processes take time, but shortcuts are seldom productive. Building trust with the faculty can shorten the time you might otherwise have to spend on the process.

Know where key faculty members stand on crucial issues.

When a controversial proposal is in process, key faculty can be persuasive allies and are better than we are at neutralizing dissent and reaching meaningful consensus.

Let the faculty know you appreciate them.

The vast majority of faculty are working hard and making sacrifices to be at our institutions. Like people everywhere, they appreciate recognition for the contribution they are making to the institution and its mission.

Resist the temptation to stereotype faculty.

People who cherish stereotypes find ample evidence to support them by the way they frame occurrences. It is tempting to gather negative information about faculty and respond to them as if they are manipulative, self-centered, and blind to the greater good of the institution. Faculty are complex, multifaceted, unique, and not reducible to a few broad categories. Further, they are our brothers and sisters within the family of faith, comrades in our mission, and the greatest resource of the institution.

There is no denying that faculty can be difficult to lead. They are more autonomous than their peers in other sectors, they are less responsive to institutional hierarchy, and their discipline specializations shape the way they interpret and respond to information. Sometimes their reasoning is opaque and their actions are bewildering, but an honest attempt to understand their perspective through intentional conversation and discussion will help academic administrators find solutions to the riddle of faculty culture.

Notes to Chapter Seven

1. Benjamin Ginsberg, *The Fall of the Faculty*.

2. Lee Bolman and Joan V. Gallos, *Reframing Academic Leadership*, 79.

3. Ibid., 71–72.

4. Ibid., 72.

5. Ibid., 65.

6. Ibid., 57.

7. Ibid., 66.

8. Stephen Covey, *The Speed of Trust*.

For Discussion

1. Think of an incident in working with faculty when you were surprised or irritated by their response. Which of the factors described in this chapter might have been at work in that situation? Does understanding the faculty perspective help you understand their response?

2. On your faculty, who has the greatest authority? How was that authority negotiated?

3. If you needed to bring about change that would affect the faculty, where would you start? Which people would you involve?

4. Do you recognize Roland as similar to someone with whom you have worked on your faculty? Explain a situation this reminds you of. If you start with the premise that all participants are people of goodwill, then using the ideas from this chapter, speculate on what might have been going on in your situation.

5. What are some strategies for moving faculty toward buying into the mission of the institution? Does faculty buy-in to mission take a different form from staff buy-in?

6. What are some new or improved strategies you might take to increase the level of trust across your institution?

Chapter Eight

BUILDING A POWERFUL LEADERSHIP TEAM

SHIRLEY H. SHOWALTER

"Choosing leaders is the most vital and important matter . . . institutions face."

—MAX DE PREE, Leadership Jazz

I was living in North Carolina, an English professor on sabbatical leave, studying the English Romantic poets as a visiting scholar at the University of North Carolina. Having just returned from spending a month in the Lake District of northern England, I was looking forward to returning to the classroom, bringing back inspiration from my travels and studies.

Then the phone rang. On the other end was the head of the presidential search committee of Goshen College in Indiana, my home campus, the place where I had taught in the English department and served in various administrative positions over the past twenty-one years. I remember taking the call in the bedroom, gazing at the blue bedspread, and thinking that I probably should remember this moment.

The journey I entered next became my teacher in the art of leadership. From the moment I allowed myself to think about the presidency, I began to envision a team of vice presidents—leaders better than myself in their areas of expertise, full of energy and joy. I saw them in my mind's eye laughing together and praying together, serving each other and the institution, acknowledging that ultimately leadership is about service to God.

When I was brought back from Chapel Hill, North Carolina, to the campus in Goshen, Indiana, as the candidate of choice for the presidency, I met with different constituency groups. The student group meeting especially touched my heart. Students were eager to engage me on many issues, but some of them expressed sadness that I was leaving the classroom. "Will you continue to teach?" asked one. I felt an immediate sense of loss, both theirs and mine, and said, simply, "Yes."

I kept the promise to teach after I took office and had completed one academic year. In developing the curriculum for the class, I did what I had often done before: I taught a class based on what I wanted to learn. Inspired by Harvard professor Robert Coles, I borrowed his course title: The Literature of Spiritual Reflection and Social Action. The reading list of the class included, among others, these texts: *Man's Search for Meaning* by Viktor Frankl, *Nine Short Stories* by J. D. Salinger, *The Song of the Lark* by Willa Cather, and a book called *Leadership Is an Art* by Max De Pree. I developed the list by asking three individuals I admired a single question: "What book changed your life?"

As an English professor, I had never heard of Max De Pree. But since I needed to learn all I could about leadership, and as fast as possible, I devoured *Leadership Is an Art* and then went on to buy all his other books as well. When I discovered the author had retired from serving as CEO and chair of the board at Herman Miller, Inc., the pioneering furniture design company, and that he lived in Holland, Michigan, I found a phone number for him and decided to give him a call. I explained that I was a new college president who was teaching a course on spiritual reflection and social action and that the course was made up of books, his included, that had changed people's lives. I then asked if he would drive the two hours to Goshen College, speak to my class, and meet the business leader and friend of the college who said the book had changed his life. Amazingly, Max said yes.

That phone call deepened and enriched my own life as a leader. After Max had talked to my class and entered into an animated conversation with friends of the college at lunch, I asked if he would consider becoming a mentor to me. I was deeply honored when he again said yes.

Ever since that day, I have had permission to call Max at any time, a privilege I have tried not to abuse but probably have on occasion. I knew that the agenda for our meetings was up to me and that Max was less likely to give advice than to ask questions—profound ones. I also learned, eventually, that Max mentored a whole group of people located on both coasts and in the middle of the country. I met a number of the others several times and was privileged to contribute to some celebrations of Max's mentorship. The Max De Pree Center for Leadership at Fuller Theological Seminary,[1] led by another mentoree, Walt Wright, carries forward the vision of leading as an art form that so attracted me and thousands of others over the years.

Max has a talent for boiling down complex ideas into a few pithy sentences. He is often quoted, for example, as saying that the first responsibility of the leader is to "define reality. The last is to say thank you. In between the two, the leader must become a servant and a debtor."[2] The reality I saw and then defined for others when I entered the presidency was the need to build a new leadership team. I knew that choosing the members of that team was my first and most important task.

Choosing Leaders

Before I sat in the president's office, I first visited the offices of almost all the faculty members and administrative units of the college. These visits made visible what had been invisible—a wide spectrum of expectations, dreams, hurts, and desires that lay under the calm surface of the college. The only way to bring these varied and sometimes contradictory messages into conversation with each other was to find leaders who connected with everyone equally and fairly and who cultivated an environment of shared respect for all. It was a difficult task, especially at the beginning, but it was the key that enabled our leadership team and the whole community to accomplish some wonderful things together in the next eight years.

I began the work of building a team, after the visits to faculty and administrator offices, by thinking about the No. 2 position first. Goshen had had a provost when I first joined the faculty. I had observed first-hand how a president could be freed to do his or her best work with external constituents if a provost was doing his or her best work at home. With board approval, Goshen returned to the earlier model, and I searched and found a provost who complemented my skills and shared my values. From there, the provost and I could plan how to find and nurture the other leaders we needed. Some members of the previous administration remained. Some left. Making changes was hard, and I made some mistakes along the way. But I kept my eyes on the prize. My goal was to leave the institution in better shape than I found it, in the strong hands of a good team steeped in common values, able to carry on the work whether I was present or not.

As a writer and speaker, I lean toward a symbolic/human relations style of leadership, as described by Lee Bolman and Terrence Deal in *Reframing Organizations*, finding helpful tools in ritual, storytelling, and metaphor. The provost, a former chemistry professor, finds an analytic/systems approach natural. Since a good liberal arts college honors both the arts and the sciences, and since a good team is diverse, we enjoyed combining our complementary gifts and searched for even more variety in backgrounds when new hiring opportunities emerged.

The provost and I spent our early conversations thinking about how to establish an atmosphere of sacred relationship in the whole team, an idea much encouraged by the board. I was fortunate to have board members who cared about people, relationships, and ideas as well as the bottom line. My last board chair served for six years, offering continuity as well as wisdom. We read and discussed a number of books about leadership, including not only those by Max De Pree but also those by Henri Nouwen, Parker Palmer, Jim Collins, Robert Greenleaf, Margaret Wheatley, and Marcus Buckingham. We also shared poetry, concerts, and chapel talks. I felt understood by my own board as I searched for ways to not only place the "right people on the right seats on the bus,"[3] but also to nurture those people to fulfill their God-given potential.

Establishing a Covenant

Over the course of eight years, the leadership team, called the President's Council, included many different members, but one thing that the first team established together during the first year remained a constant. We called it our covenant. After reading *Leadership Is an Art*, I wanted to take the advice to look upon leadership as a trust rather than as an entitlement, a sacred obligation to followers rather than a privilege to maintain. Max never describes a literal covenant in the book; he may have been speaking metaphorically rather than literally. But our team decided to take the idea literally by writing out our high expectations of ourselves and each other and naming the document a covenant.[4] We deliberately chose sacramental language rather than legal language to describe the high bar of honesty, transparency, and excellence for which we strove.

How Did the Covenant Function in Practice?

Looking back, I would give high marks to the covenant. It spelled out significant behaviors often glossed over in organizational life—in particular, how to honor and respect each other, and how to "fight fair." The covenant focused especially on the relationships of vice presidents to each other in the weekly meetings and outside of the meetings. It encouraged fun and humor while stressing accountability and appropriate confidentiality in certain settings.

We worked on the "who" first and the "what" later. We also described the "how"—not as in how to do your work, but as in how we want to relate to each other, challenge each other, and support each other. All of us had observed teams where unresolved bickering had led to distrust, which had led to barely civil reserve. We didn't want that disintegration to happen for us. Just writing the covenant document with all vice presidents participating did a lot to help name dysfunctions we wanted to avoid and gave us language like "angel advocate," for helping ideas get an airing, "yours, mine, and ours" for clarifying territories, and "consensus minus one" as a way to describe an acceptable alternative to consensus when only one person in the group agrees to subordinate his or her perspective after others disagree. Interestingly, most decisions became a consensus in the end. Was it because everyone had the covenant to back up both individual and team rights and responsibilities? Perhaps.

Unquestionably, the covenant became a touchstone. It helped build a culture of trust at the center, recruit new people to the group, and shape and reshape the culture. Every year, we reviewed the covenant in the fall retreat and referred to it when we had difficult decisions in front of us. The team formed the covenant, and then the covenant formed the team.

Beyond the Covenant: Five Practices

While the covenant helped set the tone and manage the agenda of the team, it couldn't do everything. Looking back, I would select five other practices that helped build the team: understanding strengths, delegation, ritual, gift-giving, and getting away together. The covenant created the foundation; these practices helped to solidify sacred relationship.

Practice One: Understanding and Valuing Diverse Strengths

Max De Pree taught me that to be a leader is to "abandon oneself to the strengths of others"[5] and that "[e]ffectiveness comes about through enabling others to reach their potential."[6] I searched and listened for ways to better recognize and encourage others' strengths.

One such method came from the Gallup organization. Members of the Council for Christian Colleges & Universities had already discovered Marcus Buckingham and the Clifton StrengthsFinder instrument.[7] Our new vice president for institutional advancement, who had served previously at George Fox University, brought her knowledge of how to use the test to help employees and students understand themselves better. She led our senior team into very fruitful conversations about our individual and collective understandings about leadership based on strengths. The entire President's Council took the StrengthsFinder assessment and then made modifications in group structure, job descriptions, and team meetings according to the findings. Some of the directors then did the same with their own teams, and some students also took the test.

Decades of research by the Gallup organization, which included more than twenty thousand in-depth interviews with senior leaders, a million work teams, and ten thousand followers, resulted in the identification of three findings:

1. The most effective leaders are always investing in strengths.
2. The most effective leaders surround themselves with the right people and then maximize their team.
3. The most effective leaders understand their followers' needs. Those needs are trust, compassion, stability, and hope.[8]

Strengths-based leadership seems like an intuitive concept, so why is it practiced so little? Why do we think we should primarily value work that is hard for us and diminish the work at which we naturally excel by thinking of it as inconsequential? Isn't such self-denigration a perversion of our God-given gifts?

When working out of our strengths, we begin to sing from the same hymnal in harmonious parts and experience the joy that comes from being part of something complete and great. My mother used to sing to us and urged us to join her when we five children had to do chores:

> "When we all work together, together, together. When we all
> work together, how happy we'll be. When your work is my work
> and our work is God's work, when we all work together, how
> happy we'll be."

I hated that song in childhood. When I sang it to the faculty, they had the same reaction. But underneath, we all knew the words described an important truth.

I enjoyed not only the increased self-knowledge that results from knowing my own top five StrengthsFinder-identified themes—Input, Achiever, Learner, Self-assurance, and Strategic but also the strengths of all the other members of my team. The strengths language allowed the whole team to appreciate the ways other people's abilities enlarged our own. It helped us know when it was wise to "hold 'em and when to fold 'em," when we were likely to be convincing and when we were not, when it was a good time to delegate or a good time to coach or a good time to do a task oneself. For example, I knew if a team member had "Responsibility" as one of his or her top five strengths, keeping to deadlines would not be a problem. Similarly, since our President's Council had a high percentage of Achievers, we could use that knowledge to encourage each other to take breaks and remember that "all work and no play makes Jack (or Jill) a dull boy (or girl)."

I loved talking with the council members who reported to me about their strengths. Awareness of their natural talents gave me clues about how to express appreciation in ways they could hear. Gary Chapman has written about "love languages"—words of affirmation, quality time, gifts, acts of service, or physical touch—all of which can apply when used appropriately in the work setting.[9] Similarly, I tried to support and challenge the team in ways they preferred.

Practice Two: Delegation

One of the best gifts a leader gives his or her team is delegation. The only things presidents should do in an organization are things only the presidents can do. That's a tautology, but think about it. Those holding vice presidential roles cover the whole gamut of the organization. Presidents will have interests and expertise that overlap with those of at least some of the vice presidents, but if they begin to get involved with projects, or communicate with the direct reports of the vice president, the authority of the VP is diminished, and people can get confused about who has final authority.

Over time, I began to recognize signs about how involved to be in a given issue or territory. Some vice presidents asked for my input or presence occasionally. Some almost never did. When I had the opportunity to appear before their divisions or to describe their work to the board, I tried always to reinforce their authority and show appreciation for their work.

Practice Three: Ritual

Like all campus cultures, especially those with more than a century of history, Goshen College has acquired its own traditions and rituals. One of these is the ceremonial dunking of a new president in Schrock Fountain. Presidents Lawrence Burkholder and Vic Stoltzfus (my predecessors) and James Brenneman (my successor) have all been baptized by the students of Goshen College in fountain water. In my case, six senior women were dispatched to carry me across campus and dump me into the fountain.

There were no similar public initiation rituals for the vice presidents, but together, we created a ritual for the whole community based on a variation of one I witnessed at Converse College when I gave the inauguration address for President Nancy Grey. We created a "Welcome Tunnel" after the first convocation of the year. The President's Council left the auditorium first, followed by all administration and faculty, followed by seniors, juniors, and sophomores. Outside the exit they created a very long "applause tunnel."

When I finally dismissed the new students to leave, they found themselves being cheered, high-fived, and applauded down a long avenue of affirmation for their presence. This tradition was so popular it continues to this day and can be viewed online.[10]

We also created some private rituals in our semi-annual President's Council retreats. I recall studying the origin of the names of all the cabinet members and creating a series of exercises out of understanding the meaning of each name. This idea arose from the concept of naming in Madeleine L'Engle's book *A Wind in the Door*. In the book, the cherubim Progo sits beside Meg and calls out the names of the stars. When L'Engle visited Goshen College, she challenged all of us to become namers, a challenge I took to heart in my philosophy of education.[11] What better place to start than with the President's Council?

Practice Four: Retreat Time

When I think about nurturing the team, I think about Merry Lea, an environmental learning center and nature preserve of 1,150 acres located along Wolf Lake between Goshen and Fort Wayne, Indiana. It is the largest privately held land reserve in the state. The gift of two local philanthropists (Lee and Mary Jane Rieth, hence the name), this land creates the perfect conditions for retreats. The President's Council met there at least once annually. I remember a meditation led by our academic dean who talked about the quality of "away-ness" the land generates, a quality that we needed in order to connect to God and each other in deeper ways than the press of daily tasks generally allows.

We used times at Merry Lea to review our covenant, learn about our strengths, discuss our strategic planning progress, chart annual goals, review and celebrate our accomplishments, and just to play. We brought food and drinks and sometimes took a meal at the only café in town. Once or twice we stayed overnight to deepen the time for personal and collective renewal. I encouraged members of the council to take personal retreats and scheduled at least one each year, either at Merry Lea or The Hermitage or Gilchrist. The latter two retreat centers offered about the same level of "awayness" as Merry Lea—both are located an hour's drive away, near Three Rivers, Michigan.

Practice Five: Giving

I remember reading about one of the talents of a luminary Goshen College leader in the mid-twentieth century, Harold S. Bender, dean of both the college and the seminary. He delighted in buying gifts for people that showed his attentiveness to their interests and tastes. I enjoyed trying to follow his good example. When I traveled to South Africa on a trip sponsored by the CCCU and funded by the Mellon Foundation and the Kellogg Foundation, I searched for gifts that would be of special meaning to each of Goshen's vice presidents. Likewise, after an extraordinarily successful fundraising weekend in New York City, I enjoyed going to Macy's and picking out ties for male VP's and scarves for female VP's. Sometimes, the gifts were not about buying anything but simply intended to reflect gratitude for each person. For example, I went to the public library one evening and just spent time thinking about each of the people in my leadership team. I checked out a book that I thought he or she might enjoy and presented it to each individual at the next meeting of the President's Council. The chief financial officer was a runner, for example, so I checked out for him Alan Sillitoe's novel *The Loneliness of the Long Distance Runner.*

Food was another way to both give and receive gifts in the team. We sometimes brought tasty treats to share from our travels. But here's a tip. If you go to Switzerland, choose a cheese other than goat cheese to bring back home! And don't store it in your office before you give it away.

I also received many gifts from the campus community. After I gave a chapel talk called "How to Organize Your Scarf Collection," I started getting scarves from around the country and the world—so many that the Physical Plant staff built a special board in my office to display them. I both received these gifts and gave them away to anyone who asked for one. They became a wonderful illustration of how energy flows in a gift economy.

One gift I continue to wear almost every day. It came in the form of a piece of jade my daughter brought back from her Goshen College Study-Service Term experience in China. The jade is an oval shape, tucked inside a unique setting designed and cast by an art faculty member. It was a present from my team, the President's Council, and I cherish it.

Conclusion:
The first and last promise

Max De Pree admonishes leaders to make few promises but to deliver faithfully on those made. I promised the students one thing—to continue teaching and learning. And, when I accepted the call to lead in 1996, I made one promise to the whole community. I adapted my pledge from these words from Bishop Joseph Bernadin:

> I hope that before my name falls from the Eucharist prayer in the silence of death, you will know well who I am. You will know because we will work together and play together, fast and pray together, dispute and be reconciled together. You will know me as a friend, fellow priest, and bishop. You will also know that I love you. For I am Joseph, your brother.[12]

Looking back on eight years as president of Goshen College, I know that I was not a perfect leader. But I also know that I kept the most important promise of all—to love. The vision of a community enjoying work and play, disputing and reconciling, began with the original vision of a team of leaders at the center and spread outward to the campus and the world.

Postscript

After I left the presidency to accept a new call—to lead the program staff of the Fetzer Institute—I placed a picture of the five vice presidents who had been part of the President's Council on my new desk. I knew these people would carry forward the vision we had shaped together. During those eight years, they had guided the whole community into the embrace of our five core values; completed one strategic plan and started another; built a world-class music building, a state-of-the-art outdoor track, and sparkling new student apartments; raised almost eighty million dollars in funds, doubled the endowment; created an endowed faculty development center; and eliminated a decade or more of deferred maintenance problems.

A snapshot of the five vice presidents standing together at our last retreat brought to mind the words of the Apostle Paul, thanking God "upon every remembrance" of the Philippians. I breathed a prayer of gratitude and blessing for them every time I looked at that picture. These were the leaders to whom, because of their strengths, I had abandoned myself. They, in turn, had abandoned themselves to the other members of the community. All of us had abandoned ourselves to the students whose energy, creativity, and insights inspired us.

As I write these words in 2011, I no longer work in an organization. I have harkened to a new call, one I heard long ago but placed aside in order to accept the call to lead. I now am a full-time writer, speaker, blogger, and consultant. My husband and I are enjoying an interlude in New York City, taking care of our new grandson by day and enjoying the culture of the city at night and on weekends. I am writing a memoir about my childhood, reflecting upon the leadership team my parents established in our home.

My husband and I are building a leadership team with our son Anthony and daughter-in-law Chelsea around the goal of creating a healthy beginning for our grandson's life. Anthony and Chelsea have abandoned themselves to our strengths, and we have participated in forming a covenant with them. The language of all good teams, at work or at home, is sacred. It's the language of love.

PRESIDENT'S COUNCIL COVENANT

Goshen College

1. President's Council Meetings
   - Bi-weekly schedule, 8:30–noon on Tuesdays.
   - Attendance required.
   - Promptness expected.
   - Meetings begun with meditation and prayer.
   - Meeting cancelled if two or more members need to be absent.

2. Purposes of President's Council Meetings
   - Primary focus is on strategic issues and decisions with **45 minutes** of reporting.
   - Individual and area agenda sent to president's assistant by the Friday before each meeting.
   - Ongoing team-building and communication.
   - Lunch afterwards—fun—relational.

3. Confidentiality
   - In general, what is discussed in PC needs to remain confidential among President's Council members.
   - Difficult issues involving personnel should be brought to the PC for counsel, for information if another area might be affected and/or for crisis management. The director of human resources should be consulted early in such cases.
   - In certain situations, it may be necessary to share information with program directors on a "need to know" basis.
   - There may be times when colleagues at a distance may be helpful in offering an outside perspective—this is a judgment call on the part of an individual vice president.

- Weekly minutes of the President's Council meetings show what is public information.

4. Process for Addressing Differences in President's Council Meetings and/or Outside of Meetings
   - Search for commonalities—what do we agree on?
   - Name differences.
   - Determine if the difference grows out of a principle held by a member or a preference of a member.
   - Consensus in decision making is our goal. However, there may be situations, when timeliness is of the essence, that it may be necessary to act without reaching complete agreement. In those cases, "consensus minus one" will be acceptable.
   - Use the "Angel Advocate Principle": The second person to speak after an idea is given will first identify strengths of the idea before offering critique.
   - If something still bothers a council member after 24 hours, go to the person with whom you have differences and have a conversation (Matthew 18). If you have not confronted the person within a short period of time (24–48 hours), agree to let go of the issue(s).
   - In general, differences should be addressed face-to-face, not through email.
   - If a PC member receives a complaint about another council member, refer the person directly to the council member with whom the person has a concern. If there is a power difference between the person and the vice president, go with this person or arrange for an advocate. In such cases, the director of human resources will usually be brought into the situation.
   - We agree not to impute motives to others.

5. Accountability
   - Continue to work on clarity of what decisions are mine, yours and ours.
   - Ask questions when you are not sure.
   - Try to identify a point person when two or more work together.
   - Unity is the responsibility of each member.
   - Each VP meets with another and discusses what's mine/yours/ours.

6. Conduct
   - Be sensitive to the feelings of others in the group.
   - Recognize that internal jokes can be easily misunderstood.
   - Practice fun, humor, trust, and honesty. Include families on occasion.

7. Mutual Support—Physical, Emotional and Spiritual
   - Share stories of our lives.
   - Regular prayer for one another.
   - Aiding one another in times of crisis.
   - Expectation that council members will ask for help when needed.

Notes to Chapter Eight

1. The website for the Max De Pree Center for Leadership is available at http://depree.org/.

2. Max De Pree, *Leadership Is an Art*, 11.

3. See Jim Collins, *Good to Great*: "The executives who ignited the transformations from good to great did not first figure out where to drive the bus and then get people to take it there. No, they first got the right people on the bus (and the wrong people off the bus) and then they figured out where to drive it," 41.

4. In choosing the word covenant over other words, like contract, we followed Max De Pree's language for the spiritual base of relationship we wanted to follow. See *Leadership Is an Art*, 15, 37, and 53–62.

5. De Pree, *Leadership Is an Art*, 9.

6. Ibid., 19.

7. See the instrument's website at http://www.strengthsfinder.com/home.aspx.

8. Tom Rath and Barry Conchie, *Strengths Based Leadership*, 82.

9. See Gary Chapman's website, http://www.5lovelanguages.com/.

10. See, for example, the 2009 Applause Tunnel, available for viewing at http://www.goshen.edu/virtualgc/videos/2009/applause-tunnel/.

11. Shirley Hershey Showalter, "Discovering an Anabaptist Voice," 41–53.

12. Joseph Bernardin, *The Gift of Peace*, 141–42.

For Discussion

1. What elements of team building do you find most difficult? Most rewarding? Why?

2. Have you ever developed a literal covenant in your organization? Why or why not? If yes, what was your experience of its value? Would you do it again?

3. Is delegation easy or difficult for you? How have you evolved a delegation style that suits you and your team best? What would you still like to learn in this area?

4. Below are ten suggestions (not commandments!) taken from the chapter. How can you improve upon them?

Ten Suggestions for Developing a Powerful Leadership Team
1. Finding the right people to name to leadership positions is the leader's number one job.
2. Placing them in the "right seats" comes next.
3. Agree on goals and expectations before beginning.
4. Once the team is assembled, develop a covenant. Talk about the group's aspirations, both how the individuals want to relate to each other and what they want to avoid.
5. Review all goals and the covenant at least annually. Adapt and amend to meet current needs.
6. Develop practices that fit your own leadership context, style, and the campus culture.
7. Lead from your own strengths and know the strengths of your team members.
8. Delegate effectively.
9. Identify rituals you want to keep and create new ones to underscore your collective dreams for the students and faculty.
10. Retreat together. Rest and play together. Abandon yourself to God and each other.

Chapter Nine

MENTORING FOR LEADERSHIP

Jeanine B. Varner

*"It's good to do uncomfortable things.
It's weight training for life."*

—ANNE LAMOTT, Plan B

When my son was about seven or eight years old, my husband and I decided that it was time to have "the talk"—the dreaded birds and bees talk. I don't remember now why we believed it was the right time or why the initial conversation came to be my responsibility. What I do remember is explaining the fundamentals of sex to him and then pausing to ask if he had any questions. And I remember his hesitant response: "Well, yes, I do have one question. . . . Why would anybody *want* to do that?!"

Perhaps the same question might be asked about higher education leadership. Consider what we communicate, intentionally or unintentionally, about higher education leadership: its long hours, its incessant demands, its petty annoyances. So, yes, to borrow the words of my son, I ask, "Why would anybody *want* to do that?!"

Apparently many others are asking the same question. Higher education institutions are facing a crisis of leadership.

A Crisis of Leadership

In 1989, Estela M. Bensimon, Anna Neumann, and Robert Birnbaum pointed out the frequent calls "for better, stronger, and bolder leadership" in higher education.[1] For the last twenty years, those calls have become increasingly frequent and frantic. Adrianna Kezar, Rozana Carducci, and Melissa Contreras-McGavin argue that "the need for leadership in higher education has only become more urgent as fat days with regular increases from state governments are long over, and the days of accountability and assessment, globalization, and competition are here to stay, providing new pressures for colleges and universities."[2]

The urgency is particularly great in Christian higher education. On many Christian university campuses, senior leaders struggle to fill positions for chairs and deans. Presidents find a limited pool of qualified candidates for chief academic officer positions, and boards find themselves with few qualified candidates for the position of chief executive officer. In the last few years, I have known of at least four presidential searches that, astonishingly, elicited only a few qualified candidates.

Searches for key leadership positions are frequent and costly. They are costly in regard to the money spent on the search and interview process, of course, but they are also costly in regard to the stress on the institution and the time so many personnel must expend on the process.

Faculty Members' Attitudes Toward Leadership

Many faculty, in particular, fear moving into positions of academic leadership. Having witnessed various turnovers in administrative positions, they are concerned—perhaps rightly—about the instability they would be accepting in taking on such a position. They also fear that in accepting an administrative position, they would be committing intellectual suicide. They fear that they would be abandoning longstanding friendships with faculty peers. They fear that they would be trading meaningful moments of lively intellectual exchange with students for days filled with repetitious administrivia.

A Problem of Our Own Making?

Why do faculty tend to think this way about administrative roles? It may be that administrators themselves are frequently guilty of emphasizing the frustrating and disappointing aspects of their work. Those of us who serve in senior administrative roles might do well to do some self-monitoring to observe how frequently we make negative comments among ourselves or to our faculty colleagues about the burdens of leadership. How often, on the other hand, do we communicate the joy of our work? In what ways do we communicate that? Have we said anything in recent days or weeks or even months that could make a faculty member perceive why our leadership work is pleasant or intellectually stimulating or in any way rewarding?

Senior administrative leaders need to consider and reconsider what makes their work satisfying. It may be obvious that the typical increase in salary is a benefit. But we need to speak openly and often about other rewards as well. We need to convey to our faculty colleagues the joy of leadership—the joy of helping to fulfill a mission in which we believe deeply, of helping shape the future of our institutions, of setting and accomplishing meaningful academic goals. We can acknowledge some of the challenges of leadership, but if we hope to encourage others to accept leadership positions, we must acknowledge the joys as well.

Some administrators do lose touch with their academic disciplines— and their faculty colleagues see that. It is true that the demands of academic leadership frequently impinge on a leader's scholarly work in his or her discipline. There may be some effective ways to avoid losing touch with one's academic discipline. Perhaps it is simply making a commitment to read regularly in one or two disciplinary journals. Making a commitment annually to attend at least one scholarly conference in one's discipline can be helpful. Some administrators make a commitment to write one article per year in their academic discipline; they may commit one month each summer, for example, to research and writing. Commitments such as these are helpful to the administrator's work and intellectual life; they also serve to show faculty colleagues that accepting an administrative position need not equate to intellectual suicide.

Some administrators do find themselves cut off from faculty and student colleagues and increasingly isolated from the very reason for the existence of the university—teaching and learning. This danger for administrators is very real. They may find that they have not had substantive academic conversations with their faculty colleagues in weeks or months. They may find that they have not had intellectually stimulating conversations—or even casual, friendly conversations—with students in weeks or months. They may indeed find that they are losing touch. But that need not be the case. In fact, that must not be the case. Administrative leaders—particularly at the dean level and above—must make opportunities for deep interaction with faculty members and students. They must schedule such interactions deliberately. Perhaps the administrator can teach a short course or team-teach a regular course. Perhaps the administrator can establish a weekly lunch with faculty groups or student groups, or reserve one lunch per week for substantive interaction with a faculty member. Finding opportunities for interaction can be soul-renewing for the administrator and can also help others to realize that leadership positions are not inevitably isolating.

Of course, some faculty don't *fear* moving into positions of academic leadership; they simply have no interest in doing so. They have worked many years to prepare themselves in their discipline, and they have honed their craft. They love their students, and they don't want to take on any leadership position that could impinge on their connection with students. I certainly don't believe faculty members should be coerced into accepting leadership roles. However, I do think it is important for senior administrators to talk frankly and concretely with faculty members who have leadership potential about how they could maintain their connection with students and, for a time, add a leadership role.

Preparing Faculty for Leadership

Obviously, not every faculty member desires or is suited for positions of academic leadership. But our institutions desperately need more leaders—and stronger leaders—for the present and for the future. In the June 2011 article "Rethinking Higher Education's Leadership Crisis," Daniel Fusch and Amit Mrig cited a survey of senior- and mid-level higher education leaders. In response to the question, "How is your institution responding to the waves of faculty and administrators who will be retiring in the next five years?" a discouraging forty percent of respondents indicated that their institutions were not preparing. Their responses included such phrases as "no institution-wide strategy, not doing anything, seat-of-pants approach, hoping problem goes away." Even more discouragingly, forty-eight percent of the respondents assigned their institutions "a C, D, or F letter grade when assessing the level of commitment they felt their institution has toward their development as a leader."[3]

Clearly, we must find more effective ways to identify, develop, and sustain academic leaders. How can senior academic leaders identify individuals who might have the potential to become future academic leaders? They can scout continuously, observe carefully, experiment cautiously, and encourage lavishly.

Scout Continuously

Senior academic leaders can and should scout continuously. They can scout even among undergraduate and graduate students for academic leadership potential. Such students will likely have years of academic preparation ahead of them before they can assume positions of academic leadership. But if we identify leadership potential early, students may begin to consider opportunities early in their graduate programs. Within the last year, I've discussed the joys of academic leadership with three undergraduate students in whom I've seen great potential. One, a senior named Jordan, told me he was interested in an internship; I asked him to intern in the provost's office, and I assigned him the task of doing a complete revision of the university's Study Abroad Handbook. It was an important task that needed to be done, and he did it well. To complete the task he had to work collaboratively with the provost, the executive director of the Office of International Education, the Legal Services Office, and a variety of support staff members. I was scouting for potential future academic leadership. I have no doubt that Jordan will complete a doctorate in communication. And I hope as he does so, he will have, from that summer's internship, a particular insight into organizational structure and communication, as well as a notion of his potential for academic leadership. The two other students I've scouted this year are Samuel and Noemi, a Hispanic brother and sister. The two are high achievers, with excellent minds and hearts and demonstrated leadership ability as undergraduates. The two aspire to earn doctorates, Samuel in communication and Noemi in biblical studies. Samuel began his graduate work in Fall 2011 at the University of Texas, while Noemi completes her undergraduate work in Spring 2012. The university needs their leadership abilities, and I believe it is not at all too soon for them to begin thinking about their potential as academic leaders.

Observe Carefully

Senior academic leaders must also observe faculty carefully to discern leadership potential. Provosts, vice presidents, and deans can take notice of faculty members who naturally use leadership gifts, sometimes in quiet ways that are hardly noticeable. Which faculty members seem to have a real understanding of institutional mission, organization, and culture? Which faculty members have a genuine interest in and appreciation for disciplines other than their own? Which faculty members have a special ability to work with groups of students or to mentor student organizations? Which faculty members have an ability to collaborate with colleagues to accomplish a task? Senior leaders who observe carefully can identify leadership potential. It may be that the time is not yet right to offer a faculty member an opportunity to move into a leadership situation. However, a senior leader can always take the opportunity to point out, privately at least, in a note or even an email, what leadership skills a faculty member has demonstrated in a particular situation.

Experiment Cautiously

Sometimes faculty members may find themselves thrust into leadership situations for which they are not at all prepared. Senior academic leaders should experiment cautiously with leadership situations, providing faculty members with leadership opportunities of increasing responsibility. Perhaps a young faculty member can be assigned to chair a departmental committee, then a college-wide task force, then a section of a university self-study. Senior academic leaders can observe and commend the faculty member's efforts, critiquing as needed. The gradually increasing responsibilities and successes can allow faculty members to experience the joy and success of leadership and prepare them to say yes as formal leadership positions become available.

Encourage Lavishly

Senior academic leaders must make the effort to encourage lavishly. Although the encouragement can be monetary—a payment delivered upon the completion of a project—often the best form of encouragement is the hand-written note, a sincere expression of thanks for a job well done, including some specific commendation of the faculty member's demeanor or insights or actions. Such notes become a written record, a sometimes-surprising account of a faculty member's increasing leadership skills and abilities.

Certainly the annual review is a good opportunity for such commendation. But often the most effective opportunity is the most immediate one—catching a faculty member in the act of demonstrating leadership, commending that individual immediately and specifically after a committee report or a faculty meeting in which he or she demonstrated some leadership skill.

Sustaining Leaders

Senior administrators must also find ways to sustain academic leaders. One reason for faculty members' reluctance to accept leadership positions is that they fear there is No Exit. They fear that if they accept a position as department chair, for example, they will find themselves stuck in that position forever. In some institutions, unfortunately, that is the case. Faculty members must be allowed to step out of leadership positions for a time or perhaps forever. Some institutions, on the other hand, have done a good job of setting renewable terms for particular leadership roles such as chair or dean. For those who are appointed to positions with expectations of long service, presidents and other senior leaders need to think about creative ways to provide sabbaticals (or mini-sabbaticals). Chairs, deans, and cabinet-level leaders can benefit greatly even from mini-sabbaticals, from a month to three months, in which they are completely freed from administrative responsibilities.

Opportunities for ongoing professional development for administrators must also be readily and regularly available, just as they must be for faculty members. Administrators may find it difficult to get away from campus for professional development. Sometimes the reason is financial; they may think of the limited professional development funds that are available and decide to forego their own professional conferences in order to send faculty members instead. Sometimes, however, the reason may be a matter of time; they may feel they simply can't get away from campus because there is just too much to do. Senior leaders need to be particularly vigilant to ensure that those in leadership roles reporting to them make the time for local, state, national, and, if possible, international professional development opportunities, which can sustain them in the leadership work they do.

If we are to address the crisis in leadership in our higher education institutions, senior leaders and boards must have the courage and the determination to address the problem. We absolutely must not assume the problem will be self-correcting. We must speak openly about the problem and consider frankly and specifically who the future leaders for our institutions will be. Senior leaders and boards must recognize that such leaders must be developed, usually over the course of many years. Senior leaders and boards must also recognize that many faculty members do not aspire to positions of administrative leadership and that even those who do will need significant encouragement and development. We must mentor future leaders.

Mentoring for Leadership

I have been the beneficiary of both informal and formal mentoring throughout my professional life, and I will forever be grateful to my mentors. I am most grateful to one mentor who has invested himself in my life for more than forty years.

I first met Dr. Bailey McBride in my first year of college. He was my academic advisor and my English professor. From the first day I met him, when I was a college freshman, he seemed to take me seriously as a student. He paid careful attention to my academic interests and my academic progress. He challenged me in my undergraduate literature classes, and he followed my progress through a master's degree and a doctorate.

My mentor recommended me for my first full-time teaching position after graduate school. Several years later, having moved into a chief academic officer's role, he hired me for my second full-time teaching position. There the mentoring continued: he placed in my path opportunity after opportunity to increase my knowledge and my experience. He encouraged me to accept positions of increasing responsibility—as department chair, as dean, eventually as chief academic officer—the very position he held at the time.

Now, more than forty years later, he remains my mentor. I am at a different university, in a different state, but I still draw upon the experiences he put in my path and the wise counsel he has given and continues to give, and I work to provide similar support for others.

Formal Mentoring Programs

In addition to benefiting from the informal personal mentoring I have received, I am grateful for two more formal, structured mentoring programs. The first of such programs was a crash course in higher education provided through a regional accrediting body. I was encouraged by my mentor to apply to become a consultant-evaluator for the Higher Learning Commission of the North Central Association. Once accepted into the consultant-evaluator corps, I benefited enormously from annual professional development programs and from serving on peer review teams alongside colleagues from institutions quite similar to and utterly different from my own. Accreditation visits allowed me to delve deeply, albeit quickly, into other institutions' policies and practices, strengths and weaknesses. They allowed me to offer advice and counsel as a peer, but they also allowed me to return to my own campus with a broader understanding of the world of higher education and a host of new ideas to consider. In my years of work as a consultant-evaluator, team chair, and trainer for the Higher Learning Commission, I encountered many academic leaders who considered their accreditation work crucial in their own professional development and their path toward leadership.

Another formal, structured mentoring program that was highly beneficial to me was one offered through the Council for Christian Colleges & Universities. Designed to develop and sustain effective leadership in Christian colleges and universities, the Leadership Development Institutes have since 1996 brought together cohorts of leaders and emerging leaders in intensive summer programs, followed by year-long one-to-one mentoring relationships. The program is structured so that less experienced leaders shadow more experienced leaders, observing them as they go about two to three days of work on their home campuses and then staying in contact by telephone and email throughout the year.

In 1993, leaders in the CCCU discussed their serious concerns about leadership development in its member institutions. As reported by Karen A. Longman and Shawna L. Lafreniere, "With supportive funding provided by a foundation, a Steering Committee was formed to oversee the development of a project called the Executive Leadership Development Initiative (ELDI); the goal was to provide professional development for newer presidents, newer chief academic officers, and emerging leaders."[4] The Executive Leadership Development Institutes began in 1996 with the Presidents' Institute, and it was followed in 1997 by a Chief Academic Officers' Institute. Leadership Development Institutes were added in 1998; resulting in "a three-year rotating cycle of leadership development programming."[5]

One of the great benefits of CCCU's Executive Leadership Development Initiative has been that the institutes allowed participants to think deeply about their leadership gifts and to consider how they might further develop and use their leadership skills and abilities. In serving as a resource person for these programs for several years, I have had a number of people, particularly women, tell me that until their participation in these institutes, away from their campuses, they had never really thought of themselves as leaders. They acknowledged that they took on important tasks on their campus, but, as they saw it, they just naturally did what needed to be done. As we reviewed and discussed the tasks they had undertaken and completed, they were often genuinely surprised to recognize their leadership work and their leadership gifts.

A number of other leadership development and mentoring programs have proven quite successful. Among these are the American Council on Education (ACE) programs, the Harvard Institutes, and the Bryn Mawr summer institutes for women. All of these programs can be enormously helpful in providing individuals crucial tools for leadership, important networks for leadership, and focused time for considering leadership opportunities.

Perhaps the most important step senior leaders can take is to mentor, both informally and formally, individuals on their own campuses and elsewhere, directing attention to their leadership potential and preparing them deliberately for effective leadership. Senior leaders should speak individually to talented faculty members who demonstrate leadership, pointing out leadership qualities of which the faculty members themselves may or may not be aware. Taking care not to take unfair advantage of faculty members' willingness, senior leaders can put in their path increasing opportunities for leadership and then find ways to support, encourage, and, as needed, constructively critique the leadership those faculty members demonstrate. It is crucial, of course, for leaders to be especially aware of and responsive to leadership qualities in women and minorities—qualities that may be different from those of the individuals typically in leadership positions.

Perhaps a president, provost, or dean could establish an ongoing reading group for emerging leaders—individuals who might volunteer for such a group or individuals recommended by their peers. Simply participating in such a reading group might encourage individuals to begin considering their potential for leadership. Over time, participating in such a reading group could provide individuals with a deep understanding of a wide range of literature on the subject of leadership. A reading group at Azusa Pacific University—a group known as Leaders Are Readers—for example, has discussed more than twenty books during lunch-hour meetings in recent years.

The Course of Leadership

An important concern for those contemplating leadership roles is the concern for what is next. Faculty members who spend a typical career in faculty positions may be quite clear about what is next; they begin, most often, as assistant professors, and they move up the faculty ranks until they reach the rank of professor, where they remain until retirement. The course of academic leadership, however, seldom is smooth. After one accepts a position as chair or dean, what is next?

If we are to develop and sustain administrative leaders, we need to speak more openly and often about what is next—that is, about the trajectories an academic career may take. If a faculty member accepts a leadership position in his thirties, for instance, should he expect to continue in that position indefinitely? Can he successfully return to a faculty position a few years later? Will he be accepted back into the ranks of faculty? Will he likely enjoy a return to a faculty position? If a faculty member becomes a dean in her forties, should she expect to move into a vice presidential or provost role in her fifties? What is next for her? What should she expect or hope?

As we seek to develop academic leadership for our institutions, we need to speak frankly about the possible trajectories of an academic career. Faculty members in the earliest stages of their professional lives can be encouraged to consider their leadership potential. Even promising undergraduate and graduate students can be identified and encouraged to think about their path toward leadership. But it is not reasonable to assume that they can or will pursue positions of academic leadership without genuine encouragement and thoughtful mentoring. If we are to develop strong leadership for the future of our institutions, we must try to answer faculty members' many questions, spoken or unspoken: Why would I want to lead? What about my career as a faculty member? What leadership qualities do I have? What leadership skills do I lack? What happens next?

Mentoring for leadership can sometimes happen informally. I am forever grateful to my mentor—the person who showed me that I had leadership potential and who encouraged me every step of the way on my path as an academic leader. We need more people like him, leaders who are continually about the task of identifying and developing the next generation of leaders. Whether formally or informally, we who are now academic leaders must mentor future leaders, preparing them for the joys as well as the challenges of leadership for our institutions.

Notes to Chapter Nine

1. Estela M. Bensimon, Anna Neumann, and Robert Birnbaum, *Making Sense of Administrative Leadership*.

2. Adrianna Kezar, Rozana Carducci, and Melissa Contreras-McGavin, *Rethinking the "L" Word in Higher Education*.

3. Daniel Fusch and Amit Mrig, *Rethinking Higher Education's Leadership Crisis*.

4. Karen A. Longman and Shawna Lafreniere, "Moving Beyond the Stained Glass Ceiling," 50.

5. Longman and Lafreniere, "Looking Back and Looking Ahead," 13–14.

For Discussion

1. Can you recall the first time when you realized you had leadership ability? How did you know?

2. Who have been some of the mentors in your life? In what ways did they mentor you?

3. Have you been a mentor to anyone in your professional life? Who? How much did you mentor that individual?

4. How much of leadership ability is a natural trait? How much is learned?

5. Can leadership really be taught? What lessons have you received related to effective leadership? How did you learn those lessons?

PART III

How Leaders Can
Shape a Thriving
Organizational Culture

Chapter Ten

METAPHORS MATTER
Organizational Culture Shaped by Image

MARIE S. MORRIS

*"It is something to be able to paint a particular picture, or to carve
a statue, and so to make a few objects beautiful; but it is far
more glorious to carve and paint the very atmosphere and medium
through which we look, which morally we can do. To affect the
quality of the day, that is the highest of arts."*

—HENRY DAVID THOREAU, Walden

*"Ring the bells that still can ring,
Forget your perfect offering.
There is a crack in everything,
That's how the light gets in."*

—LEONARD COHEN, "Anthem"

Metaphors matter. Metaphors guide our individual expression of leadership. As we lead, we affect the educational approach taken at our institution, and ultimately, the institution's organizational culture. Our academic institutions are structured, informed, and guided by distinct organizational cultures, all of which are shaped by metaphors. Activities of strategic planning, budgeting, and our core purpose of educating students are carried out within these metaphor-informed organizational cultures. Visibly, each institution has a mission and vision statement, strategic plan, bylaws, policies, procedures, and rules that give operational guidance. Less visible, underneath all the written documents, are assumptions that are informed by deeply embedded images.

Frequently, we look to sports metaphors to illustrate leadership concepts, pedagogical approaches, and/or organizational cultures. Sports metaphors provide powerful images. In this chapter, however, I encourage the reader to examine other images that can shed light on our work in the academy. Whether one believes that leadership comes naturally or is developed (the long-standing nature versus nurture argument), leadership does not exist in a vacuum, and neither does our educational philosophy or our distinct organizational culture. How we lead, the pedagogical approach we foster, and our institution's culture, become the embodiment of our "root metaphors."[1]

Personal Guiding Metaphors— Creating Atmosphere and Yielding to Light

Metaphors inform my leadership. In the summer of 2000, through supportive funding from a Bennett, Kellogg, and Mellon Scholarship, I had the opportunity to attend the HERS Bryn Mawr Summer Institute for Women in Higher Education Administration. Each HERS summer cohort develops a motto that can then be printed on T-shirts, sweatshirts, or canvas bags as a memento of that particular cohort's experience. My cohort's motto was "Administration as a creative act." I believe it was either at Bryn Mawr, or shortly thereafter, that I discovered the Thoreau quote set as an epigraph for this chapter. To this day, this quote guides my leadership and the environment I seek to create. Conceptualizing the leader as an artist who sculpts and paints the atmosphere of the organization in a way that positively affects the quality of daily work life is indeed a high art. I suspect that those institutions that make it into "best places to work" rankings have at least some element of sculpting an atmosphere that facilitates an environment for creativity and innovation.

Turning to another metaphor, I've yet to meet a higher education leader, or to see an academic institution, that has not experienced pitfalls along the way. It is during the valleys of institutional life that I find Leonard Cohen's image of a crack so very helpful; that is, the purpose of the crack is to let in light. The resulting sliver of light can help us notice what we hadn't seen before. Many who find their way into higher education are perfectionists, and

Cohen reminds us to relax, for often, it is in the imperfections or cracks that wisdom or a new approach can emerge.

Metaphors Inform the Leader

Images conjured by metaphors can help us understand leadership moments in ways that words may fail to convey. In their book, *Metaphors We Live By,* George Lakoff and Mark Johnson enlighten us to the notion that metaphors go beyond "poetic imagination" and "rhetorical flourish"; rather, metaphors inform our thoughts and actions.[2] Metaphors not only inform our intellect but also all the little choices we make each day, even influencing seemingly insignificant activities. While these operative metaphors may not be explicit, they affect our perceptions, our way of being in the world, and our relationships with others. Metaphors define our everyday functioning much more than we may realize. Lakoff and Johnson contend that because "our conceptual system is largely metaphorical, then the way we think, what we experience, and what we do every day is very much a matter of metaphor." Metaphors inform our leadership behaviors, which in turn impact the environment we create. *A metaphor and a paradigm are not the same thing*

In my years in the academy, as a faculty member and as an academic administrator, I have seen a number of metaphors informing the work of individual leaders, who then help shape the organizational culture of the institution. Individual leader responses to simple life choices can reveal competing metaphors. For example, one leader's way of responding in a situation may fit a hierarchical metaphor where a "pecking order" exists and various roles or positions hold different value. When operating by a hierarchical metaphor (i.e., boss vs. subordinate), a leader may believe it is highly appropriate to expect her or his subordinate to perform menial tasks for the leader. From a hierarchical paradigm, the leader's role may be viewed as more significant to the organization, the leader's time as more valuable, and certain tasks as beneath the leader's position. Contrast this with a leader who reflects a non-hierarchical or democratic metaphor, perhaps a web, where all members are viewed as filling an important role. For this leader, one employee is not valued more highly than another; rather, all are viewed as fulfilling different roles in the organization. A leader operating by such a metaphor may understand that her or his subordinates have equally valid deadlines to meet, and interrupting their work to perform a basic task for the leader does not respect the relevant contribution of those individuals to the organization. The following real-world example may seem simplistic; however, I believe that it illustrates responses of two leaders informed by differing metaphors:

> One day, the director of international students held a lunch meeting in the conference room just outside the Administrative Suite. At the end of the meeting, there were several leftover sandwiches. The director invited Sue and Candace, two of the executive leadership staff, to help themselves, saying, "They'll just spoil." Since Sue and Candace had yet to break for lunch, they each ate a sandwich. When finished, Candace began to clean up their mess, but Sue stopped her with the words: "Don't bother with that. I'll just get my assistant to clean up." Candace responded, "But your assistant didn't eat anything, so why should she have to clean up our mess?" Sue retorted, "That's why we have assistants."

Lee G. Bolman and Terrence E. Deal, in *Reframing Organizations: Artistry, Choice, & Leadership,* contribute to our understanding of leadership through their examination of Structural, Political, Human Resource, and Symbolic frames used by leaders.[3] When Sue took Bolman and Deal's leadership inventory, she was found to operate within the Structural and Political frames, while Candace operated within the Human Resource and Symbolic frames. As such, Candace viewed the organization as an extended family or tribe where the feelings and needs of individuals (such as Alice, Sue's assistant) ought to be considered. From her structural/political lens of formal relationships and specialized roles, Sue thought it reasonable to request that Alice clean up the mess that she herself had made, given a structural order to relationships. Therefore, cleaning up after the supervisor would appear to be a legitimate part of an assistant's role.

In a discussion of the differences and benefits of "broad-spectrum notice" and "focused-notice," Sally Helgesen and Julie Johnson's recent book, *The Female Vision,* includes the story of a speechwriter who was invited by the company CEO to participate in a brainstorming session to resolve a particular

I think a metaphor is a tool to be used, not a place to operate from

problem.[4] The speechwriter offered a possible solution for consideration. Upon leaving the meeting, feeling good about her contribution, "the head of corporate communications pulled her aside and scolded her for bringing the matter up. In part he was annoyed because she hadn't mentioned the idea to him before the meeting; he was her superior and information was supposed to be channeled through him." Although Helgesen and Johnson use this story to illustrate broad versus focused noticing, it also provides an interesting example of a leader who operates out of a hierarchical metaphor. For such a leader, proper channels and reporting lines take precedence over finding the best possible solution to a problem by involving all members of the institution in a collaborative process.

Even when a leader like Candace, who operates according to a web metaphor rather than a hierarchical one, may strive first and foremost to be inclusive and to attempt reweaving broken relationships, the two departmental situations below illustrate how differing outcomes may still result:

> In Department A, Samantha is struggling to effectively lead her department, which results in disillusion among departmental colleagues. Her supervisor is faced with terminating or reassigning her for failure to build a healthy department. However, the supervisor contemplates a web-based approach to leadership and searches for a way to "reweave" the web of relationships and thus build a stronger team. It turns out that Samantha is dealing with a personal situation that is influencing her relationships with her staff. With appropriate support, Samantha seeks professional counseling and is able to rebuild relationships with colleagues.
>
> Meanwhile, in Department B, Robert's teaching effectiveness is in question. Other departments that rely on Robert to provide critical prerequisite knowledge for their majors have lost confidence in him and are frustrated with his department for not addressing the deficiencies. Opportunities are given to develop Robert's pedagogical skills and to "reweave" the confidence across departments, but to no avail. Robert's dean considers the web metaphor, and although his preference would be to positively resolve

the situation, he realizes that there does not seem to be a way to meet the educational needs of the students by retaining Robert; consequently, a decision is made not to renew his contract.

Leadership author Max De Pree's counsel is beneficial in understanding how effective leadership can help persons realize their fullest potential. De Pree says that the art of leadership is really about "liberating people to do what is required of them in the most effective and humane way possible."[5] In situations such as those described above, a leader may desire positive outcomes such that the web of relationships can be rewoven in ways that result in realized potential for all. The unfortunate reality, however, is that wounds can run deep, resulting in severed relationships. Leadership, regardless of how idealistic or positive one's operating metaphor may be, or how sincere one's intention, comes with costs.

Clearly, the metaphors that inform our thinking shape individuals' behavior. As leaders we have the privilege and the power to affect our organization's environment. Imagine the confusion created in an institution when two senior leaders operate by competing metaphors, such as a hierarchical and a web metaphor. For example, when Sue and Candace work together collegially, they bring to their work all four frames identified by Bolman and Deal, thereby allowing for maximum effectiveness. However, the competing metaphors that inform their leadership approaches create conflicting environments, which can result in incoherence and employee confusion.

Metaphors Inform an Institution's Pedagogy

Not only do metaphors inform an individual's way of being in the world, they also inform an institution's pedagogy. In its infancy, the American university was informed by the metaphor of a "disciplinary citadel" where numerous regulations, carried out by a highly paternalistic administration and faculty, created a controlling environment so young collegians would be matured, molded, and shaped.[6] Learners were viewed as empty vessels, and the professor constructed his masterful lecture in private as he was, indeed, the "sage on the stage."

Another metaphor informing some faith-based institutions has been that of a monastery, which aims at faithfulness through orthodoxy and is structured with superiors and novitiates, not unlike the early citadels of education. What is the impact of such a structure on academic freedom and the creation of a learning environment to support truth-seeking by the learner? At an academic institution where orthodoxy dominates, are young learners granted the freedom to wrestle with life's tough questions, or are there some topics that are off limits?

Over the years, the American university has continued to develop, evolving from a protective fortress to more of an assemblage of bastions with pervasive individualism and disciplinary silos that exist on most campuses. Years ago, when I was interviewing for a dean's position, a group of students asked me, "Dr. Morris, if you were to be our dean, what would you do to help there to be better connections between disciplines? You see, we have professors who don't seem to have a clue what others are teaching, and we are left to sort it all out and make connections by ourselves. It would help if the faculty talked to each other!" They were articulating the isolation that comes as a result of those discipline-specific bastions.

Then again, in these times of economic uncertainty, with an increased focus on efficiency, many universities may be tempted to operate by a factory metaphor. Traditionally, factories focus on cost-efficiency in producing a consumable good. Translate this to higher education and the "consumable good" may be a career-prepared graduate versus one who is educated by a foundational liberal arts education with encouragement to follow a vocational calling. Universities informed by a factory metaphor will structure themselves with managers, line workers, and customers in mind. Workers in a factory are not hired to think, but rather to do. The "higher ups" set the machine in motion, and the workers are simply on the production line with repetitive tasks to produce the factory's particular brand of widget. Line workers do not need, nor are they encouraged, to think creatively or otherwise about developing the widget.

A factory metaphor applied to an academic institution reveals a pedagogical approach where students are viewed as widgets to be passed along a production line with faculty serving as the line workers. A factory metaphor may be useful in structuring for efficiency and cost-effectiveness, and our institutions certainly need to be fiscally viable; however, if it's taken too far, we stand to lose the heart of higher education, which is to prepare well-educated individuals able to positively impact a complex and diverse world. A human widget will not have the depth of critical and creative thinking, the wisdom of reflection, and the soul of the kind of citizen who can address the challenges ahead.

I believe a pedagogical approach shaped primarily by a factory metaphor will be inadequate for achieving what will be necessary in the future. In his book *A Whole New Mind,* Daniel Pink suggests that a significant learning outcome for graduates will be the ability to read and interpret human interaction in all its subtleties.[7] "Student as learner" must trump "student as widget" if we are to educate tomorrow's leaders.

Today's college students, however, are coming to us having grown up in a consumer-oriented environment, resulting in many of our academic institutions feeling pressured to cater to the wants and likes of this consumer orientation. Such pressures prompted Professor Deborah Miller Fox at Anderson University to share the following metaphor with her faculty colleagues. Deborah sent an email to the faculty following a meeting she had with several students earlier in the semester. She reported that, "I heard one student suggest that an undergraduate education is (or should be) like a meal at a nice buffet. His point was this: 'If I am the paying guest, then I should have the freedom to choose whatever I want from the buffet. If I ignore some of the things that are good but just not suited to my taste, then who cares? It's my meal.'" In response, Deborah, shared with her colleagues "A Parable: The Hungry Young Consumers." The following is an excerpt from that parable:

> Once there was a young man and a young woman who said to their parents, "You have provided us meals and a table at which to eat for 18 years, but now we want to taste other foods and learn to feed ourselves." So the young man's parents sold half their livestock and gave the gold they earned to the boy. "Take this," they insisted. "Go to The American Bistro and eat heartily from its buffet."
>
> Similarly, the young woman's parents sold for a sack of gold a chest of linen they had worked years to weave and dye and

embroider. "Take this," they insisted. "Go to The American Bistro so that you may feed your hunger and instruct your tongue."

So the young man and the young woman left their respective homes and set off in search of the culinary education they said they desired. Now, The American Bistro was a fine restaurant, offering its guests an expensive buffet of fine foods. The meal was pricey, though—$2,000 for one four-hour, eight-course feast. It was not the only restaurant of its kind. Many restaurants promised a feast for the same or even lesser fee. The American Bistro, however, invited its guests to bring more than just money to the table. This restaurant asked its dinner guests to participate in the preparation and the celebration of its entrees.[8]

Through this image of a bistro, Deborah explores the challenge of being an educational mentor for students when they are so conditioned by a consumer mentality that they only want to expose themselves to their particular "likes." Just as it is difficult to expand one's palate by only eating pizza or macaroni and cheese, so too is it difficult to build a sturdy, multi-textured conceptual understanding of life that can withstand the storms of life if only exposed to select material. Deborah further intimates that learning is not unidirectional and that full enjoyment of the feast of knowledge comes from engaging the learner in preparation at the table of learning.

What metaphor might better inform a pedagogical approach to address the learning needs of today's students? In a discussion about the relational and educational purpose of today's university and this generation of learners, Christian Early, a professor of philosphy, encouraged me to consider a workshop metaphor for shaping our pedagogy.[9] Certainly during the many hours spent together in the workshop, the apprentice learns more from the master craftsperson than the basic trade. Many of the mission statements of our church-related colleges and universities are informed by following Jesus' way of being on this earth—why not an apprenticeship model, as Jesus would have experienced in carpentry? Would our students be better served if we adopted a workshop metaphor with a focus on creativity, where students were developed in ways that demonstrate the excellence of the Creator craftsman? The university that embodied a workshop culture as its learning paradigm would not be one of producing widgets but rather would view learners as apprentices, mentoring them through periods of vigorous artistic and intellectual activity where head, heart, and hands are equally engaged.

Citadel, monastery, bastion, factory, buffet, bistro, workshop—these or other metaphors inform institutions' pedagogical approaches. But metaphors are also helpful in bringing clarity and motivating others.

Metaphors—Coherence and Motivation

Often metaphors are used to help motivate a team or bring about coherence of purpose. For example, I've heard colleagues use an image of a train in an effort to motivate members in their department and bring about a coherent mission. One school dean said recently, "This train is pulling out of the station and my department members either need to get on the train and come along or get off now. We're not sitting here any longer. It's full steam ahead!" This image of a train elicits a sense of momentum in a focused direction, making clear that the choice is to either "board and travel the path we're headed down" or "disembark now."

Another use of the train metaphor might be, "That department or institution is a train wreck and needs a turnaround leader." Train wrecks happen when forward motion is thwarted, forcing the train off track. Perhaps a train switch was not properly engaged, directing the train down the wrong track. Maybe something on the track forces the train off balance. Possibly, the engineer is impaired or even incompetent, taking a curve too fast or steering the train off the tracks. Similar derailments or collisions can happen to an academic department or institution, creating a train wreck situation. When this happens, it's either "change or die." A turnaround leader may be called in to get things back on track, a situation Carol Taylor describes in her chapter in this volume. Today's books and articles on leadership have many examples of turnaround stories for departments and institutions. For example, a particular department at an institution had gotten off track, resulting in a significant weakening of core competencies for its program graduates. A new chair was appointed and given the charge to "turn that program around!" As the new chair examined the situation, he recognized that clarity of focus and getting the right faculty in the department and focused on a common goal of academic rigor was critical. By making difficult personnel decisions, revising curriculum and policies, and navigating the difficult terrain of turning around a struggling program, this department realized significant improvement in student outcomes.

Many institutions have adopted the bus metaphor proposed by Jim Collins in his book, *Good to Great*. That is, we think about getting the right people on the bus, people in the right seats on the bus, and getting the wrong people off the bus.[10] Often, personnel decisions are influenced by our guiding metaphors. Images of trains or buses quickly convey what Edgar Schein writes about in *Organizational Culture and Leadership* regarding the importance of owning shared values for a healthy organizational culture.[11] The dominant operating metaphor of an institution reflects its true core values. If these values are incongruent with my values, there will not be a good fit, and institutional fit contributes to coherence that leads to institutional success. Whether one should even be "on the bus" and, if so, in a particular seat on the bus, has a good deal to do with buy-in to the institution's core values and strategic direction. Motivation toward a coherent mission can be illuminated through the application of metaphorical concepts.

Metaphors Shape Organizational Culture

Higher education institutions today are confronted with a changing landscape affected by economic, technological, and global challenges. These challenges result in a formidable competition, not unlike a battlefield. With declining endowments, donors' waning confidence in their ability to carry through with pledged funds, cuts to federal and state financial aid, and families demanding affordability, a greater focus on efficiency is required as institutions engage the battle for limited resources. As a result, some leaders (and perhaps institutions) take on a warrior metaphor. Consider, for example, the following vignette:

> Middle University, in a small midwestern city, began an adult degree completion program when the city had a large automobile manufacturing presence. Many adult learners had enjoyed

the encouragement and financial support of their employers to pursue a college degree. Because the state had an underdeveloped community college system, four-year institutions in the area were the only real option for a college education. Administrators believed the adult studies program at the university was going to be a rising star and generate much-needed revenue. But the landscape changed—the main manufacturer moved out of the city, leaving many unemployed; the state developed an increasingly strong community college system; the governor regularly promoted a new online university; and other competing adult studies programs were vying for a dwindling adult education population. A strategy to increase online program offerings was tricky because of the accrediting agency's new distance delivery policy as well as the USDOE's new regulation regarding individual state approval for distance learning. These shifting sands threatened the revenue base of the adult studies program. One administrator suggested, "Well, let's just directly compete with the community college!" Charge! Let the battle begin.

Efficiency and financial viability are important. Making payroll, maintaining facilities, being competitive with faculty salaries, adequately resourcing academic programs, and funding new initiatives are critical. Interestingly though, even factories, with concerns about productivity and profits, do not have to be informed by a mechanistic, hierarchical, or warrior metaphor. For example, in the forward of Max De Pree's book, *Leadership Is an Art,* James O'Toole shares an interesting alternative observed at a Herman Miller factory:

> I was given *carte blanche* to go anywhere and talk to anyone, managers and workers. The only problem was that I couldn't tell one from the other! People who seemed to be production workers were engaged in solving the "managerial" problems of improving productivity and quality. People who seemed to be managers had their sleeves rolled up and were working, side by side, with everybody else in an all-out effort to produce the best products in the most effective way.[12]

As families rethink whether or not they can afford a private liberal arts education for their children, they are considering the value-added promises made by institutions, particularly private institutions. Academic organizational cultures informed by metaphors such as a factory, hierarchy, silo, or battleground do not create an environment for the creative, flexible, collaborative, and innovative problem-solving resourcefulness needed for institutions to thrive financially and for members to realize the full range of their gifts. Educators such as Parker Palmer and Lee Shulman have observed that the process of learning is best conceived of as a communal process, and not as a battle of the fittest.[13] Without a healthy and empowering community culture, the academy becomes little more than a group of individuals preoccupied with ensuring their own advancement and preserving their own little corner of the world. Shulman said it well:

> Learning is least useful when it is private and hidden; it is most powerful when it becomes public and communal. Learning flourishes when we take what we think we know and offer it as community property among fellow learners so that it can be tested, examined, challenged, and improved before we internalize it.[14]

For the health of our academic community, to promote robust student learning and faculty scholarship, we need to release ourselves from the silos, build better connections, and create learning organizations in which all members are viewed as critical to achieving the core purpose of education. Leadership author Sally Helgesen has noted that, in today's knowledge-based world, we need an operating metaphor that recognizes that people, with their ability to function at their optimum level of creativity and giftedness, are our greatest human resource.[15] A web metaphor encapsulates both structure and process. Drawing from research, Helgesen gives numerous examples of the flexibility and agility afforded an organization when all employees are valued for their unique contributions and are given the opportunity to contribute their greatest assets. Helgesen states that "the best organizations have tried to adapt to the new environment by becoming more weblike and inclusive, and adopting a less compartmentalized approach to structure and operations."[16]

Margaret Wheatley, in *Finding Our Way: Leadership for an Uncertain Time*, reflects,

> Most of us have had the experience of touching a spider web, feeling its resiliency, noticing how slight pressure in one area jiggles the entire web. If a web breaks and needs repair, the spider doesn't cut out a piece, terminate it, or tear the entire web apart and reorganize it. She reweaves it, using the silken relationships that are already there, creating stronger connections across the weakened spaces.[17]

Wheatley goes on:

> In order to counter the negative organizational dynamics stimulated by stress and uncertainty, we must give full attention to the quality of our relationships. Nothing else works, no new tools or technical applications, no redesigned organizational chart. The solution is each other. If we can rely on one another, we can cope with almost anything. Without each other, we retreat into fear. . . . People must be engaged in meaningful work together if they are to transcend individual concerns and develop new capacities.[18]

The rigidity of hierarchical relationships cannot compete with the elasticity of a web of relationships built on mutual respect for the contributions of all.

In writing about professional collegiality in today's academy, provost emeritus at Quinnipiac University John Bennett observed that "overall, organizational structures lean toward aggregations of individualists rather than vibrant intellectual communities."[19] A highly competitive system of promotion and tenure, as well as competition for enrollments, creates a battleground. The common idiom of "the best defense is a good offense" prevails as academic institutions and individuals within those institutions are predisposed to attacking their opponents rather than building a collegial community. While Bennett uses a construction metaphor to examine teaching and learning, I believe this metaphor is also beneficial in thinking about an organizational culture that facilitates the kind of collegial environment for optimal learning and for creating together a financially viable institution with integrity to its mission. Like a web metaphor, the construction metaphor calls our attention to connectivity and the value of relationships as we build a strong institution.

The construction metaphor helps us understand the value of building a firm foundation, recognizing the importance of bearing one part on another. Each part serves a meaningful purpose as the building becomes more than the sum of its individual parts. A construction metaphor emphasizes connections, stability, and building on the foundation of the past even as we create a new future. When we construct, we assemble, remodel, and strive to become "at home" in our dwelling. No part of the institution is independent of the other parts or of the larger whole. Bennett suggests that if our institutions were to be informed by a construction metaphor, the liberal arts curriculum would be integrated with study in the majors, what happens inside the classroom would not be isolated from what happens outside the classroom, faculty would provide constructive collegial feedback to one another rather than become isolationists or battle each other for resources, and everyone in the institution would be a valued subcontractor in the construction of the university. Likewise, an institution informed by a construction metaphor, where mission is tied to assessment-informing strategic planning and budgeting, will have the sturdiest dwelling. Coherence leads to stability.

A healthy organizational culture is one that offers a vibrant community of engagement for all members. In *Drive: The Surprising Truth about What Motivates Us,* Daniel Pink reveals three key elements of true motivation: autonomy, mastery, and purpose.[20] Those called to the academy generally have a desire to direct their own lives, to grow and develop in areas that matter, and to be part of something larger than themselves. An organizational culture that fosters healthy autonomy, mastery, and purpose will foster motivation. Institutional success is connected to the ability of an institution's members to think beyond their specific department, to engage institution-wide realities and possibilities, and together develop strategies for furthering institutional mission and purpose. Our academic environments must encourage and reward innovation, creativity, and change. Conducting business in the same way we always have is as unhealthy as eating the same thing every day. Our institutional palates need stretching to survive these turbulent times.

Metaphors for the Future of Higher Education

Metaphors help to shed light on our work. Both our leadership and our influence on the institutions where we serve are framed by our institution's culture, by our operating metaphors. Innovative pedagogical approaches and emerging career avenues call for interdisciplinary collaborative partnering among faculty and across institutions. The educational experience of the future university is best informed by metaphors that call us toward connectivity, creativity, and collegiality, and by focusing on the common good. The organizational culture of the successful university of the future is best built on a web of relationships, understanding that our primary purpose—our core business—is to help our students engage others and the world in constructive and redemptive ways. An institution's foundation and its web of relationships must be strong and resilient enough to cope with the stress and uncertainty of the future.

What conditions will we create for the very best growth of our students and ourselves? On the institutional seal of Anderson University are these words: *veritas, fidelitas, utilitas.* Truth-seeking, faithfulness, and usefulness inform Anderson's organizational culture and our distinct approach to higher education. As the chief academic officer, my personal operating metaphors will merge with, and influence, our institutional culture.

It is critical that we hire for fit with institutional mission and culture. Perhaps asking applicants to reflect on metaphors that inform how they inhabit this world and approach their role would be beneficial. I think again of the two operating metaphors with which I opened this chapter. The leader as artist, creating an atmosphere for growth, is for me an act of faithfulness (*fidelitas*) to my calling. Maintaining openness to truth (*veritas*), looking for the slivers of light shining through cracks, is what helps me live with the imperfections and uncertainties that come with such work.

For all of us, metaphors inform our leadership and in turn shape our organizations. As we anticipate the future in higher education, we need to recognize and choose carefully the metaphors that will shape our organizational cultures.

Notes to Chapter Ten

1. Edgar H. Schein, *Organizational Culture and Leadership*.

2. George Lakoff and Mark Johnson, *Metaphors We Live By*, 3.

3. Lee G. Bolman and Terrence E. Deal, *Reframing Organizations*.

4. Sally Helgesen and Julie Johnson, *The Female Vision*, 45.

5. Max De Pree, *Leadership Is an Art*.

6. Laurence R. Veysey, *The Emergence of the American University*.

7. Daniel Pink, *A Whole New Mind*, 1–3, 52.

8. Deborah Miller Fox, assistant professor of English, in an email on April 28, 2011, to the Anderson University faculty.

9. I enjoyed many stimulating conversations with Dr. Christian Early, a philosophy professor at Eastern Mennonite University, as we talked about how various metaphors inform the work of the academy. He first introduced me to this notion of the academy as workshop.

10. Jim Collins, *Good to Great*.

11. Schein, *Organizational Culture and Leadership*.

12. De Pree, *Leadership Is an Art*, xxii, 1

13. Parker J. Palmer, *The Courage to Teach;* Lee S. Shulman, "Taking Learning Seriously."

14. Shulman, "Taking Learning Seriously," 2.

15. Sally Helgesen, *The Web of Inclusion*, 48.

16. Ibid.

17. Margaret Wheatley, *Finding Our Way*, 106–107, 118.

18. Ibid., 118.

19. John Bennett, *Collegial Professionalism*, 165.

20. Daniel H. Pink, *Drive*.

For Discussion

1. As you reflect on your own leadership journey, what metaphors or images best depict how you personally carry out your leadership? How might your leadership differ if it was informed by an alternative metaphor?

2. If you were to use an image or metaphor to describe your area of responsibility, what might that be? How is the operating metaphor for your area similar to or different from those of your colleagues in other areas?

3. In what ways have the various metaphors introduced in the chapter (e.g., factory, web, train, etc.) been applied at your institution or in conversations across your campus? Are there additional metaphors or images that have informed your understandings of your organization's culture?

4. If you were to describe your institution's dominant operating metaphor, what would that be? How does that metaphor inform the operations of various leaders throughout your institution? In what ways does this metaphor facilitate achievement of your institution's mission?

5. Do you see competing metaphors at play on your leadership team or in your institution? If so, in what ways is that competition influencing institutional effectiveness?

Chapter Eleven

BEYOND "HOSPITALITY"
Moving out of the Host-Guest Metaphor into an Intercultural "World House"

Rebecca R. Hernandez

"We have inherited a large house, a great 'world house' in which we have to live together—black and white, Easterner and Westerner, Gentile and Jew, Catholic and Protestant, Muslim and Hindu—a family unduly separated in ideas, culture and interest, who, because we can never again live apart, must learn somehow to live with each other in peace."

—DR. MARTIN LUTHER KING, JR., Where Do We Go from Here: Chaos or Community?

One of the most often-cited job duties of a leader is to envision a compelling future and a purpose yet unknown for an organization. Based on existing work, assets, past performance, and mission, a leader then determines a strategic plan to move the organization toward that new future. The art of projecting the long view and yet working day-to-day in the short term are both necessary skills for a trailblazer. Among administrative leaders in Christian higher education, many propose that the future and the present vision must include creating and sustaining an intercultural worldview—that is, caring deeply about diverse populations and the needs of diverse students in the United States who, if we are proactive, will be our students. The Calvin College *Comprehensive Plan for Racial Justice, Reconciliation, and Cross-cultural Engagement* states that "[w]orking toward a multicultural Kingdom of God is not simply a high-minded ideal; it is a dictate of biblical justice."[1] We know that this is work that educational leaders must undertake now to assure a future that is inclusive and meets the growing demand for change.

"We Invited Them, but They Didn't Come."

If one phrase could sum up the attitude that I have often heard in higher education when it comes to explaining—or asking for an explanation about— why institutions have not attracted a more diverse student body or faculty, this would be it: "We invited them, but they didn't come." An invitation is just fine; it's a wonderful and needed first step. But just because we beckon others to come toward us doesn't mean that we understand how to truly welcome them, to make them feel at home, or to share the space we've invited them to inhabit. To have diverse campuses does not mean simply that non-White persons are present. Christian colleges and universities must be willing to grapple with the cultural, systematic, logistical, pedagogical, and personal changes needed to create the sense that everyone is living and learning alongside one another, rather than fostering a sense that there are permanent members of the community and then there are outsiders who are welcomed in but are unconsciously asked to fit into existing structures.

While many Christian colleges and universities understand this distinction in a general sense, few make the changes necessary to ensure that all students are welcomed into an environment that allows them to flourish. Few are prepared to accept the critique necessary to do the hard work of examining long-held attitudes and assumptions, to be humble and also open, in the face of broader societal and global change—to make shifts in power structures and understandings of the "new normal" in the classroom and community. As an academic administrator with "change agent" practically written into the job description, I have found the role of bridge-builder to be an exciting one that has its roots in my own experiences as someone who was once a higher education outsider, literally speaking a different language.

Knocking on an Unknown Door

When I received my first financial statement from Southeastern College, I was stunned. It was 1984, and while I had received a scholarship from Junior

Achievement to help fund my education, I had arrived on the Florida campus with very little understanding of where I had landed. Arriving meant already having taken a huge leap from my close-knit Mexican-American community in Idaho to this Southeastern college. My parents and I were comforted by the fact that I was attending a school affiliated with our Assemblies of God church, yet it quickly became clear to me that I was in a completely new place, having to find my own way.

I had been determined to go to college after high school, having discovered a love of learning. I also knew, to put it bluntly, that this was what White kids did, and there was no reason that I couldn't go to college too, despite the fact that I'd met only one Mexican-American (an admired elementary school teacher) who had taken that path of dreams. My parents, neither of whom had completed high school, were very supportive of my interest in higher education. They had traveled the United States as migrant workers, but made a commitment to settle in one community so that my siblings and I could go to school. While I spent many a summer working alongside them in the fields, I discovered a love of learning in the classroom. The guidance counselor at my high school offered no encouragement. He recognized that I was bright; however, his limited sense of what I could achieve led him to tell me that I had the potential to become a supervisor at one of the local factories. But I was college bound.

As a young person stepping onto the Southeastern College campus, I felt I had landed in another world where everything was different: the independence from my close-knit Mexican-American family and community, the Southern U.S. accents of my roommate and classmates, the food, even the worship styles. I felt lost. As a first-generation student, everything about college was new, from the administrative paperwork and the financial aid process to the culture of living with strangers. I was particularly surprised by the expectation for interaction with professors both in and out of the classroom. My past experience in my predominantly White high school was one in which my teachers did not encourage questions, nor seem to either care about me as a person or welcome my family into school activities. We were discouraged from sharing any of our culture in the classroom or the school and felt clearly that we were not wanted in this school. So to be expected to interact with professors was one of the most challenging experiences I had in that first semester. It was also the most compelling. While we were different, we were bound together by a faith perspective. This idea of the way in which the larger body of Christ could include us all and encompass our worship resonated with me and kept me engaged.

I persevered, not for myself alone, but for my family. All of my experiences—those that were painful as well as those where I found success—were collectively owned. My family didn't understand most of what I was encountering, but I knew they were proud of me even as they missed me. I missed them, too. Once, early in my first year, I called home in tears and told my mother that I wanted to come home. She listened to my frustrations but firmly insisted that I stay at college. It was only later that I learned from siblings that my mother, after hanging up the phone at the end of that conversation, also cried.

I can look back on that time with profound joy and profound sadness and still feel an overall sense of accomplishment. I left Southeastern with an academic degree, but also with a growing sense of the opportunity I had to be a bridge-builder between my cultural community and the majority White culture. There are so many assumptions made about the basic understandings that new undergraduates bring to their first day at college, but I had very little knowledge of academic culture and the processes needed to navigate easily.

After having made my way through the systems and culture of academia, I knew there was so much information that Latino families needed to not only access higher education but also to thrive there. I wanted colleges and universities to make changes that would do more than merely open the door to Latino students. I felt my life's path was to be a translator, interpreter, and agent of change—to make a difference in the lives of people in the communities I straddled. My call to lead was birthed from my goal of making a home in higher education for Latinos.

In the pursuit of graduate degrees, I chose state schools based on location. Making my way through a master's degree program and then moving on to doctoral work, I found professors who were wonderfully supportive, but none of them looked like me, nor had they had experiences like mine. The challenges were very much the same as those I had met in my undergraduate program. I continued to see a need for the art of interpretation, and I was soon tapped to work on creating and assessing interventions for diverse communities. My family and community membership, as well as my professional knowledge, have combined to propel me into the arena of academic leadership. Now, I believe, is the time to unpack these experiences and see what can be learned about change in institutions to create better opportunities for diverse students to be successful.

Pushing beyond the Host-Guest Model

The call of Christ is real, and many institutions have taken seriously the implications of Christ's invitation for transformation as it applies to the way in which the body of Christ can operate within academic communities. Calvin College, Goshen College, and others have built on a foundation of faith and theology to make the case for changes in our Christian institutions toward building a multicultural kingdom of God. Yet while the theological impetus for true change is recognized by many, I question the "host-guest" model, one of the central images used in discussing issues of diversity and inclusion. This image, based in the biblical language of hospitality, is often cited as the ideal model for our engagement of persons and ideas that have not been part of our culture, tradition, or practices. In this model, the host is to open the door and welcome the guests to the comfort of the interior—a home, a church, a campus, a community. This model falls short in several ways.

First, if you are the host, much can be kept at the surface level. We engage hospitality on our terms. The host can make accommodation for differences in some areas without really touching fundamental differences that would mean a significant change in behavior, purpose, or in power and control. Wherever change is made, the host decides how and when that change is made. Having the control to decide how much change, what resources to give to change, and who will do the work of change, is firmly in the hands of the host.

The guest, on the other hand, is dependent on the host for any accommodation or adaptation done to make the guest feel welcome. Guests know this is not their house nor is it their home in which to be fully comfortable. They must watch and listen carefully to the spoken words or the behavioral cues of the host to determine their level of comfort and entry into different areas of the space. The guest knows that to enter those spaces requires personal change. In order to make those changes, the guest must know the host well, while the host—who makes no change—never has to truly know the guest. On a college campus, students of color watch and listen to the cues of the leadership, faculty, staff, and others to determine to what level they are truly welcome. The pamphlets that feature smiling students of color engaged in various activities throughout the campus are not always the reality once a student arrives. They find fewer students of color than advertised, and the "welcome" sign doesn't really extend to the classroom, the dorms, or even the chapel services. All colleges and universities have a set culture, some of which is still deeply rooted in theological tradition. While this is not wrong, it must be understood that as the host, the institution and its leadership are in the driver's seat. Leaders, who are still predominantly White, are fully responsible for how students and faculty of color read the institution and know their place as the guest in it.

If We Want Change

We say we want diversity in our colleges. We want to engage a broader range of students to more fully represent our values and missions. So what options do we have in light of current realities? Throw up our hands and say there is nothing we can do to change this culture? No, I believe we can start with a new image. As articulated so clearly in the chapter by Marie Morris, we need to work individually and collectively through changing the metaphor that guides this dimension of institutional life.

In his book *Where Do We Go from Here: Chaos or Community?* Dr. Martin Luther King, Jr., wrote,

> Some years ago a famous novelist died. Among his papers was found a list of suggested plots for future stories, the most prominently underscored being this one: "A widely separated family inherits a house in which they have to live together." This is the great new problem of mankind. We have inherited a large house, a great "world house" in which we have to live together—black

and white, Easterner and Westerner, Gentile and Jew, Catholic and Protestant, Muslim and Hindu—a family unduly separated in ideas, culture and interest, who, because we can never again live apart, must learn somehow to live with each other in peace.[2]

The idea of a world house is a strong model for diversity in higher education. A big house where we live together, where we "work out" our nuanced and not-so-nuanced differences to create a new culture that is large enough for the "other" to become "us." Where we care for the other as we care for ourselves. In higher education, we live out our faith and ideals together in a place—a campus—where we work, eat, live, and learn together. So this ideal of "the creation of a truly diverse campus requires a commitment to God's vision of building a World House *of Learning*."[3] In the context to higher education, we can see that building such a house demands a process of learning and takes focused effort. It requires a significant shift in our thinking and our approach to creating an intercultural campus where all students and faculty are supported and successful.

Institutional Change

What exactly needs to change in institutions to make diverse students welcome as true members of the community rather than guests—*at home* in our predominately White institutions? Before we get to the what, we need to talk about why. Why do we need to make diverse students welcome? Several reasons are most often cited. The first is based in our moral call as human beings. We care for each other as a part of living in community with others and with the goal of bettering life for all members. Cesar Chavez once said: "We cannot seek achievement for ourselves and forget about progress and prosperity for our community. . . . Our ambitions must be broad enough to include the aspirations and needs of others, for their sakes and for our own."[4] In today's harsh political and divisive environment, this advocacy on behalf of others is important, but we must go further. As Christians, we are called to be like Christ and be his witnesses.

And so in addition to our basic human responsibilities, our second reason for embracing diversity as part of our collective identity is our Christian witness. The words of Christ reflect his call for diversity as described in the New Testament. Specifically, consider Revelation 7:9–10:

> After this I looked, and there before me was a great multitude that no one could count, from every nation, tribe, people and language, standing before the throne and before the Lamb. They were wearing white robes and were holding palm branches in their hands. And they cried out in a loud voice:
> "Salvation belongs to our God,
> who sits on the throne,
> and to the Lamb."

This idea of being a family together means we must care for one another and that, in caring, we grow in understanding of and appreciation for the similarities *and* the differences we bring to one another. Some would say that our responsibility to support the call for greater diversity in all aspects of campus life lies in our biblical calling to more accurately reflect God's kingdom here on earth. The call for biblical justice is described by Professor Tom Thompson as he reflects on the extent to which even sincere Christians can become witting or unwitting carriers of racism. He concludes that "if we in the Christian church are ungraceful about affirming others because we stumble over distinctions of race, ethnicity, or culture, then it is quite possible that we have too tight of a grip on our lives, a false (i.e., insecure) image of ourselves, which we may have to learn to ungrasp."[5] In response, Thompson suggests that multicultural encounters should be seen as "an imperative of basic Christian discipleship," rooted in the life of Christ, "who, being in very nature God, did not consider equality with God something to be used to his own advantage; rather he made himself nothing by taking the very nature of a servant."[6]

The third reason is much more pragmatic, with demographic shifts raising issues for strategic planning and resource allocation for certain colleges and universities. I point out these issues with caution, as some have happened in the past with no alterations to our structures. However, it is important to identify, for those not aware, the dynamic changes happening across the United States. The contemporary shifts in our country clearly demonstrate the growth of diverse populations in the school systems across the country, bringing new market opportunities for our colleges and universities. The U.S. Census Bureau's 2010 Census brief on the national Hispanic population reported that "the Hispanic population increased by 15.2 million between 2000 and 2010 and accounted for more than half of the total U.S. population increase of 27.3 million. Between 2000 and 2010, the Hispanic population grew by 43 percent, or four times the nation's 9.7 percent growth rate."[7] The growth among Latino school-age children is also expected to grow. According to the Pew Research Center, these are the future college students we must prepare for:

> Strong growth in Hispanic enrollment is expected to continue for decades, according to a recently released U.S. Census Bureau population projection. The bureau projects that the Hispanic school-age population will increase by 166% by 2050 (to 28 million from 11 million in 2006), while the non-Hispanic school-age population will grow by just 4% (to 45 million from 43 million) over this same period. In 2050, there will be more school-age Hispanic children than school-age non-Hispanic white children.[8]

We know that for our own survival, we must change to welcome these new groups, not as guests but as full members who share in the creation and lives of our institutions at every level, as students, faculty, and administrators. But are these reasons enough to compel us to change? Some would say yes, but the evidence of change is not there . . . yet. Why are we so slow to change? The challenge of institutions is that at the same time we want to make change, we also feel a desire to keep things the same. We hold onto traditions, processes, and systems even when they aren't working in the new realities facing today's colleges and universities. This holding on and letting go at the same time brings frustration and undermines our efforts as we also lose energy. We want to be welcoming but somehow miss the boat as our efforts lack sustained results.

If we are to make changes, perhaps we ought to take a step back and look at what we want in our institutions. Most institutions have statements that articulate their overarching vision and mission. These vision and mission statements, while forward-thinking, are coupled with traditions that hold onto the past. The long-term vision we cast and the identity we hold must be renewed and flexible enough to allow for new symbols that encompass the vision and provides a space for the diversity of people to come together. We don't seek to destroy the old but to allow a renewal of ways to express the vision and the mission of a Christian institution. Dr. Vincent Harding, friend, colleague, and former speechwriter of Dr. Martin Luther King, Jr., spoke recently at Goshen College. He was asked about the concern some individuals had regarding the potential loss of Mennonite identity "if we open our doors too wide or are too open to change." Dr. Harding replied:

> Identity is not something that is most valuable to us when we are grasping it and saying don't lose it! Identity is most helpful and useful to us when we are saying, how do we join what we have with what others have? Yes, you might have to do something different in order to open this space so that someone else can come here, but we must be ready to look at the possibility that something new needs to be born. And what we call Mennonite identity cannot, must not . . . be a block of stone that is set down and we are told this is Mennonite identity and will not be anything else ever! NO! . . . if we are alive . . . life is always going through transmutation, changes, development that we did not expect. I think that all of us that have "identities" must recognize that identities are meant to be engaged with other identities in order to create new identities. Mennonite identity is not as something to grasp and therefore almost choke to death but something to open up and say this is what I have, what do you have? What can we make new together?[9]

Creating a World House of Learning

A few Christian colleges and universities have a burgeoning awareness that as the country and the church diversifies, we too must be prepared and in fact convivial to diverse students if we are to be relevant. These colleges have taken on the challenge to recruit diverse students and provide intentional support to them. But many more institutions have experienced the frustration of recruiting diverse students, only to lose these students as they fall away after a semester or two. The reasons vary but usually students report "not feeling at home" and not feeling "connected to the institution."[10] Since we know the growing diversity is coming, how do we prepare? How will we survive and be relevant institutions? We must change, and the time for change is now.

So how do institutions enact change? Many institutions start by looking for a leader to help them move toward becoming the diverse and intercultural campus they want to be. They look for and hire a change agent, the person whose job it is to lead diversity change. This position is called many things—diversity officer, multicultural director, inclusion specialist, etc. Whatever the name, the work is similar. An individual—usually a person of color—is hired to lead change, to work with diverse students, to engage in activities that will expand the learning of all students across campus and to engage change within the institution. They are tasked with making the college welcoming so that diverse students will come and partake in what the campus has to offer. This sounds like a worthy goal; however, some fallacies need to be addressed.

First, no diversity officer can make an institution what it is not. Change must be internal, deep, far-reaching, and the work of *everyone* in leadership and on the ground. For the change agent, this is not a new concept. Their job is isolating; they are asked to make changes but not call out too much—don't touch the "sacred cows," stubborn loyalties to long-standing traditions or processes, even when those traditions and processes impede progress. They are familiar with being labeled "oversensitive" and "troublemakers," people who don't understand the whole but rather are focused only on a small minority. These labels and minimizations are often applied by some who are resistant to change, who might say, "We don't want to lower our standards," "We are fine as we are," "Why do we need to worry about engaging diversity?" and finally, "We are all humans and that should be enough." The implications are that we are aiming for the wrong things. Others in the institution, however, are eager to change but lack the knowledge they need to do so. They may also fear what the institution will look like in the end, and this holds them back. If they can see a new and compelling future, they will move forward a bit more.

Second, many people think this change is a finite process. That is, if we address certain areas, moving around pieces and hiring diverse people, that will be enough. We will be diverse, and we can move on to other things. The reality is, this work is ongoing, challenging, and demanding.

In order to make the changes we want, for the reasons we articulate, we must get the right people working on this. Who are the right people to help make colleges and universities the kinds of places we want them to be? It's all of us, from the leaders at the top to the staff person in the back room. All of us together must work to change how we "have always done things" to how we "will operate today." Organizations are not replacements for people and interpersonal relationships. Those interpersonal relationships *inside* organizations will determine how we live and work out our beliefs together.

Goshen College Story

In taking seriously the mandate to model God's kingdom in all of its rich diversity, perhaps some lessons from one story can be helpful to others. Goshen College, a small, Mennonite church-owned institution, has a deep commitment to the idea of diversity. Like other colleges and universities, having a cross-cultural commitment has meant work around the world and at home. Most recently, Goshen College developed the Center for Intercultural Teaching and Learning. The goals of the Center are to (1) recruit and retain local Latino students in our private Christian college; (2) transform our curriculum and faculty development to better meet the needs of all students, preparing them to live in an intercultural world; and (3) research the regional demographic shifts and document the experiences of the Latino students we recruit for program improvement and success.

This initiative is still a work in progress, but we have learned some things since launching in 2006 that we believe can help other institutions. The creation of the Center, funded by a generous Lilly Endowment grant, resulted in fast changes—hiring new staff (several being people of color), the creation of a leadership program, new academic center space, advertising to a new market, and the development of a research agenda with a large team and the resources to engage faculty and staff in training and continued education. In fact, large changes were made quickly. But these changes represented what might be called gathering the "low-hanging fruit"; that is, while intensive, they were fairly easy to create when there is a significant budget (as some critics point out). However, the changes that are deep and long-lasting—marking a significant change in the way we view the other and ourselves—are harder to make. This kind of change is starting at Goshen, after a long period of time, challenge, and struggle. Are we there yet? No! But I am cautiously optimistic and can say that many faculty and administrators are willing to engage in the hard work of transformation to a new model of diversity, that of a world house of learning that requires a change in the campus culture, a new way of thinking about who we are and what we do, and changes in the relationships and stances we take with each other and the local community.

Some of the lessons we have learned thus far in our journey include the following:

1. ***Decide if this vision is tied to the mission.***
   The first lesson is perhaps the most important and is directed to key leaders individually. Why are you doing this? Is there a deep commitment and agreement to the biblical mandate of justice and reconciliation? Without this personal commitment on the part of the leadership, little will be sustained and few will follow. This is hard work and leaders must believe this is the right thing to do. Personal work must precede the public work At Goshen College, like many other colleges in our CCCU fellowship, our leaders believe in and hold to God's call for change.

2. ***Recognize the critical role of leaders.***
   Essential to establishing an environment that encourages the shift from a host-guest to a world house perspective is a close look at the mission, vision, and desired outcomes of the organization's work. The leadership—its board of directors, president, and other key administrators—needs to take the organization through a strategic plan that specifically details what the institution will look like when its mission and goals are reached. Throughout the process, all participants must be willing to be learners and open to hearing what areas of the institution need to change so that all students have the opportunity to become equal participants.

3. *Take stock.*

   Institutions need to invest in a professional or in-house audit to take stock of the current environment. But if we're honest, we know that sometimes it is easier for an outsider to communicate the truth than those inside the organization. It is often difficult to hear about current practices across the institution that continue to uphold historical and cultural perspectives. Taking an open rather than a defensive stance throughout this process will help colleges and universities reach their goals.

4. *Examine internal policies, procedures, and practices.*

   One of the challenges in this work is that we had perfectly sensible reasons for the existing policies and procedures that guide our institutions. They were developed to resolve specific and immediate issues at the time they were created. The question we have had to face is, are these still the right policies and procedures to help us in the current environment, or are they now simply tradition? The practices have developed over time to make work processes easier. So we also have to ask, for whom do they make things easier? Many times, we fall into habits that have served a particular group of people well but represent barriers for other groups and need to be reviewed. The holding on and letting go process is a challenge, filled with emotions that wise leaders must recognize and embrace.

5. *Focus on hiring.*

   One area where we know change is needed is in hiring diverse faculty, staff, and administrators. Many colleges want diverse faculty, staff, and administrators, but few know how to attract candidates who bring diversity. Many institutions try advertising in targeted newspapers or journals, but we need to start changes closer to home. What does the job description really ask for? One area is that of qualifications required and preferred. We describe the person we want, and it turns out to be that we want someone just like us, only in a different color! I'm not saying we don't have essential requirements for the job, but

we must look at the intangible and additional skills that we
need as well—skills that include understanding and compe-
tently moving between majority culture and particular types
of communities: immigrant communities, Latino, African
American, or Asian subcultures, specific faith traditions, etc.
These are skills that can help organizations thrive and students
flourish. We do not value such skills often enough, yet in reality, they are exactly what we need. Institutional leaders need to
remember that even though they are successful in recruiting
persons of color, additional work needs to be done to retain
them. Engaging in ongoing conversation and support plans is
invaluable to the retention of faculty and staff of color.

There are many other recommendations that we could list, but the most critical element doesn't take new money to implement: it is leaders' honest and
critical self-examination, which is necessary to lead into change at all levels.

The Challenges

This work is hard, and it takes effort to sustain people to keep moving forward.
In reality, moving forward uncovers more areas that need to be addressed.
Thus, the challenge is to create short-term wins that are celebrated genuinely
and then build on the changes one-by-one. Additionally, we must anchor
changes in the culture so that despite changes in personnel or priorities, we
don't forget where constructive changes have occurred. Institutional memory
must include these changes so we don't slip back into old patterns.

Finally, how do we do all the great things we want to do as an institution?
There are plenty of good ideas, new interest areas, and initiatives proposed by
creative people. These new ideas, coupled with old programs and initiatives,
make the field of opportunities and possibilities too crowded. People don't
know what to focus on. So we may need to give up some things from the past
in order to be more effective with the resources and the people we have available now. The idea of "planned abandonment" that was proposed by leadership guru Peter Drucker suggests that if we say yes to one thing, we are saying
no to something else.[11] Frankly, there are good things we have been doing
that may need to be released in order to move forward with something better.

Conclusion

What have we learned? For leaders, this work is personal and internal as much as it is external. Leaders must commit to constant humbling, letting go, and sharing the work of change. Because the work is ongoing. Goshen College is like other colleges, trying to respond to the social and demographic shifts in this country by preparing students to live and thrive in a global world. We are not alone nor are we always successful, but we are working on it. There are no quick solutions, no hard and fast changes that colleges can employ and "be done with" this process. We must stay committed and know that the work of engaging each other is never finished. We do this because we know that it's the nature of higher education institutions to change and respond to the needs of the community. It's slow but necessary, important work.

David's Story

Developing and maintaining a commitment to diversity on any campus requires organizational ownership at all levels. But as my own story from the beginning of this chapter illustrates, the joy in this work is found in the lives of students who benefit from our commitment and efforts to this worthy cause. One such story belongs to David, a Goshen College graduate who was a middle schooler when he came to the United States with his parents. His first experience in a U.S. public school was a painful one of feeling like an outsider, lacking the language skills to engage in his education. His English class consisted of students who wanted to learn Spanish in exchange for some English instruction. David felt powerless and decided then that he wanted to be a teacher so that other non-English students would have an opportunity to learn, feel a part of the classroom community, and experience success. In coming to Goshen College where he was encouraged to explore his identity, to connect that identity to others, and to develop himself as a servant leader, David realized his dream. He stated, "I always felt that since I came to the States that I needed to give back or somehow be that person that I lacked in teaching me English, I needed to be that person, that support somehow. . . . I felt that teaching would be the most immediate support. And now coming through college, through CITL [the Center for Intercultural Teaching and

Learning] and helping me evolve as a leader, I knew my purpose and what I wanted, and now I know how to do it and how to be that person of support!"

By providing a place for David to excel, to connect his purpose with his education, he was able to reach his goal to serve others through his vocation and life. This is not unusual for students; this is what Christian institutions of higher learning do. But the reality for David was, as a first-generation immigrant student, he was welcomed in and found barriers removed and programs in place that made him feel at home and connected to this college. This was his house—he was not here as a guest but as a member of the family, where his unique identity was honored and he was able to bring that as a gift to the campus and was given the gift of others' uniqueness in return. This story is more an exception than the norm. The tragedy for leaders in higher education today is that they too often miss the changing diversity in our communities and deprive promising students of the opportunity to excel at our Christian institutions.

In conclusion, consider this passage from Martin Luther King, Jr.'s *Where Do We Go from Here: Chaos or Community?*:

> Nothing could be more tragic than for men to live in these revolutionary times and fail to achieve the new attitudes and the new mental outlooks that the new situation demands. In Washington Irving's familiar story of Rip Van Winkle, the one thing that we usually remember is that Rip slept twenty years. There is another important point, however, that is almost always overlooked. It was the sign on the inn in the little town on the Hudson from which Rip departed and scaled the mountain for his long sleep. When he went up, the sign had a picture of King George III of England. When he came down, twenty years later, the sign had a picture of George Washington. As he looked at the picture of the first President of the United States, Rip was confused, flustered, and lost. He knew not who Washington was. The most striking thing about this story is not that Rip slept twenty years, but that he slept through a revolution that would alter the course of human history. One of the great liabilities of

history is that all too many people fail to remain awake through great periods of social change. Every society has its protectors of the status quo and its fraternities of the indifferent who are notorious for sleeping through revolutions. But today our very survival depends on our ability to stay awake, to adjust to new ideas, to remain vigilant and to face the challenge of change. The large house in which we live demands that we transform this world-wide neighborhood into a world-wide brotherhood. Together we must learn to live as brothers or together we will be forced to perish as fools.[12]

Notes to Chapter Eleven

1. *From Every Nation: Revised Comprehensive Plan for Racial Justice, Reconciliation, and Cross-cultural Engagement at Calvin College.*

2. Martin Luther King, Jr., *Where Do We Go from Here?* 177.

3. "Intercultural Teaching and Learning at Goshen College," YouTube video, created by the Center for Intercultural Teaching and Learning, Goshen College.

4. Quoted on the website of the United Farmworkers of America, http://www.ufw.org/_page.php?menu=research&inc=history/09.html.

5. Thomas R. Thompson, "Ungrasping Ourselves."

6. Ibid., and Phil. 2:6.

7. "2010 Census Shows Nation's Hispanic Population Grew Four Times Faster Than Total U.S. Population," U.S. Census Bureau.

8. Richard Fry and Felisa Gonzales, "One-in-Five and Growing Fast: A Profile of Hispanic Public School Students."

9. Vincent Harding, "Martin Luther King—Servant Leader."

10. John W. Lounsbury and Daniel DeNeui, "Psychological Sense of Community on Campus."

11. Peter Drucker, *Management.*

12. King, *Where Do We Go from Here?* 180.

For Discussion

1. What metaphor or model fits your institution in regard to cultivating a diverse campus? (World house of learning, host-guest, or other?)

2. How many students on your campus are culturally different? What would they say about their experience on your campus? Do you have ways of getting honest feedback from these students? How do you receive feedback on campus climate?

3. What three things would you need to change on your campus in order to model a world house of learning?

4. How will you measure your efforts in becoming a campus that effectively supports diverse students?

5. There will be resistance to change. What kinds can you expect? How will that resistance likely be expressed, and what is behind the resistance?

6. What steps would you need to take to bring about change? What issues of loss must you potentially address in order to engage a new paradigm of thinking?

Chapter Twelve

TOWARD A DISTINCTIVE, CHRIST-HONORING CAMPUS CULTURE
Working the Vision

CARLA D. SANDERSON

"A [college] community is perhaps the single most powerful influence in shaping a person's values. It is therefore of major importance that we shape the community well."

—ARTHUR HOLMES, The Idea of a Christian College

"The calling to move [toward] . . . strengthening a place of belonging in which scholars, educators, staff, leaders and learners live, share, serve and relate together in authentic community is a high and noble calling. It is one not only worthy of envisioning, not only of choosing, but one worthy of our full pursuit and commitment."

—DAVID DOCKERY, Renewing Minds

In 1992, the United States men's Olympic basketball team earned the name the "Dream Team." They were a group of professional basketball players allowed to compete in the Olympics for the first time.

In 1995, wearing white T-shirts with big red Dream Team lettering, our administrative team began its work, new kids on the block, rookies in our

30s and 40s, eager, energized. No one was in it "for a job," not one person on the team was the least bit apathetic. Some members of the team were highly inductive, others highly intuitive. We all felt bold. We had been given a new vision by a new president. We were deeply committed to a new day for our university as a matter of personal calling. We felt committed to one another. It was joyful.

We laughed together, watched movies, played ping-pong. We read volumes on Christian higher education, contemporary culture, history, globalization, leadership, and the like. We were data-driven. We knew we had to create value. And we asked the question, "For what kind of place do we want to work twenty-five years from now?" We saw ourselves as a part of a larger team of colleges and universities with the same ultimate mission, and we knew that we needed every one of them to be strong. With a vision for Christ-centeredness and with yieldedness to God's best, we knew we were not alone.

The relationship between a strong and compelling vision and the kind of organizational culture it takes to see that vision become reality is worthy of reflection. In my estimation from having experienced the emergence of a highly distinctive campus culture, two factors are critical: a strong "missional" center around which everything connects and a "can do" ethos of industry to get the work done. It is only in looking back that I fully realize the strategic role that "working the vision" plays in creating the desired campus culture. The purpose of this chapter is to inspire other academic leadership teams to work the vision by giving deliberate attention to all that defines and contributes to campus culture.

Campus culture reflects the complex whole of the institution's mission, identity, core values, relationships, traditions, customs, and patterns as experienced by its people. Creating a vibrant and productive campus culture is a daily task, not a one-time or periodic management decision. College and university leaders hold responsibility for developing and nurturing a strong and vibrant campus culture—its philosophy, ethos, values, attitudes, and practices, the principles and beliefs that give the campus its identity. Creating campus culture starts at the top, but the work is in the hands of every member of the community. Guardianship of the culture is a shared responsibility, a strategic choice.

The work that takes place on the nation's college and university campuses is purposed to ensure a strong and prosperous American and global society. Research in teaching-learning strategies and the co-curriculum has given us new knowledge about how students learn, and how they develop into leaders and community servants. But as a rule, the nation's campuses are not flourishing and are not well-respected for offering a positive environment for students. It takes only an occasional review of the national news to see that Americans are losing trust in higher education's ability to prepare an effective workforce for tomorrow.

Writing from the context of private, Christian higher education, let me begin with a description of what a vibrant Christian campus culture capable of ensuring the nation's preferred future might look like.

A thriving campus culture begins with a sense of community that is emboldened by an unapologetic mission that drives academic and student life programs of exceptional quality. The focus is on students and parents as customers, face-to-face and one-on-one. The goal is faithful living and learning in relationship, with faculty as torchbearers for knowledge and staff as "guides at the side."

A strong sense of place draws students to campus cultures—traditions you can feel and touch, such as alumni walks, bell towers, beautiful lawns, winning playing fields, historic chapel buildings, appealing and well-designed learning facilities, and student apartments not so far removed from the luxuries of home. A strong sense of purpose is the ultimate draw—a curriculum that holds together through the truth found in Holy Scripture and is worthy to bear the name Christian education; a dynamic student life program characterized by leadership development, residential life programs, a robust freshman year experience, student travel programs, varsity and intramural athletics, and a culture of praise and worship.

All of the above is accomplished through the right people living and working in community together. Mission-fit faculty hiring and faculty orientation, development, and mentoring lead to a culture of strong and diligent faculty teaching and scholarship, learning innovation, and faculty advancement. Service-minded staff members are the backbone of the institution, competent problem solvers who know objectively what students need and do their work intuitively.

In sum, campus culture is bold and confident authenticity, with a collective faithfulness—the campus that "feels good in its own skin." Such campuses are special places that offer distinctive experiences, places that are relevant and worthy of preserving.

Returning to my 1995 administrative team: At the outset of our work as a leadership team, we knew that our work was about advancing a new vision for a denominational institution about to celebrate its 175th anniversary. Our work was to recreate our university starting with a fresh and clear definition of our true center. Strong and complex influences ebb and flow with changing campus circumstances, reminding us of how easily culture can be altered or lost. We face governmental regulations and funding shortfalls, accreditation demands, greater accountability, well-financed competition, game-changing learning technologies, local community needs, student interests, parent expectations, and faculty voices. Alongside this array of pressures, shifting societal influences bring added significance and challenge. We find ourselves leading during urgent moral times as depicted in Tom Wolfe's fictional DuPont University in *I Am Charlotte Simmons* and in Christian Smith's research findings about the beliefs and attitudes of emerging adults described in *Souls in Transition*. Each new circumstance and shift has been met with questioning. "How does this impact the vision for our university?" "What can we do about this and still stay on center?" "Where are our opportunities to advance the vision in the face of new realities?"

Looking forward into the twenty-first century, Christian higher education aspires to a cultural model that enables its campuses to withstand the ideological shifts and operational threats happening in the larger culture in which we live. The demand has never been higher for Americans with postsecondary degrees. Today's world calls for significant expertise to bring about short-term economic recovery and a promising future. Forecasters say that America's contribution to meeting the challenges of the new global economy will not just be knowledge but also context, meaning, and wisdom.

Therefore, the demand has increased for the traditional American model of higher education, and for the life-changing influence of a liberal arts education in particular.

I suggest we take it a step further. One could claim that the demand for a new model is a calling specifically for Christian higher education. We have been presented with the opportunity to do what we do best: prepare graduates to understand context, find meaning, and act wisely. I believe in distinctive, mission-driven liberal arts education delivered through strong, tightly woven, God-honoring campus cultures, and I believe we can find hope for the future therein. Christian higher education is the academic arm of kingdom-building work. We draw strength from remembering the providential hand of God at work on and through our campuses across the years. We are a people of hope, resiliency, and strength, because we are a people of faith and vision. Working the vision together, Christian higher education can indeed continue to be a part of the solution for what the world needs—relevant, worthy, and highly effective institutions that produce graduates who invest their lives in the cause of Christ and the good of society.

A True Center

The word culture comes from the Latin word *cultura*, stemming from *colere*, which means to cultivate. The first step in carrying out vision is adopting a "work in process" approach, the idea that the vision has to be cultivated every step of the way.

Inhabiting a strong sense of purpose on campus requires strategic effort involving trustees, administration, faculty, staff, students, invested alumni, and other key constituents, all pulling in the same direction to find the true center, the distinctive institutional mission and cultural identity. Distinctive ideological identities have from the beginning characterized American campus cultures and are often found in the university seal. The seal of Union University carries the motto: *religio et eruditio*. Religion and erudition. Faith and learning. Leaders bring such words to life. They cultivate meaning out of them.

Higher education is headed toward a time when an institution's right to grant degrees will be related to how well it demonstrates accountability to institutional mission. Gone is the time when we can rely on our time-honored campus traditions or historical roots as stated in university seals. Distinctive campus cultures must line up everyday policies and procedures with clearly stated convictions so that hiring practices and community values statements, for instance, will stand up against threats of discrimination or claims of intolerance. Without a distinctive identity and practices that match, our colleges will be powerless in our claims to be who we espouse to be.

Mission distinctiveness in and out of the classroom has been key to transforming the culture on the campus where I serve. Today's mission to prepare graduates to serve church and society flows from a clear grasp of our time-honored historical purpose of religion and erudition. We find our charge from Romans 12:2: "Do not conform to the pattern of this world, but be transformed by the renewing of your mind. Then you will be able to test and approve what God's will is—his good, pleasing and perfect will." Our current motto, strategic plan, and capital campaign all bear the title "Renewing Minds."

As in the founding days of American higher education, a Christian vision for education comes from the call to love God with our minds; it can be cultivated across campus to create a distinctive Great Commandment culture. One of the best examples on my campus of how culture can be cultivated is the university's last core curriculum review. Months and months of work went in to the development of a document, "Why we have a core." Words and phrases such as "a love of virtuous thinking and living," "to know God and to love God's creation," and "to provide an opportunity for understanding, action and faith to dwell together," are used to guide the development of teaching and learning.

Christian cultures are not going to look the same from one campus to the next. Theological and educational foundations have been shaped and influenced by different traditions, and those traditions bring variety to the landscape of Christian higher education. In *Models for Christian Higher Education*, scholars Richard T. Hughes and William B. Adrian consider a variety of approaches:

- The Reformed tradition takes a cerebral approach, stressing the sovereignty of God over all creation so that scholarship and learning are subject to God.

- The Mennonite tradition takes an activist approach, stressing radical discipleship to Christ that includes service to the poor and needy.
- The Roman Catholic tradition is rooted in incarnational and sacramental theology concerned with the presence of Christ in the midst of suffering, poverty, and injustice.
- The evangelical/interdenominational tradition places major emphasis on biblicism, conversionism, and an evangelistic orientation.
- The Wesleyan/Holiness tradition refers to the attempt to reclaim Scripture, tradition, reason, experience, sanctification, and social holiness.
- The Baptist tradition focuses on biblical authority, freedom of conscience, centralized missions, autonomy of the local church, personal religion, and a tendency toward separatism.

Whatever specific theology and tradition, Christian higher education can offer a sound, interdisciplinary framework for finding answers to life's persistent questions, a particularly fitting and meaningful framework for higher education in the twenty-first century.

Christian college campuses aspire to cultivate in graduates the ability to engage the world for good and for the advancement of the kingdom of God. This new century provides a strong sense of fit for our graduates. Daniel Pink, in his book *A Whole New Mind,* writes about the need for people who "insist on seeing the big picture" as they attempt to impact society for good. We need people who are good at synthesizing, who pursue new ways of knowing, such as personal experience, and who allow an ethic of caring and empathy to help shape their work. The future will continue to demand people with a high intelligence quotient but also those with a high emotional quotient. Emotionally intelligent solutions will come from a study of the great ideas of humanity, many coming from our great Christian intellectual tradition.

"Meaning is the new money," says Pink. What is needed is the ability to place new information in context, to deliver the escalating number of facts in a new design complete with emotional impact. Design, Pink says, is interdisciplinary, "utility enhanced by significance," "a renaissance attitude that combines technology, cognitive science, human need, and beauty to produce something that the world didn't know it was missing."[1] Pink calls it combinational thinking. When we bring the truth of Jesus Christ to bear on all of the above, we call it thinking Christianly, faith and learning integration, intellectual discipleship, faith-informed academic excellence or vocational holiness. This is what Christian liberal arts colleges do best. We teach students to search for meaning and significance, informed by a Christ-centered perspective.

Coming alongside the projections of a futurist like Pink, top teaching-learning scholars are saying similar things. In *A New Agenda for Higher Education*, William Sullivan, Matthew Rosin, and Gary Fenstermacher reach new conclusions for our consideration, saying, "College is, indeed, concerned centrally with developing in students a 'life of the mind.' Students should become enabled and disposed to join others respectfully to explore, probe, and engage in our increasingly global cultural and intellectual heritage. This is the long-standing ideal of liberal education." But, the authors also state firmly, "students also need to develop a life of the mind *for practice* .... a disciplined activity that is informed, skillful, and exercised with care for a profession's purposes and the welfare of those the profession is pledged to serve."[2] A life of the mind for practice draws on the skills of reflection and criticism taken from liberal learning and combines them with deliberative judgment and action, the ability to pull apart through critical thinking and reconnect through judgment and responsibility. The desired higher education outcome is "an engaged and consequential person who will take up a place and a stance in the ongoing formation of their society and culture."

A recent email conversation among a few colleagues on my campus pulled all of this together in making a strong case for Christian liberal arts education for practice. Forwarding a newly published article in *The New Yorker*, "Live and Learn: Why We Have College,"[3] my colleague Ben Mitchell typed into the subject line, "Can you testify?" Ben challenged us to give public testimonies about how a liberal arts education "saved our lives, our sanity, or both." "It's well and good to be able to say where our graduates get jobs, etc.," Mitchell said, "but if a liberal arts education—especially a Christian liberal arts education—is what we claim it is, then we should be able to testify to its value quite apart from its utility." So Ben asked his email list of colleagues, "Can you testify?" Here are two responses:

> From Dickens, Melville, and others I learned that paying attention to details and being able to recount them in a meaningful way makes for a good story, but it is also an essential skill for managing projects and presenting information and ideas. From grammar I learned the order and mechanics of how we speak and write; order and clarity contribute to productivity and reduce the likelihood for misunderstandings. From what used to be called music appreciation I learned to listen for patterns and melodies. From that experience I gleaned that listening well does more than just enhance recall; it fosters discovery. This is a lesson that I draw from on a daily basis. From history I learned about cause and effect, or stated another way, I learned that understanding the "why's" of the past impact one's ability to address the circumstances of the present.
>
> —BARBARA MCMILLIN

> I cannot tell you how many times I sit in a leadership meeting talking about capital allocations or contract fine points and think, "Thank goodness I took that seminar in Shakespeare." I am not being ironic, even if I am being a bit practical. From Shakespeare I learned how to deal with people and understand them, even loving their individual quirks. From Shakespeare and others I learned to ponder on how financial decisions can radiate out into other areas. From history I learned to predict. From science, I learned how to scrutinize and not be a sucker for anything that comes down the pike. From math, I learned that right/wrong exist and cannot be fudged. The liberal arts tradition teaches us to read, to talk with others, and to reflect on both as connective/corrective/creative communities.
>
> —GENE FANT

Both Barbara and Gene are leaders with a testimony that the liberal arts and the life of the mind are preparation for the good of society, in their cases for the practice of good leadership.

Neal Plantinga says that the life of the mind is a *spiritual* calling, "properly done, it attaches us to God," that through learning we have "more to be Christian with."[4] Plantinga reminds us that Christian higher education must also be cultivating virtue—honesty, compassion, diligence, patience, charity, and stewardship, good things that come to us from the Holy Spirit working in us, intended to be put to good use for God's good purpose.

Listed here are a few "take-away strategies" for leaders to consider when helping their campuses focus on their true centers:

- **Guardianship over a solid message.** Help people connect the dots across the ideological landscape; help them reconcile any contradictions to staying on message. Our president uses the annual Convocation Chapel, among other venues, to keep our community on message, reprinted thereafter for distribution for further reading and reflection.

- **An image makeover.** An important first step is to believe the vision. Next comes the task of matching vision and image. Assert and communicate the image to which your vision takes you.

- **Faculty who fit.** Find faculty who can teach, mentor, coach, relate, and espouse a shared world- and lifeview. Having the right faculty is key for staying on center. I look for candidates to voice how they can advance the ethos and set of values that have been cultivated by our campus community. I have learned that saying no to the so-so candidate is always the right thing to do—repeatedly, our "no" has been blessed by the subsequent appointment of an excellent faculty member. The goal is for every member of the community to do their part in advancing the culture, starting with key people in every department. In an exit interview with Arthur Holmes (author of *The Idea of a Christian College*) during his month-long as Scholar-in-Residence with us, I asked the question, "What is the one action step that can best solidify what it means to be a Christian college?" His response, "In every department, hire a philosopher who cares about Truth in the context of his or her discipline." We have made that a hiring goal.

- **Faculty development.** Invest in the scholarship and discipleship of your faculty, both individually and collectively. Develop their talent. View them as valuable assets that create value. Champion them. At our institution, the president's desk is lined from one bookend to other with the publications of Union University faculty.

- **Faculty engagement with one another.** In *The Intellectual Life*, A. G. Sertillanges writes about the joy in "consorting in wise measure with well-chosen associates." Faculty working together bring forth amazing outcomes and provides deep satisfaction. Foster faculty colleagueship around the table, at a coffee shop, in reading groups, and through special projects.

- **Staff who fit.** Realize the important role young professional staff members play in creating culture—in the residence halls, on the intramural fields, in the coffee houses—anywhere students are. View them especially as culture-making assets by placing them on key committees, giving them new programs to develop, and including them in "think tank" sessions.

A "Can Do" Ethos of Industry

It is important for leaders to know how to grow stronger and become more excellent, navigating processes along the way. It takes a "can do" attitude to cultivate vision, an ethos of industry.

The college campus culture is what people say it is, not what the strategic plan espouses it to be. You can tell prospective students and parents what you want them to believe about your campus, but none of that matters. What matters are the feelings, emotions, and images that are evoked by their interactions with your community, primarily with your other students, faculty, and staff.

The organizational leadership literature refers to one's trademark.[5] What is the trademark of your college campus culture? What can be said about your campus that cannot be said about all the others? Every campus has something unique to offer. Defining and delivering that trademark image into every aspect of your campus in a "can do" way helps define the students' experience, which then defines your culture. It is not enough to simply tell people what your institution is about, you then have to show them. Ultimately, they have to experience it.

I have long understood the truth that in the absence of information, people will make things up. It is also true that in the absence of a clear and compelling image of your college's identity and purpose, people will make something up, whether your label becomes "the party school," "an egghead campus," or even "the school for preacher boys." Don't leave your trademark up to the definition of others. Message your trademark. For instance, delivering on a Great Commandment image drives faculty scholarship, an academically rigorous chapel program, student achievement, and student leadership development. It also motivates faculty and staff service, international and intercultural study, and a robust campus ministries program.

The college experience is about quality time inside and outside the classroom, engagement with others, and countless experiences that will change students' emotions, their attitudes, and even their lives. The "feel" of campus life is about the intrinsic elements that reside in the places where students live, study, play, dine. It's about the huge oak that provides shade on warm afternoons, the grove where picnics form, "the pit" where undergraduate research takes place, or the Frisbee golf course where people play late in the day. These places are culture-making places where impressions are formed and campus life is experienced.

The ethos is even more about the people, their actions, words, and "can do" attitudes. It is about the impact people make on students' lives. It is about the missional tie that binds the university's people together.

I have profited much in my understanding of the ultimate aims, benefits, and joy of community life from Wendell Berry's novels. His characters hold "membership" in the lives of one another, much like the concept of "the communion of the saints" in the Apostles' Creed.[6] Community life happens on

Christian college campuses where there is "common ground," "a centrality of place," "a place where membership is given rather than earned." Belonging on our campuses always comes as a gift at the point when the faculty contract is signed, the employment letter is accepted, or the student unpacks. Theologian D. Brent Laytham writes, "Berry's members are held together by powerful bonds that run deeper than affection and intention. . . . It is their common life of shared place and labor and love that binds them together. . . . because they belonged to the place, they belonged to one another."[7] Membership is a belonging that is given through shared place, shared labor, and shared love.

The love that binds us in our work on Christian college campuses is the love of Jesus Christ in us. The apostle Paul describes this approach to work in Philippians when he writes of people "[standing] firm in the one Spirit, striving together as one for the faith of the gospel" (Phil. 1:27). When we overcome our selfishness and pettiness and hold to a "one spirit" approach, we find ourselves in genuine community. There has been astonishingly little turnover among faculty and staff where I work. Membership is valued. The "one spirit" goal is compelling.

During the benediction at a recent commencement ceremony, the father of a graduating senior voiced an important goal of campus culture-making. He claimed before God that the graduates were "now the sons and daughters of Union University." In our graduates, we find the genetic makeup of our campuses, its customs, traditions, patterns, identities, and core values. Through the sum total of their experiences, we see our institutions advance and go forth through their lives. There is no greater compliment than the one from a graduate who says to me, "I am more proud of my alma mater with each passing year." In a healthy campus culture, we are a part of them, and they of us, for life, like sons and daughters.

Creating the experience is hard work. Strategic planning and new program development become the way of life. Rather than seeing review and reform as something that happens when it is time for reaffirmation of accreditation, creating the experience means living in a spirit of betterment all the time, creating a continual learning atmosphere. It means delivering academic and student life programs at a higher level that are more excellent and more relevant. It means honing the message afresh and anew. It means connecting with more prospective families, relating to more alumni, and befriending more donors. It means thicker grass, faster technology, and more customer-oriented service. It means having the courage to continually reinvent and even "disinvent" in order to create a campus culture that will be excellent into its future. As marketing executive Sergio Zyman has commented, it means changing the old saying "There is no finish line" from a cliché to a reality.[8]

Managing the experience requires a strong group of leaders who are good at knowing what data to collect, spotting trends, drawing connections, and discerning the big picture—leaders who can think deeply about the myriad of complexities facing Christian higher education. An inclusive approach has been used on my campus, where academic deans sit on the cabinet with functional leaders over student life, finances, operations, advancement, enrollment, and academics. The work is in part data-driven, where numbers become a matter of dialogue and interpretation, in part systematic where objective information is analyzed and evaluated, and in part intuitive where the subjective and moral imagination are valued. An inclusive approach fosters multiple ways of thinking and planning.

Leaders stay in their lanes most of the time, academic and student leaders advocating for academic excellence among faculty and students, delivering on academic and student life targets, serving the president with information and perspective about campus morale. Operating, financial, enrollment, and advancement leaders work on getting and giving the facts, promoting strategic thinking, being credible with and trusted by the trustees and faculty, resourcing the president with data, perspective, and "the big picture." On occasion, the lanes are set aside and a "dream team" mentality prevails. Cultivating the campus experience becomes the work of the team as a whole. Always central to the team's work is managing the ever-challenging financial aspects of campus life.

Creating campus cultures that will thrive in the future will require strategic planning that starts with narrative to give meaning and significance to the work, followed by business and financial plans. No longer can our campuses rely on rough estimates or "wing and a prayer" planning. Needed are feasibility studies, pro forma budgets, and balance sheets. No longer is it enough to balance the budget from year to year. Managing campus culture includes distilling the complex financial operations of a university in order to understand one's true financial condition and engaging in a broad, systematic review of one's finances over the long-term. Working with more information than in the past will bolster effective planning and budgetary decision making.

The economic downturn of the early twenty-first century has taught us to live with contingency expense reduction plans. The leader learns to live in the ebb and flow of ensuring a healthy budget. The process starts with an explicit statement of budget priority, set long before any budget reductions become necessary. When starting with identified budget priorities, managing reductions becomes an activity that follows a plan.

Ensuring the financial health and well-being of our campus cultures is a shared responsibility and involves intelligent leadership risk-taking with a watchdog management mentality. It takes prudent spending on the part of budget unit heads and patience on the part of the faculty and the staff where the operational resources are most directly applied. A culture of wise financial management can model excellence for a campus community in a way that gives a sense of security and respect.

Listed below are a few "take away strategies" for leaders to consider when helping their campuses work the vision:

- **Deliver.** Deliver on students' and parents' expectations, and those of faculty and staff as well. Learn to react quickly. Assess and reassess the impact of your efforts.
- **Manage from the center.** People need leadership from the top, but a "can do" ethos spreads across campus from the center. "Can do" department chairs invent new programs. "Can do" student life teams pack the house. "Can do" facility managers turn the flowerbeds into showcases.
- **Give stretch assignments.** Pose "what if" ideas. Look for small wins and make them bigger. Don't be afraid of uncharted waters.
- **Know what an excellent student experience looks like.** Visit other campuses. Serve on accreditation teams. Talk to others who can help define an excellent student experience. Learn best practices.

- **Be agile.** Be able to turn on a dime. Seize new opportunities for excellence—new friends, funding sources, town and gown relationships, academic programs, and student life initiatives.
- **Benchmark.** Identify variables. Let data help guide the decision making on your campus. But don't stop with data. Apply the subjective. Put yourself in the other person's shoes to fully understand what facts may not show.
- **Avoid disaggregated decision making.** Plans to increase enrollment may mean plans for more student housing and classrooms, which could cost more than the added tuition dollars would provide.
- **Fund retention.** Increasing student retention even by five percent can impact the budget in significant ways. The added benefit is found in satisfied students and parents.
- **Notice emotional cues.** Anticipate needs. Read tone. Mitigate stress. Translate cynicism into action.
- **Tend the social fabric.** Practice hospitality. Measure morale. Bring people together. Celebrate major steps forward. Recognize all steps forward. Communicate, communicate, communicate.
- **Monitor the toll the work is taking.** Acknowledge the hard work that is going on. Cut the workday short. Give unexpected days off if there is ever a strong reason to do so.
- **Think comprehensively; plan incrementally.** Vision casting requires patience. I have heard our president warn against overestimating what can be done in one year while giving encouragement to what can be accomplished in five to seven years.
- **Exceed expectations.** Establish goals and objectives; plan to reach them ahead of schedule and with greater markers of excellence than expected.

Hard work is satisfying work, made rewarding by working together as a team toward a widely held vision. As the dream team, we learned to solve problems and find solutions through experimentation, risk-taking, and creative thinking, all done in collaboration.

In 2008, a crisis came that allowed us to put these leadership skills to the test. Climbing out of the rubble created by a devastating tornado that destroyed seventy percent of our residence halls and damaged almost every building on campus, our leadership team rebounded by doing what we had always done—working the vision through experimentation, risk-taking, and creative thinking. Our president fostered in us a belief that a renewal of vision for our campus would come from the physical rubble that was left of its buildings. All of our work has been accomplished through strong collaboration, an essential leadership skill for the future.

It seems that the word crisis is used more and more frequently to describe higher education in general. Future leadership will require the time-tested core leadership qualities of character, competence, compassion, integrity, and data-driven decision making. Times of crisis demand more: the ability to tolerate ambiguity when faced with complexity and the drive to bring forth solutions from confusion. New core leadership traits are emerging—intuition, transparency, talent management, participation, adaptability, and inclusion.

The future calls for leaders who can cast forward-thinking vision within a framework that combines experience with reflection, leaders who are aware of present-day instabilities and changing realities. We need leaders who can then work the vision, turning today's confusion into a resource. In *Embracing Confusion*, Barry C. Jentz and Jerome T. Murphy describe confusion not as "a quicksand from which to escape but rather the potter's clay of leadership."

Today, our team is largely still together; we are writing our fifth strategic plan in an era of significant change in the life of our university. We remain eager and energized, now for new reasons. Our ping-pong games have given way to keeping up with Twitter feeds and the like. We work to build on the institution's value and relevance in new ways. We ask questions like, "What kind of place will the world need our institution to be ten, fifteen, or twenty-five years from now?" Yet the vision for academic excellence and Christ-centeredness has not changed, nor has the fact that we are not alone. We stand firm because of an unchanging God who enables us to dream well, to cultivate the vision He has given us, and to partner with other Christian colleges to model strong campus cultures for a watching world.

Notes to Chapter Twelve

1. Daniel H. Pink, *A Whole New Mind*.
2. William M. Sullivan, Matthew S. Rosin, and Gary D. Fenstermacher, *A New Agenda for Higher Education*.
3. Louis Menand, "Live and Learn: Why We Have College."
4. Cornelius Plantinga, *Engaging God's World*, xi.
5. Sergio Zyman, *Renovate Before You Innovate*.
6. Brent D. Laytham, "The Membership Includes the Dead."
7. Ibid., 174.
8. Zyman, *Renovate Before You Innovate*.

For Discussion

1. Identify areas within your institution where the work may be off-center.

2. Examine where there are torchbearers for the vision of your institution. In which departments and service areas are they located?

3. In what areas of your campus can you find an ethos of industry? Is that area exceeding expectations?

4. What is the trademark of your campus culture?

5. Are people with natural "can do" attitudes serving in positions of significance?

6. How agile is your institution in its ability to seize new opportunities when they arise?

Chapter Thirteen

LEADING A TURNAROUND AND THE JOY OF A THIRD-CLASS TICKET

Carol A. Taylor

"'What am I to do then?' he cried again, and now he seemed plainly to know the hard answer: see it through."

—*Sam in* The Two Towers, J. R. R. TOLKIEN

"Congratulations, President Taylor. You now have a third-class ticket."

So announced Dr. George Wood, General Superintendent of the Assemblies of God, just before the closing benediction of his address at my inauguration as the ninth president of Vanguard University of Southern California. He was referring to the story he had just told of the daring adventure of stagecoach travel in the 1800s.

For those willing to risk highway robbery, Indian attacks, and runaway horses, the nine-passenger Concord stagecoach offered three classes of tickets. Holders of a first-class ticket paid the highest price and had the privilege of being served and remaining comfortably seated inside the coach if it got bogged down in the mud. First-class passengers were spared any actual labor and, depending on the location of their seat, may have also been spared the sight of others laboring to enable their travel. Those holding a second-class ticket would disembark and either walk or stand along the roadside while others pushed the coach. Although they may have experienced some discomfort by standing in the rain or having to walk alongside the coach, these passengers remained observers and critics as others did the actual work. Those who possessed a third-class ticket were expected to disembark, roll up their sleeves, and push the stagecoach out of the mud or uphill if necessary. They were expected to help without complaint.

Contemporary author William Secrest paints a colorful history of the era of stagecoach travel, including the details above. He cites eight rules of stagecoach etiquette published by the *Omaha Herald* in 1877, including, "Don't imagine for a moment you are going on a picnic. Expect annoyance, discomfort, and some hardships. If you are disappointed, thank heaven."[1] At my inauguration, I publicly accepted a third-class ticket.

In January 2009, I was asked to step in as Acting President at a time of crisis that threatened the life of Vanguard University. We had gone from being a fully accredited institution to one facing possible termination of accreditation. By June 2009, we had improved enough to avoid loss of accreditation but were issued a public sanction of probation.

In July 2009, a new board of trustees asked me to continue serving as president, and I asked to defer my inauguration so that we could continue to work through the issues that resulted in our probation. Fifteen months later, with the public sanction of probation removed, we used the occasion of the inauguration to celebrate our accrediting commission's declaration of "phenomenal progress" and "a significant institutional turnaround."

Leading an institutional turnaround is a perilous journey filled with annoyance, discomfort, exhaustion, terror, sacrifice, and hardship. For those who choose to take the journey with a third-class ticket, there is also the paradox of joy, hope, companionship, elation, and the very real possibility of a grand quest that experiences a moment when the plot turns and shows hope in calamity.

I write this chapter with some trepidation. The closeness of our recent events offers the perspective of immediacy. At the same time, reflections today lack the perspective that is only possible with the distance of time. At the time of this writing, the university where I serve is in its second year since being taken off probation. While tracking positively on all indicators for financial sustainability and health, we are still fragile and vulnerable to an unanticipated crisis, such as a major loss of federal or state financial aid. The deep cultural change in the way we do business is still in process, and some see professionalizing our business models as threatening the very essence of what has made our university community special. Despite the stark realities of previous financial reports and the brutality of an unvarnished negative accreditation report and two accreditation commission letters, not everyone in the community believed the situation was dire.

Looking back at the miracles unfolding in Vanguard University's recent history, I relish my mother's wisdom, which prevailed in my decision to take the risk of telling the story of my institution at this point in time. Her words? "What happened, happened." The Israelites crossed the Red Sea and then wandered in the wilderness for the next forty years. Their wilderness journey did not change the fact that they had crossed the Red Sea, and that story needed to be told and remembered. In the same way, whatever lies ahead does not change the fact that Vanguard University came through a crisis, and that story needs to be told as an expression of gratitude and witness to God's faithfulness to a community that worked hard, prayed hard, and effected a dramatic turnaround.

This chapter is the story of some of the leadership principles that guided one institution's turnaround. Accordingly, rather than a chronological rendering, the story unfolds around that set of core leadership principles. The events and lessons learned did not occur in a neat, linear progression. Turnarounds are noisy, chaotic, perilous, and messy. The challenge for the leader is to find and maintain a quiet center from which clarity, focus, and calm sustain not only the leader but also others in the midst of the storm.

Commit to the Journey

In the face of a serious crisis, the first decision a leader has to make is whether or not to personally commit to the journey. There is the possibility of success and professional recognition. There is also the very real possibility of failure and damage to professional reputation. There are at least three options when a leader is asked to take on the challenge of leading a turnaround. One is to flee. Making this choice can start an exodus and create a panic among those who would otherwise invest in saving the institution. A second option is to cautiously step forward while developing a contingency plan. You can give it your best shot and, if failure appears imminent, make a quick exit. This inevitably drains focus from the work that needs to be done, and although unstated, communicates to others a lack of commitment and belief in the possibility of a turnaround. The third option is to give yourself fully to the journey, wherever it leads, without looking back. The obvious challenge is that at the beginning of the journey, the path is unclear and the outcome uncertain.

During the months of transition into my presidency, there were many references to the story of Esther and messages that I might have been put into my position "for such a time as this." I took these as words of intended encouragement, but I couldn't help but think that when Esther made her famous "if I perish, I perish" declaration, she likely thought she *would* perish in the quest to save her people.[2] Her willingness literally to risk her life is a model of risk-taking, sense of calling, and commitment at great personal cost.

In his book *Take the Risk: Learning to Identify, Choose, and Live with Acceptable Risk*, renowned pediatric neurosurgeon Ben Carson writes that after all of his thinking, analysis, planning, and prayer, his most difficult decisions can be boiled down to thinking through four simple questions: (1) What is the best thing that can happen if I do this? (2) What is the worst thing that can happen if I do this? (3) What is the best thing that can happen if I don't do this? (4) What is the worst thing that can happen if I don't do this?[3]

A friend counseled Dr. Carson not to participate in the case of the adult Bijani twins, sisters conjoined at the head who wished to separate and live independently, because the surgery had little likelihood of success and could harm his reputation. Dr. Carson chose to risk his professional reputation because he knew that he had more experience with craniopagus twins than any other neurosurgeon in the world and therefore could be of help to the surgical team. Despite months of preparation and the involvement of nearly thirty specialists working on the surgery, both twenty-nine-year-old women died from complications shortly after their separation, confirming detractors' concerns. But Dr. Carson had not made his decision based on desires for his own reputation; he had chosen to honor the twins' request because he knew of the potential for real help.

In the face of a crisis, a leader who believes in the distinct contribution of his or her institution to the world must set aside consideration of personal reputation and fully commit to the journey. The greater the risk of failure, the greater the necessity of determining whether you are called to the task and, if so, to come to peace with your own "if I perish, I perish" decision.

Confront Reality with Hope

In a time of crisis, a leader must have the courage to face the brutal reality of the present situation but do so while sustaining hope. The challenge is to be unflinchingly honest and transparent, while providing a vision for a way forward with a well-founded hope.

In his preface to *Transparency*, Warren Bennis reminds us that "organizations need candor the way the heart needs oxygen."[4] The temptation is to minimize the bleakness of the situation, soften the language of the crisis, ignore reality, hope the situation will get better on its own, or make modest changes around the fringes while avoiding the magnitude of issues that contributed to the crisis and the magnitude of changes that will be required for sustainability.

In *Good to Great*, Jim Collins found that leaders who led great companies "all maintained unwavering faith that they would not just survive, but prevail as a great company. And yet, at the same time, they became relentlessly disciplined at confronting the most brutal facts of their current reality."[5]

Institutions Facing Financial Crisis

It is difficult to pick up any higher education publication or newspaper without reading another dire report of massive budget cuts, the merger or closure of another college, and challenges on every front, especially for smaller independent colleges and universities.

Many university presidents, cabinets, and trustees were reading *Turnaround: Leading Stressed Colleges and Universities to Excellence* as soon as it was released in 2009. James Martin, James E. Samels, and Associates estimate that as many as a thousand of our nation's more than four thousand colleges and universities can be described as stressed. The authors also note that financial difficulties are the foremost reason that institutions become stressed.[6]

Sandra Elman, president of the Northwest Commission on Colleges and Universities, went further and observed that an increasing number of private colleges and universities are facing insolvency, and she projects that number will grow in the next twenty years. Elman believes that there are two reasons why presidents and boards are unable to see their institutional vulnerability—a failure to recognize the complexity of factors that contribute to an institution's health and a failure to recognize warning signs of impending doom. She states that "at risk institutions tend to fall into two categories: those that are smart and know how to seek and pursue viable venues for changing their circumstances, and those that become insular, focus on discrete rather than holistic components of the problems, and face further decline."[7]

In 2005 Robert Andringa, former president of the Council for Christian Colleges & Universities (CCCU), created a national profile of nine hundred religiously affiliated and nondenominational faith-based schools. He concluded that the majority of them, and especially those with endowments under ten million dollars, were at increasing risk of failure.[8]

A good indicator of the financial health of an institution is the Composite Financial Index (CFI), which provides a weighted measure of 4 core financial ratios—primary reserve, net income, return on net assets, and viability. The index ranges from 10 (strong health; able to deploy resources) to 1 (weak health; needs an assessment of viability to survive). Of the CCCU institutions that reported their CFI data in 2010, the 25th percentile was 1.6, which put these institutions in the category of needing to reengineer the institution for financial health. The 50th percentile was 2.9, still within the range to reengineer the institution for financial health, and the 75th percentile was 4.6, at the level of needing to direct resources for transformation. These ratings illustrate the fragility of the majority of the Christian colleges and universities that comprise the CCCU, an association that draws its membership from nearly 30 denominations. Few institutions were ranked between a 5 and 10, where resources could be used to create a healthy financial margin and invest in innovative new programs. In short, according to the CFI indicators, many of the CCCU institutions are a major enrollment or financial crisis away from not surviving.[9]

One University's Way Forward

If you cannot face or define the reality of your situation, eventually another group will define it for you. It may be your faculty and staff, donors, students, alumni, financial institution, or accrediting body. Our reality began to emerge in the spring of 2008 with the realization that, once again, the university would not make it through the summer without an infusion of funds. The board of trustees called for a special review to get at the heart of the issues that contributed to the institution being so fragile. This review, along with our regularly scheduled accreditation review, clearly defined the breadth and depth of the urgency of our situation.

Our accrediting commission granted a small window of time for us to demonstrate substantial progress on eight major issues. The university would have to: (1) demonstrate that we grasped the magnitude and severity of our problems, (2) restructure our board of trustees, (3) present a detailed financial plan that included an academic restructuring, (4) complete and share the results of a forensic audit, (5) demonstrate a qualified leadership team, (6) demonstrate integrity in communication, (7) demonstrate continued progress with respect to educational effectiveness, and (8) reaffirm our commitment to diversity. Depending on our ability to respond adequately, the commission reserved the right to terminate our accreditation or issue a Show Cause Order in June.

Our reality had just been defined in no uncertain terms. After reading the commission's letter on a Friday, for the first time I said out loud, "We may not make it." In fact, I wondered if I would be providing hospice care for an entire institution. What possible hope was there that we could achieve what appeared to be an impossible set of tasks given the timeline mandated by the accrediting association? The answer to Ben Carson's fourth question—"What is the worst that can happen if I don't do this?"—became clear. Vanguard University, after ninety years of impacting the world through its Christ-centered education and mission, would close its doors forever. And that indeed would be tragic.

There are times in a perilous journey when sheer grit and determination are insufficient to produce the will to persevere against all odds. Sometimes in such moments, hope arises unbidden. For me, hope came in the wee hours of the next morning. In the darkness of my room, I recalled two stories.

The first was the ancient story of a Jewish prophet who prayed for rain after a severe drought. Elijah had climbed Mount Carmel to pray for rain and sent his servant out six times to look toward the sea for evidence of rain. Finally, on the seventh time, his servant reported, "A cloud as small as a man's hand is rising from the sea" (1 Kings 18:44). The answer to a prophet's desperate prayer, in the midst of a severe drought, an angry king, and an even angrier queen, was one miniscule cloud. But from that tiny cloud, a storm arose that ended the drought. It occurred to me in the wee hours of the morning that our small window of time to make huge changes was our equivalent of a tiny cloud, and sometimes a tiny cloud on the far horizon is enough.

The second story was more immediate and personal. The previous spring, I had sat with a friend as her husband endured over nine hours of surgery to repair an aortic dissection. Later, his doctor told him that he had been given a three percent chance of survival when taken into surgery. Five months after surgery, he returned to work against all odds. Writing about their journey months later, this couple credited the doctors, the nurses, the myriad of medical staff and technicians, the well-equipped hospital, and a community of friends and family that prayed fervently for David's recovery. They wrote that at many moments along the way the only explanation for David's survival was "but God." Their tiny cloud of hope was a three percent chance of survival surrounded with exceptional care and faithful prayers.

Both stories reminded me of J. R. R. Tolkein's *eucatastrophe*, a term he coined to refer to the sudden turn of events at the end of a story that resulted in the leading character's good fortune.[10] By affixing the Greek "eu," meaning "good," to catastrophe, Tolkien captured the essence of the best of all cliff-hangers—an impossible situation suddenly turning to good. This is repeated throughout Tolkien's Lord of the Rings series until finally, against all odds, two unlikely hobbits achieve the ultimate quest to destroy the One Ring that was malevolent and save the mythical Middle-earth. The element of eucatastrophe makes for the best and most gripping stories.

We had the catastrophe, and perhaps like the ancient prophet, my friend David, and Sam and Frodo, we too would experience the "eu." But only if a board, a sponsoring denomination, the administration, and a significant number within the institution would be willing to take the difficult journey with faith and confidence.

Find the Why

When confronted with the full weight of a brutal reality, what inspires a leader and community to do the hard work necessary to turn around an institution? To stay the course, a leader needs to have a compelling answer to the question of why this specific organization needs to exist. In his book *Start with Why*, Simon Sinek writes that great leaders work from the inside out with a particular clarity with respect to why their organizations exist, rather than beginning with what they do or how they do it. They have an undying belief in a purpose or cause that is larger than themselves.[11]

Sinek reminds us that when Dr. Martin Luther King, Jr., delivered his seventeen-minute "I Have a Dream" speech on the steps of the Lincoln Memorial, he inspired a nation.[12] The refrain of "I have a dream"—not "I have a plan"—inspired others to embrace the dream as their own. King had presented a powerful case for why the civil rights movement should be a compelling vision for the nation.

At an institutional level, each leader must find the compelling reason for why the fight for survival is a worthy one. For me, the deep why took shape as I looked at the lives of our graduates and then back at the community that had equipped them for roles of significant service. A pivotal moment for me was the evening of a gender and justice conference hosted by Vanguard's Global Center for Women and Justice. I had been asked to introduce the opening keynote speaker, Esther Ntoto. Esther and her husband, Camille, had returned to their alma mater from the eastern Democratic Republic of Congo, where in the past decade more than five million have died in what is the world's deadliest war since the second world war. Since their graduation, this couple has worked with several missions and relief and development agencies.

I listened to Esther's account of extreme sexual violence in the war-torn region and the work she and Camille are doing, where their own lives are at risk on a daily basis. I listened to a woman share about believing and seeing that God continues to do the miraculous in the midst of unimaginable suffering. One powerful story involved an orphaned infant born out of a violent rape and an African American couple from New York who felt called to the Congo to adopt this infant, with the infant's skin disorder and breathing problem disappearing before their eyes when the adoptive mother held the baby to her chest.

As I drove up the freeway later that night, I wept for the victims of such horrific violence. I wept for a beautiful couple willing to live at risk to bring hope and healing to the wounded, and I wept for a university at risk of no longer providing graduates like the Ntotos to bring hope and healing into our world. And I knew this was a key reason that Vanguard had to continue to exist.

About the same time, I picked up Jim Collins's new book *How the Mighty Fall and Why Some Companies Never Give In* in an airport bookstore. After reading through his five stages of how organizations decline and fail, Collins stated that not all companies deserved to last. He then asked a piercing question—"When should a company continue to fight, and when does refusal to capitulate become just another form of denial?"[13] His next statement crystalized for me why Vanguard should not fail:

> If you cannot marshal a compelling answer to the question, "What would be lost, and how would the world be worse off, if we ceased to exist?" then perhaps capitulation is the wise path. But if you have a clear and inspired purpose built upon solid core values, then the noble course may be to fight on, to reverse decline, and to try to rekindle greatness.
>
> The point of the struggle is not just to survive, but to build an enterprise that makes such a distinctive impact on the world it touches, and does so with such superior performance, that it would leave a gaping hole—a hole that could not be easily filled by any other institution—if it ceased to exist. To accomplish this requires leaders who retain faith that they can find a way to prevail in pursuit of a cause larger than mere survival (and larger than themselves), while also maintaining the stoic will needed to take whatever actions must be taken, however excruciating, for the sake of that cause. This is the very type of leader who finds a path out of the darkness and gives us well-founded hope.[14]

The Ntotos had provided a tangible example of embodying the mission of Vanguard University to equip students for a Spirit-empowered life of Christ-centered leadership and service. Encouraged by the witness of their lives, I began reading through years of alumni magazines, inspired by what the graduates of Vanguard were doing around the globe as corporate leaders, founders of NGOs, teachers, attorneys, surgeons, vocational ministers, chaplains—men and women serving in every conceivable area of for-profit and not-for-profit work, being the presence of Christ and making a difference in the worlds where they lived and served. I looked at our faculty and staff and our current students and was convinced that these men and women deserved the best that could be done to ensure that the mission of Vanguard lived well beyond its first ninety years. In the process, I became convinced that there would indeed be a gaping hole in the world if Vanguard ceased to exist and that the best course of action would be to do whatever hard work was necessary to ensure the institution's future.

Pray, but Move Your Feet

A frequently quoted African proverb says, "When you pray, move your feet." Nine months after the university had been placed on probation, I sat in my office across from the accreditation visiting team that had come to campus to review our progress on each of the eight major issues that had been identified. I had prepared some comments to highlight the dramatic changes we had made, reference the evidence that we were now living within our means and making progress on our key financial performance indicators, and make the case that the team should have confidence in our ability to sustain the momentum evidenced in our work and consider a recommendation to reduce or remove the sanction of probation.

Before I could make the case, the chair of the team put down her pen, the room became quiet, and her face took on an inquisitive look. I was not at all prepared for her next question. She looked across the table at me and asked, "How did you do this?" She went on to state that universities do not change this dramatically or this fast and hold together.

I thought of the many mornings commuting down the California freeways to Vanguard. Most mornings my prayer had been, "God, *when* we come through this, there will be amazing stories to tell for your glory." Occasionally, the prayer was, "God, *if* we come through this, we will have stories to tell for your glory." And at least one morning I prayed, "Dear God, have you called me to give hospice care to an entire university? How do I do that?" I looked at my scripted notes and then explained that I had not done this. An entire community—administration, faculty, staff, former and new trustees, students, donors, parents, alumni, and other friends of the university—pulled together in sacrificial ways to ensure the future of an institution with a rich ninety-year legacy. And then I said, "Depending on your perspective, we were either extraordinarily lucky or we had providential help. As you can see from the evidence of the work before you, many people worked very hard to achieve a turnaround. But I will also tell you that we prayed as hard as we worked, and things happened at each critical juncture for which my only explanation is that God helped us."

In retrospect, there were many leadership principles that guided how we moved our feet. In particular, seven were most influential: call for help, engage the board, focus on sustainability first, embrace change, grieve the losses, keep perspective, and love the community.

Call for help.

Effective leaders know that leading an institutional turnaround is not a solo journey, and they aren't afraid to ask for help. Help comes in the form of professional, human, and fiscal resources.

Professional resources are widely available in the form of professional associations, publications, association meetings and conferences, books from the higher education and business sectors, and various journals. Of equal value are the resources that come in the form of human expertise, assistance, and encouragement. Wise leaders seek the best expertise available to come alongside and give perspective and guidance.

We found strategic partners and encouragement in external experts, denominational leaders and pastors, trustees, key donors and alumni, community leaders, and parents. We also received encouragement from leaders at other institutions, from the leadership of the CCCU, and from strangers who were reading the dramatic headlines in the local papers and sent books and words of encouragement and support.

Internally, an entire community of administrators, faculty, staff, and student leaders engaged in the daunting task of addressing the set of critical issues identified as essential to sustaining accreditation. Some of our immediate activities included creating new bylaws and restructuring the board of trustees, determining how we would live within our means, obtaining new auditors with demonstrated higher education experience, restructuring the academic house from multiple schools to an undergraduate college and a group of graduate programs, establishing a number of new or improved university policies, and communicating openly with the community and key stakeholders.

Engage the board.

Ultimately, the board of trustees bears responsibility to guard the mission of the university, select and evaluate the president, ensure fiscal integrity and educational quality, and ensure appropriate institutional policies and processes. Our board at the time of the crisis provided bold and courageous leadership in response to our accrediting association's requirement to create a new board that could retain denominational affiliation but with its own elected chair. A nationally recognized expert in governance assisted a task group in the formation of new board bylaws with a matrix for a board membership that would protect our denominational affiliation while strengthening the range of expertise needed to provide strong board-level governance and fiduciary oversight. This board made the ultimate sacrifice in stepping aside to allow for the creation of a new, more streamlined board. In the process, they went from being judged harshly by our accrediting association to being commended for their sacrificial leadership.

Once the new board was formed, each trustee received a copy of *Effective Governing Boards* and a subscription to *Trusteeship*, the Association of Governing Boards (AGB) bimonthly magazine that "reports trends, issues, and practices in higher education to help board members and chief executives better understand their distinctive and complementary roles and to strengthen board performance."[15]

In its first year of service, the new board of trustees adopted over seventy resolutions that put into place important board and institutional policies and procedures, from committee charters to a detailed Gift Acceptance Policy. They also committed to a professional development session as part of each board meeting, and they have maintained this practice. Since their initial retreat together, the board has benefited from sessions with association leaders, other successful university presidents with expertise in governance, and leading consultants.

Focus on sustainability first.

An institution in crisis is not unlike a patient in an emergency room. The first priority is to stop the bleeding and sustain vital functions. Addressing other concerns is postponed until the patient is stabilized and vital signs indicate sustainability of life.

To ensure survival, we focused first on the hard decisions that would allow us to live within our means, ensure the quality of academic programs and services, and build effective and efficient systems. In his book *Academic Turnarounds: Restoring Vitality to Challenged American Colleges and Universities*, Terrence MacTaggart stresses that restoring financial stability is the first step for colleges and universities in distress. Step two is developing a clear marketing message supported by consistent branding efforts, and step three is strengthening academic programs and transforming institutional culture.[16] We began the process by creating a balanced budget, which meant cutting significant dollars from our expense budget. It also involved making the hard decisions to reduce staff positions, cut some academic programs, and incentivize employees to retire early.

In the second year of the turnaround, we strengthened our mission statement, launched a new website, created a new marketing campaign, and developed a comprehensive set of brand guidelines.

Our board declared a state of financial exigency and adopted a set of key performance indicators that identified where we were and would allow us to track progress on each performance indicator through three stages: (1) exit financial exigency, (2) recovery, and (3) financial health. We have now made significant progress on all indicators and on several are well into the recovery stage. Achieving financial sustainability represented one of the vital functions that would allow us to continue the turnaround journey.

Embrace change.

The very word turnaround implies change. Among a collection of small motivational books on the shelf near my desk is one titled *Change is Good ... You Go First.*[17] Whether we call it adaptive leadership or change management, leading change is hard. That may be why there are so many leadership books on the subject.

Turnaround leadership is about mobilizing people for change. Harvard professor Ronald Heifetz believes that the most successful change does three things: (1) preserves the best of an institution's history, (2) discards what is no longer relevant, and (3) innovates in ways that allow the institution to thrive in the face of new challenges.[18] That sounds simple, but doing it successfully is anything but simple. Heifetz states that, when engaging people in the work of change, one is begging for conflict. He makes the point that "the tough issues are tough because they often involve losses when roles need redefinition, areas of incompetence need exposure, and loyalties require refashioning. Those stakes generate conflict, because adaptive solutions are often not wholly positive in sum."[19]

An excellent resource on the challenges of and strategies for effectively leading change is Chip and Dan Heath's *Switch: How to Change Things When Change is Hard.*[20] A crisis that threatens an institution's continued existence can provide powerful motivation to accept change. However, accepting and embracing change are not the same thing. The Heaths helped me understand that for individuals to sustain change, the leader has to influence their hearts and minds as well as the environment. They also reminded me that change is hard because it is exhausting, especially in turnaround situations where the stakes are high and dramatic and immediate change is often necessary.

Grieve the losses.

On one particularly exhausting day, I thought of two ancient Jewish stories. The first was the story of the Israelites after their exodus from Egypt. They were tired of manna, tired of the journey, tired of their leader, and longing to return to the familiarity of Egypt. The second story was of the group of Israelites that returned from Babylonian exile to Jerusalem to restore their temple. When the new foundation was laid, some shouted for joy while others wept loudly. The book of Ezra records that the shouting and the weeping could be heard far away.

These stories remind me that turnarounds are exhausting, tedious, and noisy. They also remind me that embracing change means accepting and grieving losses. It may be the loss of resources, a colleague, a program, a way of doing business, privileges once held, the familiarity of traditions, or a sense of security. While some celebrate change, others grieve very real losses. The challenge for a leader is to live with the paradox of a community's legitimate and concurrent expressions of joy and sorrow while moving forward.

Keep perspective.

One of the challenges of a third-class ticket is the limited view, which makes it difficult to gain perspective, to cultivate and create space for reflection that allows a leader to see the bigger picture. In *Leadership on the Line*, Ronald Heifetz and Marty Linsky use the metaphor of a dance floor and refer to the iterative process of being on the dance floor, getting on the balcony to observe the dance, and then returning to the floor.[21]

There are several things that help to gain and keep perspective—reading through an institution's history and stories of the alumni, remembering that the story of a university is more often an epic than a short story, listening to various members of the community and campus leaders. It can be helpful to process the work with some key advisors outside the university, who can bring a fresh perspective and expertise to the work without personal agendas.

I have also found it personally helpful to schedule periodic retreat days during the academic year for a day of guided solitude and reflection. Heifetz and Linsky note that self-reflection, or what the Jesuits call "contemplation in action," does not come naturally and needs to be nurtured.[22] Often perspective, insights, and clarity of direction follow several hours or days of contemplative reflection.

Love the community.

As I prepared my inaugural address in the fall of 2010, I was taken aback by a recurring question that intruded into my thoughts as I pondered my institution's legacy and the vision for its future. Our recent journey had been traumatic, but also inspiring. I reflected on the kind of community that Vanguard University is—a community of Christ followers, a community of learners, a community with a global reach, and a community with a special home in Costa Mesa, California. The question that kept interrupting my thoughts was, "Do you, will you, love Vanguard?"

I talked with a friend who shared her own story of serving fifteen years with Wycliffe Bible Translators in Malaysia among the Tagal people. It was in her fifth year of service that she joined a remembrance ceremony in a remote village to honor a village chief who had died. On the third day of the ceremony, her heart broke as she wept with her friends, and at that moment realized that God had given her a deep love for the Tagal people. She then said, "My prayer is that you will realize how much you already love Vanguard." A few weeks later, as I stood looking out at the members of the Vanguard community, my heart was gripped with how much they had invested and sacrificed and endured to ensure the continued legacy of our institution. I was not prepared for the overwhelming sense of love for the Vanguard community that I felt at that moment.

In their latest book on leadership, James M. Kouzes and Barry Z. Posner present ten truths about leadership. Their final truth is that leadership is an affair of the heart, that love is the soul of leadership.[23] Loving the community is not a strategy or cloak that a leader can put on like academic regalia and then return to its storage bag until required for the next official event. It is a daily choice. It is costly. It motivates and inspires a leader to work hard, persevere, sacrifice, weep, laugh, and make the hard decisions necessary to sustain the daily efforts to rebuild an institution with the deep conviction that the institution must not only survive but thrive. When a leader opens his or her heart to loving the community deeply, a turnaround journey takes on a more profound significance, motivation, and joy.

Commit to Transformation

Vanguard has traveled through the first two stages of an institutional turnaround—financial recovery and marketing/branding. As we continue to gain financial strength and see the benefits of renewed marketing with more strategic enrollment gains, we are entering the third and, according to Terrence

MacTaggart, the most difficult, most time-consuming, and least-often accomplished stage—strengthening academic programs and transforming institutional culture.[24]

When Vanguard University entered what became a major crisis in the fall of 2008, few knew the depth of the crisis or the measures that would be necessary to rebuild an institution approaching its 90th anniversary. Few would have predicted the magnitude of change that the institution would undergo. Many remained resolute in their efforts to ensure Vanguard's future and in the process discovered an institution and board that demonstrated an adaptive capacity beyond what any of us would have imagined. Today Vanguard is adding its name to other resilient organizations that have emerged through a crisis with renewed vision and commitment to its mission. Jim Collins writes,

> The path out of darkness begins with those exasperatingly persistent individuals who are constitutionally incapable of capitulation. It's one thing to suffer a staggering defeat—as will likely happen to every enduring business and social enterprise at some point in its history—and entirely another to give up on the values and aspirations that make the protracted struggle worthwhile. Failure is not so much a physical state as a state of mind; success is falling down, and getting up one more time, without end.[25]

I began this chapter with a sense of trepidation given the immediacy of our journey at Vanguard and the fact that we are an institution still in the process of transformation. I conclude with a profound sense of gratitude for those who have sacrificed so much and for the compelling evidence of God's gracious hand on this university. My prayer is that others who find themselves called to lead their institutions through a turnaround may take hope and courage and also discover the joy of a third-class ticket. I am convinced that preserving a Christian college or university whose mission it is to equip students for Christ-centered service in a world in desperate need of hope is a cause worthy of our best efforts. May we cherish our third-class tickets as we continue to pray and move our feet and rely on the One who does immeasurably more than we can think or imagine for his purposes and his glory.

Notes to Chapter Thirteen

1. William B. Secrest, *Perilous Trails, Dangerous Men*.

2. Should you want a refresher, you'll find these verses in Esther 4:14 and 16.

3. Ben Carson with Gregg Lewis, *Take the Risk*.

4. Warren Bennis, Daniel Goleman, and James O'Toole, x.

5. Jim Collins, *Good to Great*, Kindle location 1624.

6. James Martin, James E. Samels, and Associates, eds, *Turnaround*.

7. Sandra Elman, "Accreditation, Fragility, and Disclosure: Maintaining the Delicate Balance," 156.

8. Robert C. Andringa, "Keeping the Faith: Leadership Challenges Unique to Religiously Affiliated Colleges and Universities."

9. *CCCU Member Institution Financial Ratios Report 2010*.

10. J. R. R. Tolkien, *The Tolkien Reader*.

11. Simon Sinek, *Start with Why*, 235.

12. Ibid., 219.

13. Jim Collins, *How the Mighty Fall and Why Some Companies Never Give In*, 111.

14. Ibid., 111–112.

15. *Trusteeship*, Washington, DC: Association of Governing Boards of Universities and Colleges. See web page at http://agb.org/publications/trusteeship. Other AGB resources of particular help:
    - The Fundamentals Set—Independent Version (six booklets for board structure and responsibilities of trusteeship)
    - Effective Governing Board: A Guide for Members of Governing Boards of Independent Colleges and Universities (for board orientation)
    - The Chair and The President Set – Independent Version
    - Presidential and Board Assessment in Higher Education: Processes, Policies and Strategies
    - Assessing Presidential Effectiveness

16. Terrence MacTaggart, ed., *Academic Turnarounds*.

17. Mac Anderson and Tom Feltenstein. *Change is Good . . . You Go First*.

18. Ronald A. Heifetz, "Leadership, Authority, and Women: A Man's Challenge."

19. Ibid., 323.

20. Chip Heath and Dan Heath. *Switch*.

21. Ronald A. Heifetz and Marty Linsky, *Leadership on the Line*.

22. Ibid., 51.

23. James M. Kouzes and Barry Z. Posner, *The Truth about Leadership*.

24. MacTaggart, *Academic Turnarounds*, 6.

25. Collins, *How the Mighty Fall*, 123.

For Discussion

1. What are the tangible benefits that you have experienced when you have led from the perspective of a third-class ticket?

2. What are some challenging decisions that you are facing, and how does your perspective change when you apply Ben Carson's four questions for risk taking?

3. If your institution is facing significant challenges and has a CFI below a 2.0, what are the brutal facts of your institution that must be faced and addressed?

4. What is the *why* of your institution? What gaping hole would be left in the world if your institution ceased to exist?

5. In what ways does your institution need to move its feet to move from challenged to thriving?

6. What inspires you to sustain your efforts to transform your institution?

7. What do you do to keep perspective and sustain your commitment to lead your institution?

8. Do you, and how will you, love your community?

Chapter Fourteen

LEADERSHIP IN THE FIFTH DIMENSION
Balancing Time with the Timeless

Lee F. Snyder

"Eternity is not perpetual future but perpetual presence. . . .
The world to come is not only a hereafter but also a here-now."

—ABRAHAM JOSHUA HESCHEL, Moral Grandeur and Spiritual Audacity

The Call in the Night and the Knock at the Door

College presidents dread those calls in the night. Sometimes it is an angry phone call. Sometimes it is a more serious campus matter. Then there are the anonymous letters, which are relatively easy to dismiss, given that there is simply not a thing one can do about them. Except fume and stew and spend an inordinate amount of time trying to figure out who might have sent the ugly note and why.

I had arrived at the office early one morning, before the lights were on in College Hall. It was peacefully quiet. It was 6:50 a.m. I noticed the red message light blinking on the phone. When I picked up, an unfamiliar voice said, "This is Max Miller at 168 Latimer Avenue. It's 12:40 a.m. There is a disturbance at the college and I am going to call the police."[1] That was it. There was no indication of a follow-up call to suggest any outcome. Nothing from the police. Thankfully, Mr. Miller had not called me at home in the middle of the night. I never did learn what that call was about.

A more distressing telephone call came one morning about 5:30 a.m. The residence director, with a tone of urgency bordering on panic, reported that there was a fire in Ropp Hall. She hastened to assure me that the women had been evacuated, that there were no fatalities, but that there were injuries. As I hastily dressed and headed down to campus, my mind was reeling. There was little time in the following hours and days to do more than deal with traumatized students, arrange for the relocation of dormitory residents, and keep close to the fourteen students who were injured. The fire marshal's finding of arson raised the stakes and increased general campus anxiety.

While classes continued and faculty offered whatever assistance they could, resting squarely on the shoulders of the administration were matters involving physicians, counselors, fearful parents, attorneys, and a very concerned community. Speculation was rampant. The discovery that the arsonist was likely another student provoked even more troubling questions. As it turned out, this matter was not to be resolved for months. Periodically, the news media felt obligated to revisit the details. Some two years later, this headline jumped out: "Bluffton College seeks release from lawsuit" with the subheading, "Fire: College claims it does not owe residents protection against criminal acts by other students." If only it were that simple, I thought, groaning inwardly.

In the large and small events that make up the daily lives of university presidents, an inescapable reality is that one dares not yield to an illusion of total control. I suspect this goes for CEOs in a wide variety of organizations, but I learned this early in a ten-year presidency. There was the campus fire, and there was another crisis that happened in my second year as president. This was July. Most students were gone for the summer. A band camp was underway, drawing high school students from around the region. Late one Friday morning, the relentless wail of sirens began to seep into the consciousness of those of us in College Hall trying to catch up with strategic planning and year-end reports. The word came shortly, as I was meeting with the vice president for finance: scaffolding erected for use by the band director had collapsed on the practice field. An undetermined number of students, contrary to regulations, had been allowed up on the scaffolding. There were serious injuries, including the band director.

Emergency teams from surrounding counties and towns poured in. Under the blaze of the noonday sun, the EMTs attended to those involved, arranging to airlift the most seriously injured. The network television crews also descended. Hovering overhead in the helicopter or arriving in communication vans, reporters saw this accident as primetime news—an extension of a just-released national news exposé of the dangers of scaffolding.

Our small campus in a tiny Midwest town was unaccustomed to the media frenzy, but that was the least of the community's concerns as medics, pastors, counselors, and campus personnel attended to the victims and their families. When it was eventually determined that there would be no fatalities, the news teams directed their attention to larger stories, including that afternoon's shooting in Washington, D.C., at the nation's capitol.

There are moments in the midst of a hectic pace, however, when evidence of the transcendent breaks in. Such was an early morning encounter shortly after the Ropp Hall fire. I had gone to the office early, hoping for a little solitude in order to gain perspective and prepare for whatever lay ahead. The complexities of crisis control, fact-finding depositions, insurance issues, and the specter of lawsuits sapped an inordinate amount of energy.

Outside College Hall, the walkway lights were still burning. I had just gotten settled at my desk when I heard a knock at the door. Startled, I went through the outer office to see who was there. I greeted Nan, our young assistant campus pastor, who apologized for interrupting at that hour. She announced that she wanted to pray with me. What had made her come just at that moment? Somehow Nan had sensed that the pressures of the office were threatening to overwhelm me. Her obedience to an impulse carried me through the day. Because she reached out, I was able to embrace both a sense of total inadequacy and wonder at God's working.

The call in the night and the knock at the door each signal opposite ends of a continuum in which college presidents live, seeking out a path to a thriving institution. This search requires consciously cultivating a space for living in a kind of fifth dimension—a metaphor for that intersection of time with the timeless. T. S. Eliot calls this the "still point of the turning world."[2]

In a frenzied, churning, whirling world that inexorably bears down on the leader, there arise these unbidden encounters that evoke such a still point, if we are but paying attention. Acknowledging connections with others underscores our need for one another. Recognizing such moments also requires comprehending that some things are out of our hands. Nan, at that early hour in College Hall, was a reminder of the individuals who filter through our lives at certain bends in the path—persons who have a word for us at a precise point in time.

Suddenly it is as though one discovers a tiny thread in a web of hidden patterns, and that one thread gives strength and meaning to our lives. Such threads represent strands of ordinary time transformed by the simplest things, by modest efforts that yield undeserved grace. With an in-breaking of deep awareness, the leader glimpses some dimension of the timeless—that spacious realm that gives focus and meaning to our work. Leaders who cultivate openness to the unexpected and the commonplace, who notice the interruptions and surprises, have a particular ability to shape a healthy institutional culture. Such leadership is not crisis oriented, but rather models a confident ability to draw on the resources of the leadership team and the community in facing whatever arises. This is leadership that demonstrates a capacity to see beyond the challenge of the moment—which is above all grounded in the larger vision, mission, and purpose of the organization.

Understanding the Demands of Leadership

In the early uncertainties of a first presidency, I was reassured by long-experienced colleagues that the job was manageable. A piece of cake, really. They did not say that exactly, but the tone of their comments conveyed that message. After all, we first-time presidents were reminded, "It's not brain surgery." One enthusiastic leader meant to reassure us new presidents when she said, "I just love the problems." Having been a university dean for a decade, I was not reassured because I did not quite believe her. I was more encouraged, I confess, when I heard an experienced CEO reflect honestly on the "terrors of the presidency," as he put it. Here was a person who was admitting fear. His candor gave me courage to admit my own fears.

While not every day presents a crisis, there are those parts of the job that require leaders to give attention to demanding and sometimes misguided constituents (including legislators, parents, students—sometimes even employees). A father, irate about the mounting fines resulting from his son's repeated parking citations, is in no mood for a rational conversation. How a college student could accumulate nine hundred dollars' worth of violations by driving from his assigned residence hall parking space to the reserved lot near the student center was inexplicable to me. That question did not seem to occur to the father. Nor did the father seem to have asked his son why the first two or three or four tickets had not triggered some reminder about parking regulations.

College leaders must have a high tolerance for the mundane, which can be simultaneously silly and fraught with emotion. Our work is often about "unremarkable stuff"—the irritated prof who bursts into the president's office apoplectic that he fell on an icy sidewalk, clearly because the grounds crew had not done their work adequately. Or the student who, having exhausted all other appeals, asks the president to overturn his sanction for an alcohol infraction because he knows of other students who have escaped punishment.

Relationships

Leaders must recognize that relationships matter, whether dealing with petty irritations or with more weighty matters. Listening to the outraged professor who lost his dignity in a fall or to the student who had to explain to his parents why he was disciplined signals another responsibility of the leader. That is, to pay attention to people. In leadership theory, a field that previously valued "strategic toughness," experts are increasingly recognizing the significance of relationships.[3] Leadership guru Margaret Wheatley, researching complex organizations as living systems, underscores the importance of relationships developed from a shared sense of purpose. Living systems—relationships— embody "exquisite capacities to create meaning together, to communicate, and to notice what's going on in the moment. These are capacities that give any organization its true aliveness," Wheatley contends.[4]

Early in my administrative career, I discovered, almost inadvertently, how paying attention to relationships shapes the culture of the institution in even the smallest ways. I had developed a pattern of writing notes to faculty and colleagues, congratulating individuals on particular achievements or commending them on a job well done. I was humbled, even surprised, at how moved faculty were by these gestures of appreciation, by the fact that someone had noticed their work. Leadership that models a culture of caring, of honoring one another, of celebrating, contributes to that quality of "true aliveness" that marks a thriving organization.

However, attending to relationships can be all-consuming for a president. Sometimes it is the sheer pace of the work that, paradoxically, both energizes and depletes. One day mid-semester, I found myself running, almost literally, with not enough hours and hardly time to think. I found myself praying:

> God, give me grace today to see each thing in its place and to tackle one thing at a time. May the press of the urgent not keep me from meeting you today, when you choose to appear—in the questions, in the people who walk in that office door, in the overwhelming tasks which I have to get done today and tomorrow.

That prayer was expressed visually for me in a bronze that was installed in a new Centennial Sculpture Garden on campus. Next to the academic center, which I passed nearly every day on my way to a meeting across campus, there stood a beautiful, graceful hound in full running motion with a monkey perched on its back. "That's my administrator dog," I told my friend Jay, the artist. The sculpture reminded me of a bit of wisdom already mentioned by my fellow author Patricia Anderson in her chapter on storytelling: that each time an individual comes into the office with some request, the president should be aware that the petitioner has a monkey on his back that he wants to unload on the CEO. For sheer survival, I was instructed, it is imperative that the president have a mindset of not accepting every monkey that comes in the door.

Another Reality

Experience teaches us also that time's melancholy inevitably descends on leaders in the normal flow of the work. Sometimes it is simply the unraveling of a plan that held much promise. Or it might be an occasion, such as I experienced in the middle of a critical capital campaign, when a donor needed to adjust a multi-million dollar commitment to one million because of a change in personal circumstances. However, it is most often in the sphere of relationships that we must confront inscrutable pain, tragedy, or loss. Leaning into the personal anguish of students, colleagues, friends, or family grounds the leader in real time. The leader's ability to give attention to the suffering of members of the community contributes in a powerful way to fostering a deep awareness of that which transcends ordinary responsibilities within the classroom or office.

I recall an achingly beautiful September day when the very season seemed to intensify a mounting sense of loss. There was the young music professor, dealing with cancer herself, whose husband had simply collapsed on the basketball floor and died. There was another colleague who must have been terrified when stricken with a malady tentatively diagnosed as Bell's Palsy. He returned to the classroom with half his face sagging and his speech halting. Then a telephone call from a close friend confirmed the worst possible news about his spouse's surgery and prognosis—that a malignancy had spread to the liver and lymph system. That autumn, the dying of the year, became a kind of metaphor for the in-your-face reality that the human condition is sometimes utterly sad—a "falling apart."

I understood anew, given such a cascading sequence of human misery and angst, that personal relationships matter most in the daily work. When one values relationship, one is more attuned to the student who is dealing with her parents' divorce or the first-year student whose father has just died, to the unspoken needs of a staff member one meets on the sidewalk or the individual who lingers to talk after a meeting.

In the midst of such realities, I struggled to remain open to the moment, to the still point that gives meaning in the face of unspeakable grief or fear. As leaders, we are called to embrace human fragility and to allow the world to stop, to linger in the present, to reach out, to hold up and pray that God's spirit would give us discernment about how best to respond.

As so often happens in the crazy time warp of the presidency, someone or something makes an appearance just when most needed. Eberhard Arnold offers this Advent encouragement, which I return to again and again:

> When we are discouraged by the apparently slow progress of all
> our honest efforts, by the failure of this or the other person, and

by the ever new reappearance of enemy powers and their apparent victories, then we should know: the time shall be fulfilled. . . . The time is being fulfilled and the light shall shine, perhaps just when it seems to us that the darkness is impenetrable.[5]

I take comfort in the desperate hope that down-to-earth, practical realities imposed in leadership responsibilities point to "time being fulfilled."

Keep Me from Stupid Sins

I have two favorite prayers. The first is really a pair of prayers borrowed from Anne Lamott, and together they cover most situations: "Help me, help me, help me" and "Thank you, thank you, thank you."[6] I heard that someone said that life is composed of both highs and lows, but that for college presidents the highs are higher, the lows lower, and they come closer together than for most people. Lamott's prayer can be breathed, shouted, or whispered, as the occasion demands. My second prayer is equally serviceable: "Keep me from stupid sins," a contemporary rendering of Psalm 19:13 (*The Message*). This is a way of expressing another psalm petition, "O LORD, save us! O LORD, grant us success!" (Psalm 118:25). But in the Mennonite tradition of humility, it somehow seems prideful to pray for success.

I was taken aback when I heard a new college president express a belief that if leaders are simply good decision makers and possess halfway decent administrative skills, they can successfully guide and direct outcomes, whatever challenges arise. That president is still doing well in his institution, so maybe he is right. But I am much less certain than he that leaders have that much control. I believe instead that circumstance and contingency are major shapers of our work, and we govern and lead by the grace of God, not discounting the responsibility to plan and provide direction.

As presidents and executives, we must find ways to come to terms with those aspects of the work that are simply out of our control. If we are fortunate, we learn through experience to value the full spectrum of human personalities. (Although if we are honest, we appreciate some more than others.) We depend on the wisdom of colleagues and the encouragement of our communities when faced with knotty dilemmas. Experience is important in a leader's success, but T. S. Eliot may have it right when he suggests that there is only a limited value in the "knowledge derived from experience." Eliot goes on: "The only wisdom we can hope to acquire / Is the wisdom of humility."[7]

One of the most difficult challenges leaders face is those instances of misjudgment or of failed relationships. Our own "stupid sins" are the hardest to forgive—when we hire the wrong person, when we are persuaded against our better judgment to back an ill-advised project, or when we fail to hold a trusted administrator accountable. And then we fall on our knees again and pray for God's grace.

"Do something you can't do."

It is in those moments of undeserved grace, which make their appearance in unexpected ways and places, that our failures and stupidities are redeemed. It is in the process of renewal—affirmation that we are part of something much larger than ourselves—that we experience hope. Sometimes it is merely the discovery of a word of wisdom that seeks one out in the midst of discouragement or doubt. For me, that word was Flannery O'Connor's advice, "Be properly scared and go on doing what you have to do."[8]

Early in my presidency, I came across the sculptor Henry Moore's thoughtful answer to the question "What is the secret of life?" At age eighty-eight, Moore observed that "the secret is to devote your whole life to one ambition . . . . But remember: Choose something you can't do." Henry Moore laughed as he said it, recalls the poet Donald Hall, who writes about this conversation.[9] And I laughed too, because most days I would not need convincing that I was engaged in a project that I could not really do. But I was also keenly aware that something larger was going on of which I had only a dim awareness—another aspect of living with a "fifth dimension" perspective.

Somewhere along the way, as leadership opportunities came my direction, I discovered that intuition and a healthy respect for the subconscious are capacities that should be honored. While reason and intellectual prowess are highly regarded, other dimensions of the mind are too often dismissed. I became aware, almost by accident, that when complex issues arise or when contentious circumstances develop, my organization was not always best served by a quick, well-calculated decision. Rather, I began noticing that being able to put aside a perplexing matter and simply let it rest—that is, allowing the subconscious to work on it—yielded more insightful and creative solutions in the long run.

I learned to pay attention to an idea that would suddenly pop up, seemingly out of nowhere, which provided direction in a particular situation or in a decision facing the administrative team. This awareness is affirmed by Peter Senge's observation that "It is through the subconscious that *all of us* deal with complexity." He goes on to say that one of the subtler aspects of a leader's discipline of "personal mastery" involves integrating reason and intuition. Senge emphasizes that leaders must not settle for choosing between reason and intuition, or "head and heart," for both are essential to effective leadership.[10]

I became aware also that my own inclinations as team builder, one who valued collaboration and consultation, was a different model than the old "command and control" mode of leadership. After he had gotten to know me that first year, a member of the president's cabinet disclosed that in the previous administration, when the leadership team left the cabinet meeting, they were not always sure what decision had been made. They would turn to the minutes to find out what the president had decided. In contrast, I observed that where a leadership team was expected to work collaboratively, remarkable creativity and synergy were unleashed. Not only did the institution experience growth and new levels of excellence, but each of the vice presidents working with his or her respective division contributed to a culture of valuing the gifts of all, as we worked toward a common vision.

Risk-taking

The path to leadership has, for me, required a willingness to make peace with uncertainty, to rest on a ledge of ambiguity. Effective leadership is more a constellation than a star, as someone has observed. For leaders to be successful, they must understand power as relational, not simply hierarchal. I have become increasingly persuaded, as one of my colleagues suggests, that the responsibility of the leader is to listen, learn, support, and respect. This offers a model of power as relationship and involves delegating authority with a respect for the needs of individuals, as well as for the fluctuations and imbalances that beset organizations.

While this model of leadership does not absolve the president of decision making, this approach overturns the old notion that leaders are responsible for controlling everyone and everything. I am convinced that being able to "let go" is one of the most difficult but essential qualities of a leader. When the leader and the administrative team are able to trust the unfolding process, they are better able to serve the organization. Such an approach may seem risky, but it is the combination of confidence and vulnerability that empowers vision and purpose.

Presidents would do well to remember, as Linda Hill of the Harvard Business School observes, that in order to be effective, leaders must keep in mind three central principles:

1. the institution is more important than any single individual,
2. the leader's job is to help others succeed, and
3. first and foremost in making decisions, the organization's future and sustainability must be considered.[11]

Basing decisions on these beliefs often places the leader in a lonely position, particularly when unpopular actions are required.

Presidents smile knowingly at the quip that leaders are either risk-takers, caretakers, or undertakers.[12] One of the most powerful images of the risk-taker that I know is found in Scripture, in the Old Testament account of Joshua as he pauses before crossing the Jordan River. As successor to Moses, Joshua faces a formidable task—to lead the Hebrew people into hostile territory, into the land promised by God. God's command is direct: "Move out.... Then you will know which way to go, since you have never been this way before" (Josh. 3:3–4 TNIV). Stepping out and moving ahead without fully knowing the direction seems counter-intuitive to the leadership principles that prescribe careful strategy and informed decision making. It is another version of that wonderful line by the poet Theodore Roethke, "I learn to go by going where I have to go."[13]

Asking the Hard Question: When Is It Time to Leave?

In finding one's way along the path of leadership, a president or senior administrator must be more than a risk-taker, more than adept at handling day-to day crises. Leaders have a responsibility to be clear-eyed about the seasons of leadership in a particular organization. Leadership transition is about timing, about looking at the big picture. When is the right time for an executive to move on? What are the factors that ought to be taken into account by the governing board? By the administrative team? By the individual executive?

Not all executives have a perfect sense of the "right time." Not all boards are helpful in recognizing the value of transition, particularly if things are going along well and if the institution is stable. The temptation is for boards to want to hang on to that stasis. On the other hand, if managed well, executive transition can be a significant time of empowerment and envisioning new possibilities for the organization.

Too often, individuals develop a sense of entitlement, partially fostered by the very loyalty that institutions prize in a close-knit and community-oriented context. As academic vice president, I had observed individuals who had lost their edge of creativity and who had simply stayed too long. I resolved that I would "leave before it's time."

Part of this determination grew out of the simple consideration of number of years on the job. How long should a top administrator stay in the position? Change can be good for an institution and for the individual. Research suggests that it is advisable as a general principle for top administrators to move on after seven to ten years.[14]

There were three realities I was attuned to when I considered the question of how long to stay. First, I wanted to leave the position on my own terms, to be in control of when and how I would make a transition. I had observed too many situations where this had gone painfully awry. For transitions to go well, advance consultation and timing need to be attended to. Second, I was also aware of weariness and fatigue in the job after twelve years in the academic dean's role and then ten years in the presidency. It was time for fresh creativity, I sensed, even though the board chair explored whether I would continue if given a sabbatical. I knew that the university would benefit from a leader with new ideas, different experiences, even a different style. Third, approaching ten years in the presidency, I knew that the institution was in an exceptionally good place with major accomplishments to point to, a superb administrative team, a noble vision, and momentum for future initiatives. I was reassured to see the university increasingly being recognized by those outside for its quality and excellence.

I had given what I could in my stint at the helm and was proud of the academic community. I had also given attention to leadership development. While it was not in my place to choose a successor, I was confident that there would be any number of well-qualified candidates who would be prepared to take the university to the next level. The timing was right; I needed to confirm with the board my decision to move on.

There is perhaps nothing more rewarding in one's work than to sense that God's call is a dynamic one, that change is good, and that being a part of something ongoing, something large and purposeful, is a privilege—but for a time. In spite of the inevitable uncertainty ushered in by the retirement of an executive, change is energizing and points to future possibilities. As Thomas Merton observes, "In transition is also fullness."[15] That fullness can be for both the individual and the organization, if change is attended to thoughtfully by the board.

Living in the Flow of the Timeless

But back to beginnings for a moment. As a first-time president new to the university and the region, I had schooled myself in the purpose of the university's founding in 1899. I had acquainted myself with the figures who had loomed large in the history of the place. Two archivists were especially helpful in ferreting out all kinds of information about the early college years and in providing me with accounts of presidential addresses and milestone events as the campus grew. There were several official histories along the way that added to my knowledge. As the campus approached its one-hundred-year anniversary, there was opportunity to re-tell the story, to celebrate and to marvel at the ways God had blessed the institution and raised up extraordinary leaders. One of the early documents recorded the first president's call to "Expect Great Things." That challenge became a theme motto as the campus reflected on the growth and reach of the academic program and celebrated the many ways the founders' vision was being carried out.

Inspiring Hope

Remembering and celebrating are two essential qualities of a vibrant community. Telling the stories of past hardship and obstacles overcome, as well as unimagined successes, is the responsibility of the leader. In this way, hope and a purposeful vision for the future are cultivated. This is where time intersects with the timeless, where the future is illuminated by the past and where the present calls out leaders—including poets, prophets, and sages—to bring into being the transformative dreams of those called to the work.

It is the primary job of the leader to inspire hope by communicating effectively the institution's mission and purpose. This task is often best achieved through traditions and ceremonies that forge a connection between past and future. In this sense, the president is often the keeper of the institutional story. The president is the person who reminds the community of the dedication of the founders and who points to the future or who, as Emily Dickinson might say, dwells in possibility.[16]

The tradition of a New Year's Recognition Dinner at our institution, for example, provided an occasion for recognizing faculty and staff achievements and years of service. This was a time for storytelling, for laughter, for enjoying a special meal. Such celebratory events reinforce a culture of saying, "Thank you, we appreciate your work, and we honor your accomplishments." As Margaret Wheatley observes in her workplace studies, "The organizations that people love to work in are those that have a sense of history, identity and purpose."[17] Remembering, celebrating, envisioning a purposeful future— these enliven the present. This is a fifth dimension perspective: one that cultivates practices that reach into the past and that set a trajectory for the future—all in the service of a vibrant present.

I smile when I hear a friend characterize administrators as "pathological optimists." Rosemarie, wife of a very successful academic dean, does not mean that as a compliment, but on second thought, it very well may be. Let us say it is a necessary affliction of the leader—being grounded in time's reality but with a capacity to envision the unimaginable, with the conviction that the work we do is not our work but God's work.

The Mundane and the Sacred

Living daily with an awareness of the timeless—dwelling in the fifth dimension—is pressed upon us in familiar routines, if we are listening. I remember the beginning of a new school year, a dazzling time of breathing in new student expectations, teachers eager to meet their classes, getting schedules organized and feeling ready to go. "Thank God it's Friday," I caught myself thinking in the flurry of the start-up. I remembered Professor Ross's comment from the day before, when I had slipped into the seat next to her at chapel. "How is the new semester going?" I had asked. "I'm trying to live in the moment," she responded. That morning she became my teacher, too, and I knew her students were in good hands.

At such times, I know the truth of Kathleen Dean Moore's observation that "the mundane—the stuff of our lives—is irreplaceable, essential, eternal and changing, beautiful and fearsome, beyond human understanding, worthy of reverence and awe. The English word for this combination of qualities is 'sacred'"[18] Time and experience have taught me that it is the ordinary "stuff of our lives" that I love; it is the mundane that surprises with sometimes startling revelations if we are open to seeing and hearing and lingering in the moment.

Again, this is T. S. Eliot's image of the *still point*, that place "where past and future are gathered. Neither movement/from nor towards." This is the point of consciousness, of dwelling in the realm of the timeless, of living in the "here-now."[19]

I recall another very ordinary example. It was at the conclusion of an academic year when the graduates had departed, proudly carrying their diplomas. Faculty had finished turning in grades and were clearing their desks. The appointment calendar had eased up, and I realized that I actually had "time," time to do some reading. On a whim, I sent out a campus email asking what books folks were reading and which ones they would recommend. Books started arriving in my office. It was as though a great feast was being laid out (well, maybe more like a potluck). I received wonderful responses, and these opened up rich conversations about what we were reading. Unexpectedly, this became a kind of celebration outside of time. We were attending to matters of heart and mind, open to exploring new thoughts and sharing discoveries— another way to dwell in the present moment.

Ask Me

Cultivating a consciousness of the timeless is essential to the health, creativity, and well-being of the leader. Such mindfulness subtly affects the culture of the institution as well. Paying attention to evidences of the sacred in the mundane is perhaps the most surprising manifestation of the power of a moment out of time. It was July. Four years into the presidency, I was no longer a novice. But I still had a lot to learn about being empowered by paying attention to the present moment. The small things, as I noted in my journal, included on that summer day an awareness that I was doing the work I love. There was the lingering memory of a rare evening alone with my spouse. A curry supper of *Pakistani kima*, yogurt, and melon. Time slowed. That evening had even allowed me to catch up on the ironing.

It is at such a time that I understood the question posed by the poet William Stafford:

> Ask me whether
> What I have done is my life . . . .[20]

Leadership is a meaningful thing to do with one's life; it is a spiritual calling that transcends day-to-day demands. We must not overlook the fact that, paradoxically, it is in those normally unattended moments of the ordinary that we are most likely to be interrupted by some deep awareness and intimation of the sacred.

Loving the work, resting in uncertainty, being open to surprise and welcoming glimpses of the timeless—these describe a quality of leadership that requires a shouting out to the question: Who, seeing the work to be done, can help wanting to do it?[21] Yes, I say. Yes.

Notes to Chapter Fourteen

1. I have, for privacy, changed this person's name.

2. The image of the "fifth dimension"—the intersection of time with the timeless—is one that has guided me in the leadership journey, although I do not recall the source. For the "still point," see T. S. Eliot, "Burnt Norton," line 62. Also, "Dry Salvages": "But to apprehend / The point of intersection of the timeless / With time, is an occupation for the saint" (lines 200–202).

3. Sally Helgesen and Julie Johnson make this observation in *The Female Vision*, 56.

4. Margaret J. Wheatley, *Finding Our Way*, 27. Margaret Wheatley's body of work offers a creative exploration of leadership with a refreshing emphasis on the practical and personal as well as on theoretical principles.

5. Eberhard Arnold, "When the Time Was Fulfilled," *Watch for the Light: Readings for Advent and Christmas*, January 1 entry.

6. Anne Lamott, *Traveling Mercies*, 82.

7. T. S. Eliot, "East Coker," lines 81–84; 97–98.

8. Flannery O'Connor in her last letter before her death from Lupus. See *The Habit of Being*, 596.

9. The Henry Moore anecdote is recorded in Donald Hall's *The Old Life*, 70.

10. Peter Senge, *The Fifth Discipline*, 162, 167–68. Helgesen and Johnson also discuss intuition in leadership (*The Female Vision*, 37); but whether it is a particularly female quality, as they suggest, might be questioned.

11. Linda Hill, "Leadership Development."

12. A truism noted by Edgar Stoesz in "Scaling Mountains," 147.

13. Theodore Roethke, "The Waking," 226?.

14. Bert Lobe, "Begin with the End in Mind," *Setting the Agenda: Meditations for the Organization's Soul*, Scottdale: Herald Press, 2011, 196–97.

15. Thomas Merton, *Contemplation in a World of Action*, 223.

16. Emily Dickinson, "I dwell in possibility," 166.

17. Wheatley, *Finding Our Way*, 74.

18. Kathleen Dean Moore, "The Eternal, Beautiful, Fearsome Mundane," 7.

19. T. S. Eliot, "Burnt Norton." Rabbi Abraham Joshua Heschel's term "here-now" is particularly apt in describing eternity not as future but as present.

20. William Stafford, "Ask Me."

21. This is a paraphrase of a wonderful line in Wendell Berry's essay "Healing."

For Discussion

1. Where have you observed leaders shaping the culture of an organization by the manner in which they approached decision making? For the good? To the detriment of the institution?

2. To be effective, leaders must balance transparency/vulnerability with confidence/decisiveness. Cite several examples in which you have seen this done well. Where have you seen leaders failing in this regard?

3. Cite an example in which you have experienced a moment of transcendent awareness interrupting the normal flow of the work.

4. Current theory stresses the importance of leaders honoring intuition, not striving solely for objectivity. Give an example in which you have paid attention to some inner sense in considering a decision—not relying completely on reason or logic.

5. Leaders must be clear-eyed about reality for themselves, but at times, they must also name that reality for their organizations in order to point the way ahead. Where have you observed a CEO doing this effectively, finding a way to confront the difficulties of the present while inspiring a future vision?

6. It has been said that the leader's first responsibility is to keep hope alive. Where have you seen this principle demonstrated in your organization— either effectively or not?

7. What are the inner sources of strength for leaders today when they must guide their institutions with courage and unflappable grace, keep the bottom line healthy, and articulate an inspired vision in an uncertain future? Give specific examples.

EPILOGUE

Karen A. Longman, to whom Christian higher education owes a massive debt that can only be repaid to future generations, suggested I conclude this book with some of my own thoughts on leadership. I will comply with her request—sort of. I will offer ten ideas for how leadership can enrich the campus climates of our Christian colleges and universities. The first section covers general leadership attributes I gathered from the Gospel-writer John's introduction of Jesus. In the second section, I offer campus culture suggestions that will position us to benefit from the kind of leadership reflected in this book's essays.

Five Leadership Characteristics from the Example of Jesus

In the summer of 2000, I took a short sabbatical after fourteen years as a college president. I decided to reflect on some of the leadership literature I had studied as a doctoral student. My reflection turned into *Leading People from the Middle*, a book that traced the history of leadership theory in the twentieth century, looking at ideas, leaders, and organizations in light of my own experience. Because the book was intended primarily for a secular audience, I did not explicitly present a Christian perspective on leadership.

On the following Christmas Eve, all the leadership ideas must still have been ringing in my ears. When the minister read the most quoted advent verse "And the word became flesh . . . ." I heard a stunning description of leadership. Instead of being background noise to whatever I was thinking about, the familiar words of John 1:14 seized me: "And the Word became flesh and dwelt among us, and we beheld His glory, the glory as of the only begotten of the Father, full of grace and truth" (NKJV). What I heard was not a Bible verse; it was the voice of a faithful follower introducing his leader to the world. I did my best to put that voice into my own words in a short book entitled *Incarnate Leadership*. The following attributes of leadership are some I've come to believe in as significant.

Nearness—"he dwelt among us"—After declaring the Word became flesh, John could have started his story by taking a news reporter's approach. A big, flashy miracle would grab everyone's attention. But instead, John began with what was probably the biggest and best miracle to him—Jesus' address. He lived with us. The Son of God pitched his tent in our camp.

I am convinced that the most powerful location from which to lead is not in front of, above, behind, under, or on a cell phone with the people God has given us to lead. It is *among* them, in their midst. In chapter ten, on the metaphors of leadership, Marie Morris lifts up what might be called "side-by-side" leadership. In chapter nine, Jeanine Varner identifies the importance of academic leaders entering into "deep interaction with faculty and students." The claim that respect comes from being perched on a pedestal is a myth perpetuated by people in high places talking to other people in high places. I heard this kind of stuff at presidents' conferences, but I'm still waiting to meet a student or employee who says to me, "Bill, you need to be a little more aloof, a little more above us, you know, detached."

A Christian college president once asked me what the best thing I've read on leadership was. I answered, "Our students." When we draw close enough to read the texts of people's lives, work, studies, and feelings, we will find ourselves reading how best to lead them.

Transparency—"and we beheld"—Jesus was a transparent leader. Evidently, you could *behold* him. He told his disciples, "I've named you friends because I've let you in on everything I've heard from the Father" (John 15:15 *The Message*)

Today's leaders are so much less open than they could be. If Jesus is the light, why do we keep our people in the dark? It's not Christian, and it's not smart. Speculations are usually worse than the truth. In a difficult turnaround situation, Carol Taylor (in chapter thirteen) found transparency an essential ingredient in building unity and trust.

A few years ago, I asked myself, "Why is our budgeting process confidential?" Every answer I could think of was a bad one. So, we invited faculty and staff representatives to join us as we built the next year's budget. They turned out to be more than observers. They were resources in the meetings and defenders when we were done.

Regrettably, Christian organizations bear a reputation of being particularly "confidential." The good work of the Evangelical Council for Financial Accountability has battled this perception, but transparent leaders will be our greatest asset in this area. Jesus stood openly in the midst of the people. He reminded them, "If it were not so, I would have told you." Openness breeds trust, and that's what Jesus wanted. If today's leaders will dwell transparently among their people, we will replace the kind of darkness into which leaders and organizations have fallen.

Humility—"His glory, the glory as of the only begotten of the Father"—If any leader has ever had the right to say, "it's all about me," it was Jesus. But what he said was, it's all about "him who sent me." Jesus claimed he could do nothing without the Father. John Calvin observed how Jesus was always careful to give credit to the Father for his divine authority. Jesus was a reflector of his mission and the one who sent him.

Leaders today need to reflect humbly the mission of their organizations. Unfortunately, self-aggrandizement seems to have a stronghold on our culture. I recently read a column about "talking smack," in which the author commented on watching professional sports in which mediocre players make routine plays and then stand over opponents, foaming at the mouth, thumping their chests and pointing to the heavens as if to high-five God, who surely gets an assist on the play. That their team is getting annihilated seems to matter little. When it's all about me, that's all it's about.

Among the more pernicious ideas in American culture is that humility represents an admission of weakness. In fact, the evidence suggests that humility unlocks the door to strength and greatness. In the research Jim Collins did for *Good to Great*, he found the characteristic most dominant in the leaders of the companies achieving greatness was a blend of extreme personal humility and intense professional will. In two-thirds of the other companies, Collins found leaders with what he called "gargantuan egos."

Before moving beyond the importance of humility, we all need to recognize that humility carries greater risk for some than it does for others. After I finished giving a speech on humility, an African American faculty member sent me a note that said essentially, "It's a lot easier for you than for me to present yourself as humble. . . ." Sure, I go by my first name, I dress casually, I make self-effacing jokes, but I'm in a power slot, not to mention that nobody has ever mistaken me for "The Help."[2] Humility is a tall order for victims of humiliation.

Underrepresented groups in higher education leadership have been implicitly and explicitly disrespected. Although humility for all of us, including those in dishonored groups, will make us more Christlike and effective, one expression does not fit all. For some, we need to create extra space to admit frailties and needs. Deborah White's chapter on honoring giftedness offers the best way to build a safe place for humility—create an environment that recognizes and honors strengths.

Generosity and Honesty (Grace and Truth)—"full of grace and truth"— These last two leadership ideas require coupling. I'm sure John recognized the extent to which grace and truth rely on each other. Grace without truth tumbles into what Dietrich Bonheoffer labeled "cheap grace."[3] In a university, it perpetuates low or broken standards. It demoralizes those who witness injustice. Its permissiveness benefits no one. But truth without grace is neither Christlike nor effective. Truth without grace creates defensiveness that shuts down hearing. It feels as though it is more for the benefit of the truth proclaimer than for the target of the truth.

Grace offers leaders opportunities to experience one of human behavior's most reliable principles: you get what you give. Human nature abhors a vacuum. When we have incomplete information, we fill in the gaps. As leaders, what valence do we use when filling the vacuum? Is it positive or negative? Generally, we can only infer the motives of those who challenge or disagree with us. Do we make the positive assumption that they want what's best for the college? Or do we assume negatively that our challenger is trying to be hurtful? As I read Shirley Hoogstra's essay on high-trust environments (chapter five), I remembered that one of my goals as a university president was to have people feel, "Bill has a generous spirit; he can be trusted to give the benefit of the doubt." And, of course, I hoped to get what I gave; I hoped they would extend the same level of trust to me.

It goes without saying that Christian leaders should tell the *truth*. Their honesty should surface not only in the discouragement of lies and deception, but also in the promotion of clear understanding. I received a letter from a well-respected Christian organization that claimed to be relocating an operation. Please send money. In truth, they were closing their current program and reopening a very different model in a different place. Clearly, their description would attract more support than a full explanation of the situation, but I don't think the Lord needs our spin in order to accomplish his purposes. I did have a chance to speak with the leaders of the organization, and to their credit, they changed the language they used to characterize the move.

Jesus united grace and truth in his very being. In a towering example of these two attributes John chose to lift up, we see the quiet exchange between Jesus and the woman caught in adultery. "What are you going to do, Jesus?" pestered the Scribes and Pharisees. "We caught this woman in the act. Moses and the law say she should be stoned." Jesus looked up from the ground where he was writing something in the sand. "Whoever among you is without sin, cast the first stone." Sheepishly, the accusers left. "Where did your accusers go?" Jesus asked the woman. "Did they condemn you?" "No," she replied. And Jesus said, "Neither do I"—grace. "Don't do it again"—truth.[1] Would that we all worked for leaders filled with grace and truth.

Five Suggestions to Improve Christian Campus Climates for Leadership

Work for positive change positively. This book focuses more on what we *can* do rather than on what we *can't* do. We need truth, information, hard facts, but haven't we seen enough carnage from the efforts of those who have tried to leverage guilt and shame? Little gain will come from scolding our campuses

In chapter eleven, Rebecca Hernandez writes,

> As an academic administrator with "change agent" practically written into the job description, I have found the role of bridge-builder to be an exciting one . . . .

Building bridges should excite all of us who take seriously Paul's declaration that God has given us the ministry of reconciliation.

In the last five years as a college president, I tried to keep track of my offense-defense ratio. How much time was I spending doing damage control, correcting, smoothing, and fixing? Was it more time than I spent advancing, creating, supporting, and promoting? I began to look for ways to convert defense to offense. When I heard from a disgruntled parent or employee, I invited that person to participate in problem solving our way through the situation. "What would be a better way to deal with this?" "How would you write the policy?" Authentically moving into positive territory always outperformed accusing and defending.

Be honest about privilege. Being a white guy should neither be strutted nor envied. It's not an earned condition. But being a white guy in the U.S. does come with a tailwind. G. K. Chesterton has been quoted as observing, "The Reformer is always right about what's wrong. However, he's often wrong about what is right." Both my observation and my research convince me that most white male administrators are right in their recognition of disadvantages faced by historically underrepresented groups in our schools, but are wrong in failing to recognize their own privilege. Rather than feeling privileged, we in the majority see ourselves "without disadvantage." Is that a distinction without a difference? Absolutely not. Feeling "without disadvantage" implies the climate has been unfair for people of color and women, but fair for the white men who sit in the seats of power. Feeling *"privilege"* implies the climate has been unfair for all involved—unfairly negative for some, and unfairly positive for others. And that distinction makes a difference. With *privilege* comes *responsibility*.

I'm convinced most of us in university leadership do recognize the challenges many have faced in advancing their careers. But I'm afraid we have *not* seen how privilege helped us *attain* our positions and awaited us *in* our positions. Hence, most of us do not see how privilege has bequeathed us with the fundamental *responsibility* to elevate those *without* privilege. In Shirley Showalter's chapter, she discusses the power of a mentoring relationship with Max De Pree, a moral titan who embraced in countless ways the responsibilities of his privileges.

All people of privilege need to leverage their standing. It is a Jesus thing to do. For example, Jesus used his standing to help fight the sexism of his culture. His initial resurrection appearances to women honored them across the ages. But beyond honor, the appearances also confronted his culture's institutional sexism. In a society that did not allow women to serve as witnesses in a court of law, Jesus commissioned these women, not Peter and John, as his eyewitnesses of the resurrection.

Jesus also attacked sexism in the Mary and Martha story. When Jesus told Martha he wasn't going to ask Mary to go to the kitchen, we twenty-first century workaholics hear how we should not only work for God, but enjoy God. But that cannot be what the seventy-two men in the room heard. What screamed loudly to them was Jesus giving Mary a chair where only men were allowed to sit. In their world, women were supposed to serve the men, not join the men. When Jesus endorsed Mary's appalling behavior, he was using his rabbinical influence, which, by the way, was unavailable to women, to attack a thick wall of cultural separation.

And those on our campuses with unearned privilege must do the same. Our campus climates will not improve until all of us understand privilege and responsibility.

Think of leadership diversity in terms of *quality* more than *equality*. Over my twenty-four years as a college and university president, almost all institutional challenges became more complex. Unintended consequences and inverse relationships stripped the simplicity out of solutions that worked pretty well in the '80s. And as complexity deepened, "groupthink" became more ineffective than ever.

Research published in 2007 confirmed earlier findings that groups do better than even expert individuals in solving complex problems.[4] Multiple perspectives, diverse assumptions, and broad ranges of experience break down complexities more effectively than a single point of view. Today's higher education world demands the kind of broad perspective found most often in diversely composed leadership groups.

I think Christian campuses should tone down their spiritual rhetoric on advancing women and persons of color. I read every published statement on diversity at one of our strongest colleges. They were thick with Christian duty, but I found not one word about the *benefits* of diversity. I am committed to biblical justice and affirmative action, but when we talk about appointments being made in the name of God and fairness, what happens? First, it diverts credit from the person who earned the job and gives it to the one doing the hiring. And second, if it looks like a person got hired on a non-merit based criterion, he or she will carry a *de*merit into a meritocracy where others have defined merit. And that mark will be hard to erase.

When existing leaders hire strong minority candidates, they cannot allow themselves to be assigned hero status simply for hiring the best candidate, because when they do, it contaminates the hire. Where men and women alike can and should take credit is in all efforts to fill their candidate pools with underrepresented applicants. But the best reason for gender and racial balance is that it makes our institutions wiser, more sensitive, more open, more humble, more curious, more cosmopolitan, and more like the multi-gifted body of Christ.

Think holistically. Few of our mission statements omit "educating the whole person" from the goals we list. But our leadership values don't always reflect that commitment. The unwritten rules of higher education have been in custody since the Enlightenment. One of those rules favors fact-finding over intuition, verifiability over instinct, cognition over affect, parsimony over beauty, and objectivity over subjectivity. This bias reached a fever pitch when the logical positivists attempted to objectify philosophy.

It is impossible to read MaryKate Morse's chapter (two) without acknowledging the heart as higher education leadership's source of oxygen. In my second presidency, I expanded the president's cabinet to include an "assistant to the president for diversity" and the dean of the chapel. It wasn't long before

I realized how easily management by objectives can become management by objectivity. Leadership is about faith and hope and heart and compassion and friendship and caring and breaking the rules and intuition; it is about truth AND grace.

Karen A. Longman introduces this book with research that identifies examples of leadership assets that lie beyond the ability to execute data driven analyses, gifts found most frequently in women leaders. But I wonder if women and other holders of these gifts find themselves in a double bind. If they play by the old rules and downplay the "soft skills" they bring to the leadership table, they're just bringing more of what we have already had in excess, and they won't be leading from their strengths. But if they accentuate their whole person sensitivities, they align themselves with values that historically have held only secondary status in higher education.

Christian campuses need to lead with the kind of heart they teach. When our colleges exalt mind over heart, facts over intuition, and certainty over mystery, we impoverish our claims of wholeness and deny the rich contributions of those who have so much with which to lead us.

Be quick to explore and slow to settle on theology and hermeneutics. It is important for us to consider not only the Holy Spirit's *inspiration* in the *writing* of Scripture, but the *illumination* of the Holy Spirit in the *reading* of Scripture. Words are symbols. They are symbolic of the objects they represent. The words in most of our Bibles are symbols translated from other languages transmitted over time. Are words trustworthy? Yes, certainly those inspired and illuminated by the Holy Spirit. But hermeneutics is not an exact science. We need humility and grace when we start explaining what God means.

It is also grace and humility that should enable Christian campuses to be relentless in *exploring* and reluctant in *settling*. Where is a better place for followers of Christ to study new and challenging ideas than on a Christian campus? Is changing our understanding of Scripture really a threat? Evangelicals have made many U-turns in their history; do we now think we've finally got it?

Discussing what the Bible says on controversial issues is hard. Every time a campus enters into serious discussions of hot topics, it feels like lose-lose to the president. Leaders take heat from every direction. I have been called "spineless" by folks on both sides of three different debates. These conversations *feel* lose-lose, but there's always a huge win. The *students* win. The students win when we show courage and respect and grace and humility as we learn about even the most contentious ideas from each other.

Beyond my professional experience with "settled" theological issues, I have been touched personally. I had the privilege of being in the congregation when our daughter candidated for her first position as an ordained minister of word and sacrament in the Presbyterian Church. As she greeted folks on their way out of the sanctuary, a man complimented her on the sermon, but went on to say he hoped she would teach their newborn son that a woman's place was not preaching; it was in the home.

Would not the tone of this remark and the tone of our campuses benefit if we all wanted to keep learning? When our daughter told me what happened, I remembered an incident from my childhood. After our pastor preached on the Sermon on the Mount, I heard my father say to him, "That was a really good sermon, but I don't agree with you. I'd love to learn how you reached your position."

For Christian higher education to keep learning about leadership, new voices, different voices, and repressed voices that need to be heard. I believe we will create a more welcoming environment for these voices when our campus cultures are ones characterized by theological humility and hermeneutical openness.

Clearly, the authors of this book can unsettle some of our most stubborn ideas about leadership. May their words and their leadership bring quality and justice and wisdom and grace and humility and salt and light to all of Christian higher education.

William P. Robinson
President Emeritus, Whitworth University
May 2012

Notes to the Epilogue

1. See John 8.
2. See Kathryn Stockett's *The Help*.
3. Dietrich Bonhoeffer, *The Cost of Discipleship*.
4. Patrick Laughlin, Erin Hatch, Jonathan Silver, and Lee Boh, "Groups Perform Better Than the Best Individuals on Letters-to-Numbers Problems: Effects of Group Size."

ABOUT THE EDITOR

Karen A. Longman serves as program director and professor of doctoral higher education at Azusa Pacific University. She earned her doctorate from the Center for the Study of Higher Education at the University of Michigan, holds master's degrees from U.M. and Trinity Evangelical Divinity School, and completed her undergraduate work in psychology at Albion College in Michigan.

While at APU, Longman has served since 2007 on Doctoral Studies Council and Faculty Senate, chairing Doctoral Studies Council for two years. She primarily teaches Higher Education Administration, Introduction to U.S. Higher Education, Policy and Politics, and Ethics. Beyond APU, Longman continues to serve as a Senior Fellow of the Council for Christian Colleges & Universities (CCCU), having directed the CCCU's Women's Leadership Development Institutes since 1998. Longman and her colleague Laurie A. Schreiner co-edit the journal *Christian Higher Education: An International Journal of Research, Theory, and Practice.*

Longman's previous professional roles have included six years as vice president for academic affairs and dean of the faculty at Greenville College (IL) and nineteen years in Washington, D.C., on the senior leadership team of the CCCU. She has traveled extensively; taught in China, Mongolia, and Vietnam; and served on several nonprofit boards. Her research and publications focus on gender issues, leadership, and Christian higher education.

ABOUT THE CONTRIBUTORS

Patricia S. Anderson served for nearly forty years in higher education, holding senior leadership roles as the provost at Fresno Pacific University and Azusa Pacific University after serving as associate provost at APU. Prior work includes leading a statewide higher education consortium, leading a five-county, multi-service, social service agency, serving in two regional educational laboratories, as well as teaching in higher education. She has also served on nonprofit boards for child care and senior retirement organizations, as well as two higher education boards of trustees. Her passion is analyzing systems and programs in order to develop success strategies. Anderson has authored numerous white papers, evaluation reports, and publications. She continues teaching graduate students in an online environment and serving as a volunteer in her church community.

Carolyn E. Dirksen has been in academic administration at Lee University for the past twenty-five years, serving as a department chair and dean before becoming the vice president for academic affairs, a position she has held for thirteen years. Before entering academic administration, she served on the faculty for seventeen years. Holding a PhD in sociolinguistics, Dirksen's research areas include gendered uses of language and second language acquisition. Although her career has centered on Lee University, she has taught in China, Mongolia, Ukraine, Russia, Vietnam, and South Africa.

Rebecca R. Hernandez completed her doctoral work in human development and family studies at Oregon State University. She earned a master's degree in public administration from Portland State University. Born in Joliet,

Illinois, as a daughter of migrant farm workers, Hernandez has been working on Latino issues throughout her career. She began as a schoolteacher, then served as a community program director, and now serves as the director of the Center for Teaching and Learning at Goshen College in Indiana. Previously, Hernandez was the director of community building for the Hacienda Community Development Corporation of Portland, Oregon. She also has held faculty appointments at Oregon State University and at Oregon Health and Sciences University, School of Nursing, where she worked to develop community-based programs to reduce health disparities among Latinos.

Shirley V. Hoogstra is an experienced vice president for student life and a trial attorney. She has been a leader in the legal profession, serving as president of the New Haven Bar Association and Foundation and also serving as chair on numerous nonprofit, school, and church boards. As a senior administrator, Hoogstra leads a team of seventy-five professionals and serves on the president's cabinet at Calvin College. She plans and speaks at leadership events for the CCCU and other organizations. She is co-host of a nationally televised program on PBS called *Inner Compass,* on which she interviews outstanding and interesting national and international culture shapers on a variety of topics that include faith and science, the healthcare conundrum, women in politics, relationships, the immigration crisis, race and reconciliation, and international political or religious conflicts.

Marie S. Morris is provost at Anderson University in Indiana. Born in Baltimore, Maryland, Marie lived in Tennessee, California, and Washington State before spending her adolescent years in Rota, Spain. With an eclectic religious upbringing, Morris is Anabaptist Mennonite in her theology. Morris's journey to academic leadership includes two fascinating years in the hollows of southeastern Kentucky working at Red Bird Hospital, after which she moved with her husband to Harrisonburg, Virginia, to continue her education. Morris earned a master's degree in primary nursing care in society from the University of Virginia and a PhD in nursing administration from George Mason University. She served for over twenty years at Eastern Mennonite University in various capacities, including faculty member, department chair, associate dean, honors program director, SACS self-study director, and vice president and undergraduate dean. Morris's community involvements include founding a transitional housing unit for low-income women and their children, serving on community and hospital boards, and volunteering at a free clinic. Interests include leadership development, mentoring, living simply, developing intercultural competency, and building connections for healing and hope in our broken world.

MaryKate Morse is professor of leadership and spiritual formation in the seminary at George Fox University in Oregon. Raised in the Air Force, Morse lived in various states and overseas. She completed her BS in secondary education and English literature at Longwood University in Virginia. With her husband, Randy, and small children, she lived in the Andes Mountains of Bolivia and Peru doing ministry and social projects with the Aymara Indians. Upon return, she completed a masters in biblical studies and an MDiv at Western Evangelical Seminary (now George Fox Evangelical Seminary). She began teaching, studied spiritual formation and direction, and was recorded as a pastor with the Evangelical Friends. Morse completed her doctorate at Gonzaga University, where she studied the characteristics of renewal leadership as modeled by Jesus. She has planted two churches and served in various administrative positions at the university including seminary associate dean, director of hybrid programs, and university director of strategic planning. She has published on spiritual formation and leadership. Morse enjoys being with family, hiking, reading, exploring Oregon, and playing with her puppy, Tess.

Deana L. Porterfield recently assumed a new role as executive vice president for Azusa Pacific Online University after several years as senior vice president for people and organizational development at Azusa Pacific University in California. In that role, Deana's charge to maintain university values and ethos undergirded her keen understanding of the university community and history. With a passion for people, Porterfield combined her sharp institutional insight with an unwavering commitment to advance the university's objectives in the area of human resources and organizational development initiatives. Previous APU positions included chief of staff and over twenty years in enrollment, including six years as vice president for enrollment management, with the university experiencing unprecedented growth under her leadership. Porterfield champions team-building and takes pride in knowing that hiring the right people increases an organization's ability to advance its mission and productivity. Nationally recognized as a leader in the enrollment field, she has served as a consultant within organizational settings. She enjoys time with family and friends and is currently completing her EdD in organizational leadership at the University of La Verne.

William P. (Bill) Robinson is president emeritus of Whitworth University in Spokane, Washington. He served as Whitworth's seventeenth president, from 1993 to 2010, after serving as president of Manchester College, in Indiana, from 1986 to 1993. Currently, he works full time speaking and consulting with universities, businesses, and ministries. Robinson serves on the board of Princeton Theological Seminary, the ING Educators Advisory Board, and the Max De Pree Center for Leadership. In 2010, a second edition of Robinson's book *Leading People from the Middle: The Universal Mission of Mind and Heart* (Executive Excellence, 2002; iUniverse 2010) was released. His second book, *Incarnate Leadership*, was released by Zondervan in February 2009. Robinson is married to Bonnie Robinson, principal organist at the First Presbyterian Church of Spokane. They have three married children—a social worker and two ministers ordained in the Presbyterian Church (U.S.A.).

Carla D. Sanderson is provost and executive vice president at Union University in Tennessee. Prepared as a nurse researcher, Sanderson draws upon many similarities between the high touch, caring role of the nurse and that of an academic administrator. Her entire thirty-year career in higher education has been in service to Union University, where she began as a nursing faculty member. She continues to contribute to the field of nursing as an author and speaker on ethical decision making in health care. She has contributed to four books on academic leadership and serves on the board of trustees for the Southern Association of Colleges and Schools and the Consortium for Global Education. Her international involvement focuses on the establishment of a new system of higher education for Kurdistan in Northern Iraq. Having grown up on the banks of the Tennessee River, her hobbies include water sports and time with her husband and young adult sons "gathered at the river."

Laurie A. Schreiner is currently professor and chair of the doctoral programs in higher education at Azusa Pacific University in California, having spent thirty years in higher education as a psychology professor and associate academic dean. A senior fellow at the Council for Christian Colleges & Universities, she is also co-author of *The Student Satisfaction Inventory*, *StrengthsQuest: Discover Your Strengths in College, Career, and Beyond* (2006, Gallup Press), and *Helping Sophomores Succeed* (2009, Jossey-Bass). She has published numerous journal articles and book chapters on positive psychology, engaged learning, sophomore success, faculty development, and advising.

Shirley H. Showalter joined Goshen College in Goshen, Indiana, straight from graduate school at the University of Texas at Austin. For twenty-one years, she taught English and played a variety of administrative roles, including chairing the English department. She published essays in numerous scholarly journals and books and in *The Chronicle of Higher Education*. In 1996, she was named the fourteenth president of Goshen College and was honored by the John S. and James L. Knight Foundation for her presidential leadership in 1999. In 2004, she accepted an invitation from the Fetzer Institute in Kalamazoo, Michigan, to lead the program development of that private foundation. In 2010, she moved with her husband Stuart back to his home community in the Shenandoah Valley of Virginia. In 2011–12, Showalter and her husband lived in Brooklyn, New York, and cared for their baby grandson, creating a new leadership team with his parents that included a covenant. Showalter is writing a childhood memoir about growing up Mennonite in the 1950s and '60s. You can read more online at www.shirleyshowalter.com.

Gordon T. Smith recently became president of Ambrose University College and Seminary and professor of Systematic Theology. He previously had served as the president of reSource Leadership International, an agency that fosters excellence in theological education in the global south. He also serves as an adjunct to the faculty of Regent College, Vancouver, where he was formerly the academic vice president and dean. He is the author of a number of publications, including *Courage and Calling* (IVP, 2011 rev. ed.), and *Transforming Conversion: Rethinking the Language and Contours of Christian Initiation* (Baker, 2010). As a theologian, he has particular interest in the character of religious experience, and he publishes and teaches on conversion and spiritual discernment, as well as vocation, work, and career. He is married to Joella, an artist; together they have two grown sons and six grandchildren.

Lee F. Snyder, president emeritus of Bluffton University in Ohio, currently resides in Harrisonburg, Virginia, and in Salem, Oregon. Born on a farm in Oregon's Willamette Valley and raised in a Mennonite community, Snyder would describe the trajectory of her life and work as unexpected but immeasurably rewarding. After several years in West Africa, Snyder continued graduate work in English literature, receiving her PhD from the University of Oregon. She has held various administrative and teaching positions, including appointment as vice president and academic dean at Eastern Mennonite University in Virginia. Following twelve years as dean, Snyder accepted the presidency at Bluffton University, where she served ten years as Bluffton's eighth president. Other professional involvements have included writing, speaking, and brief education assignments in China, Central America, Egypt, and South Africa. Her publications are in the areas of leadership development, board governance, and spiritual memoir. She currently serves on several national and regional boards. Snyder—always with a stack of books awaiting—enjoys travel and spending time with family.

Carol A. Taylor is president of Vanguard University of Southern California. Taylor came to Vanguard University as provost in 2007 and became president in 2009; in 2011, she received the *Orange County Business Journal*'s Women in Business Award in recognition of leading a significant institutional turnaround. Taylor has over thirty years of experience in education and higher education—including seven years at Biola University as the vice provost for undergraduate education, twelve years in research and administration at Educational Testing Service in Princeton, with additional experience at various state universities and public schools. Taylor has taught and lectured internationally and has served on various national commissions for assessment, study abroad programs, women's leadership development, and women in ministry. She holds a PhD in multilingual/multicultural education from Florida State University.

Taylor enjoys entertaining, traveling, home decorating and gardening, music, a good read, exploring back roads and out-of-the-way places, and anyone with a good sense of humor.

Jeanine B. Varner most recently served as provost for Abilene Christian University. Prior to that role, she held the role of dean of the College of Arts and Sciences at ACU and spent eleven years as vice president of academic affairs for Oklahoma Christian University. Earlier in her career, she also served as English department chair and the dean of the College of Liberal Arts at Oklahoma Christian. Varner holds a PhD in English from the University of Tennessee in Knoxville, and has worked as a consultant-evaluator for the North Central Association of Colleges and Schools (NCA), working with the Accreditation Review Council, Assessment Task Force, and Consultant-Evaluator Core Team. Varner also has been an active participant in the CCCU, particularly in the Executive Leadership Development Initiative and through serving as a mentor for emerging leaders. She currently lives with her husband, Paul, in Abilene, Texas, and the two travel frequently to visit their children in Alabama and Oklahoma.

Deborah J. White currently resides in New Jersey, teaching online courses for Lee University in Tennessee and the Clifton Strengths School. She also serves as a Strengths Education Consultant for Gallup, Inc. Previously, she served as faculty member and accreditation self-study chair at Northwest University in Washington, vice president for academic affairs at Sterling College in Kansas, and director of the Lilly Endowment's theological exploration of vocation program at Lee University. Interests include mentoring, leadership development, strengths coaching, and spiritual direction.

BIBLIOGRAPHY

Anderson, Mac, and Tom Feltenstein. *Change is Good . . . You Go First: 21 Ways to Inspire Change*. Naperville: Simple Truths, LLC, 2007.

Andringa, Robert C. "Keeping the Faith: Leadership Challenges Unique to Religiously Affiliated Colleges and Universities." In *Turnaround: Leading Stressed Colleges and Universities to Excellence*, eds. James Martin, James E. Samels, and Associates. Baltimore: Johns Hopkins University Press, 2009.

Angelou, Maya. *I Know Why the Caged Bird Sings*. New York: Random House, 1969.

Arnold, Eberhard. "When the Time Was Fulfilled." *Watch for the Light: Readings for Advent and Christmas*. Farmington: Plough Publishing House, 2001.

Avolio, B. J., and Fred Luthans. *The High Impact Leader*. New York: McGraw-Hill, 2006.

Ayman, Roya, Karen Korabik, and Scott Morris. "Is Transformational Leadership Always Perceived as Effective? Male Subordinates' Devaluation of Female Transformational Leaders." *Journal of Applied Social Psychology* 39.4 (2009): 852–79.

Barash, David, and Judith Lipton. *Gender Gap: The Biology of Male-Female Differences*. New Brunswick: Transaction Publishers, 2002.

Barker, Randolph T., and Kim Gower. "Strategic Application of Storytelling in Organizations: Toward Effective Communication in a Diverse World." *Journal of Business Communication* 47.3 (July 2010).

Bennett, John. *Collegial Professionalism: The Academy, Individualism, and the Common Good*. Phoenix: ACE-Oryx Press, 1998.

Bennis, Warren, Daniel Goleman, and James O'Toole. *Transparency: How Leaders Create a Culture of Candor*. San Francisco: Jossey-Bass, 2008.

Bennis, Warren G., and Robert J. Thomas. *Leading for a Lifetime*. Boston: Harvard Business School Publishing, 2007.

Bensimon, Estela M., Anna Neumann, and Robert Birnbaum. *Making Sense of Administrative Leadership (ASHE-ERIC Higher Education Report)*. Washington, DC: School of Education, George Washington University, 1989.

Bernardin, Joseph. *The Gift of Peace: Personal Reflections*. Chicago: Loyola, 1997.

Berry, Wendell. "Healing." *What are People For?* San Francisco: North Point Press, 1990: 12.

Bergquist, William H., and Kenneth Pawlak. *Engaging the Six Cultures of the Academy*. San Francisco: Jossey-Bass, 2006.

Blum, Deborah. *Sex on the Brain: The Biological Difference between Men + Women*. New York: Penguin Books, 1997.

Bolman, Lee G., and Terrence E. Deal. *Reframing Organizations: Artistry, Choice, & Leadership*, 4th edition. San Francisco: Jossey-Bass, 2008.

Bolman, Lee, and Joan V. Gallos. *Reframing Academic Leadership*. San Francisco: Jossey-Bass, 2011.

Bonhoeffer, Dietrich. *The Cost of Discipleship*. Clearwater: Touchstone, 1995.

Boyatzis, Richard E., and Annie McKee. *Resonant Leadership: Renewing Yourself and Connecting with Others through Mindfulness, Hope, and Compassion*. Boston: Harvard Business School Press, 2005.

Braxton, John, ed. *The Role of the Classroom in College Student Persistence: New Directions for Teaching and Learning*. San Francisco: Jossey-Bass, 2008.

Brenneman, James. "A World House of Learning." *Bulletin: The Magazine of Goshen College* (Winter/Spring 2007).

Buckingham, Marcus. *Go Put Your Strengths to Work: Six Powerful Steps to Achieve Outstanding Performance*. New York: Free Press, 2007.

———, *StandOut: The Groundbreaking New Strengths Assessment from the Leader of the Strengths Revolution*. Nashville: Thomas Nelson, 2011.

Buckingham, Marcus, and Donald O. Clifton. *Now, Discover your Strengths*. New York: Free Press, 2001.

Buckingham, Marcus, and Curt Coffman. *First, Break All the Rules: What the World's Greatest Managers do Differently*. New York: Simon & Schuster, 1999.

Buechner, Frederick. *Wishful Thinking: A Theological ABC*. New York: Harper & Row, 1973.

Burns, James MacGregor. *Leadership*. New York: Harper & Row, 1978.

Cameron, Kim S., and Robert E. Quinn. *Diagnosing and Changing Organizational Culture*. San Francisco: Jossey-Bass, 2006.

Campbell, Andrew, Jo Whitehead, and Sydney Finkelstein. "Why Good Leaders Make Bad Decisions." *Harvard Business Review* (February 2009): 60–66.

Camus, Albert, "Return to Tipasa." *The Myth of Sisyphus and Other Essays.* New York: Knopf, 1955.

Carr-Ruffino, Norma. *The Promotable Woman.* Belmont: Wadsworth, 1993.

Carson, Ben, with Gregg Lewis. *Take the Risk: Learning to Identify, Choose, and Live with Acceptable Risk.* Grand Rapids: Zondervan, 2008.

Cashman, Kevin. *Leadership from the Inside Out.* San Francisco: Berrett-Koehler Publishers, 2008.

CCCU Member Institution Financial Ratios Report 2010. Washington, DC: The Council for Christian Colleges & Universities, 2010.

Clifton, Donald O., Edward "Chip" Anderson, and Laurie A. Schreiner. *StrengthQuest: Discover and Develop Your Strengths in Academics, Career, and Beyond.* New York: Gallup Press, 2006.

Clifton, Donald O., and James K. Harter. "Investing in Strengths." In *Positive Organizational Scholarship: Foundations of a New Discipline,* eds. Kim S. Cameron, Jane E. Dutton, and Robert E. Quinn. San Francisco: Berrett-Kohler, 2003.

"Clinton: disclosure classified information an attack on international community." *PanArmenian.net.* Nov. 30, 2010. Available online at http://www.panarmenian.net/eng/world/news/57591/.

Cloud, Henry. *Integrity: The Courage to Meet the Demands of Reality.* New York: HarperCollins, 2006.

Cohen, Leonard. "Anthem." New York: Sony/ATV, 1992.

Collins, Jim, *Good to Great: Why Some Companies Make the Leap . . . and Others Don't.* New York: HarperCollins, 2001.

_____. *How the Mighty Fall and Why Some Companies Never Give In.* New York: HarperCollins, 2009.

Cooperrider, David L., and Diana Whitney. *Appreciative Inquiry.* San Francisco: Berrett-Koehler, 1999.

Covey, Stephen. *The Speed of Trust: The One Thing That Changes Everything.* New York: Free Press, 2008.

Cunningham, Loren, and David Joel Hamilton, eds. *Why Not Women?* Seattle: YWAM Publishing, 2000.

Denning, Stephen. *The Leader's Guide to Storytelling: Mastering the Art and Discipline of Business Narrative.* San Francisco: Jossey-Bass, 2011.

_____. *The Secret Language of Leadership: How Leaders Inspire Action Through Narrative.* San Francisco: Jossey-Bass, 2007.

De Pree, Max. *Leadership Is an Art*. New York: Dell Publishing, 1989.

———. *Leadership Jazz*. New York: Doubleday, 1992.

Dickinson, Emily. "I dwell in possibility." In *Final Harvest: Emily Dickinson's Poems*, selection and introduction by Thomas H. Johnson. Boston: Little, Brown, 1961.

Dockery, David S. *Renewing Minds: Serving Church and Society Through Christian Higher Education*. Nashville: Broadman and Holman, 2008.

Drucker, Peter. *Classic Drucker*. Boston: Harvard Business Press, 2006.

———. *Management: Tasks, Responsibilities, Practices*. New York: HarperCollins, 1974.

Dweck, Carol S. *Mindset: The New Psychology of Succes*. New York: Random House Publishing Group, 2006.

Eagly, Alice H., and Linda L. Carli. *Through the Labyrinth: The Truth about How Women Become Leaders*. Boston: Harvard Business School Press, 2007.

———. "Women and the Labyrinth of Leadership." In *Harvard Business Review* (September 2007): 63–71.

Eliot, T. S. "Burnt Norton." *Four Quartets*. New York: Harcourt Brace Jovanovich, 1971: 15.

———. "Dry Salvages." *Four Quartets*. New York: Harcourt Brace Jovanovich, 1971: 44.

———. "East Coker." *Four Quartets*. New York: Harcourt Brace Jovanovich, 1971: 26–27.

Elman, Sandra. "Accreditation, Fragility, and Disclosure: Maintaining the Delicate Balance." In *Turnaround: Leading Stressed Colleges and Universities to Excellence*, eds. James Martin, James E. Samels, and Associates. Baltimore: Johns Hopkins University Press, 2009.

Ewert, D. Merrill. "Fired: Seven Lessons of Unemployment." US Mennonite Brethren 2008. Available online at http://www.usmb.org/fired-seven-lessons.

Fels, Anna. "Do Women Lack Ambition?" in *Harvard Business Review* (April 2004): 50–60.

Folkenflik, David. "Hopkins student's disappearance, other cases linked. Suspect may have tried to trick female motorists." *Baltimore Sun* (March 7, 1996). Available online at http://articles.baltimoresun.com/1996-03-07/news/1996067089_1_reynolds-mrs-hopkins.

Frankel, Lois. *Nice Girls Don't Get the Corner Office.* New York: Warner Business Books, 2004.

Frederickson, Barbara L., and Marcial F. Losada. "Positive Affect and the Complex Dynamics of Human Flourishing." *American Psychologist* 60 (2005): 678–686.

Freeman, Sue, Susan Bourque, and Christine Shelton, eds. *Women on Power: Leadership Redefined.* Boston: Northeastern University Press, 2001.

From Every Nation: Revised Comprehensive Plan for Racial Justice, Reconciliation, and Cross-cultural Engagement at Calvin College, Calvin College provost's office, February 2004. Available online at http://www.calvin.edu/admin/provost/multicultural/documents/FEN.pdf.

Fry, Richard, and Felisa Gonzales "One-in-Five and Growing Fast: A Profile of Hispanic Public School Students." Pew Hispanic Center, Aug. 26, 2008. Available online at http://www.pewhispanic.org/files/reports/92.pdf.

Fusch, Daniel, and Amit Mrig. "Rethinking Higher Education's Leadership Crisis." *Higher Ed Impact: Monthly Diagnostic* (June 2011).

Gardner, Howard. *Leading Minds: An Anatomy of Leadership.* New York: Basic Books, 1995.

Gersick, Connie, Jean Bartunek, and Jane Dutton. "Learning from Academia: The Importance of Relationships in Professional Life." *Academy of Management Journal* 43.6 (2000): 1026–1044.

Gibb, Jack. *Trust: A New View of Personal and Organizational Development.* Los Angeles: Guild of Tutors Press, 1978.

Gibson, Sharon K. "The Developmental Relationships of Women Leaders in Career Transition: Implications for Leader Development." *Advances in Developing Human Resources* 10.5 (2008): 651–671.

Ginsberg, Benjamin. *The Fall of the Faculty: The Rise of the All-Administrative University and Why It Matters.* Oxford: Oxford University Press, 2011.

Goldsmith, Marshall. *Mojo: How to Get It, How to Keep It, How to Get it Back if You Lose It.* New York: Hyperion, 2010.

Goleman, Daniel, Richard E. Boyatzis, and Annie McKee. *Primal Leadership: Realizing the Power of Emotional Intelligence.* Boston: Harvard Business School, 2002.

Gonzales, Laurence. *Deep Survival: Who Lives, Who Dies, and Why.* New York: W. W. Norton, 2003.

Gunsalus, C. K. *The College Administrator's Survival Guide*. Boston: Harvard University Press, 2006.

Gurien, Michael. *The Wonder of Boys: What Parents, Mentors, and Educators Can Do to Shape Boys into Exceptional Men*. New York: Penguin, 1997.

———. *The Wonder of Girls: Understanding the Hidden Nature of Our Daughters*. New York: Penguin Putnam, 2002.

Hall, Donald. *The Old Life*. Boston: Houghton Mifflin Company, 1996.

Hall, Edward T. *The Hidden Dimension*. New York: Anchor Books, 1966.

Harding, Vincent, convocation. "Martin Luther King—Servant Leader." Goshen College convocation, podcast, Mon, Jan 16, 2012.

Heath, Chip, and Dan Heath. *Switch: How to Change Things When Change is Hard*. New York: Broadway Books, 2010.

Heifetz, Ronald A. "Leadership, Authority, and Women: A Man's Challenge." In *Women and Leadership: The State of Play and Strategies for Change*, eds. Barbara Kellerman and Deborah L. Rhode. San Francisco: John Wiley & Sons, 2007.

Heifetz, Ronald A., and Marty Linsky. *Leadership on the Line: Staying Alive through the Dangers of Leading*. Boston: Harvard Business School, 2002.

———. "Managing Yourself: A Survival Guide for Leaders." *Harvard Business Review* (June 2002): 65–74.

Helgesen, Sally. *The Female Advantage: Women's Ways of Leadership*. New York: Currency Doubleday, 1995.

———. *The Web of Inclusion: Architecture for Building Great Organizations*, reprint edition. Washington, DC: Beard Books, 2005.

Helgesen, Sally, and Julie Johnson. *The Female Vision: Women's Real Power at Work*. San Francisco: Berrett-Koehler, 2010.

Heschel, Abraham Joshua. *Moral Grandeur and Spiritual Audacity*, ed. Susannah Heschel. New York: Farrar, Straus and Giroux, 1997.

Hestenes, Roberta. "Leadership and the Christian Woman." Plenary address, Christians for Biblical Equality conference, San Diego, 1999.

Hill, Linda. "Leadership Development: A Strategic Imperative for Higher Education." Harvard Business School Working Paper, No. 06–023, 2005.

Holmes, Arthur. *The Idea of a Christian College*. Grand Rapids: Eerdmans, 1987.

Ibarra, Herminia, and Otilia Obodaru. "Women and the Vision Thing." *Harvard Business Review* (January 2009): 62–70.

"Intercultural Teaching and Learning at Goshen College." YouTube video. Created by the Center for Intercultural Teaching and Learning. Posted by GoshenCollege, Nov. 2, 2009. http://youtu.be/sCHQbbQ8z48.

Jaschik, Scott. "Too Nice to Land a Job." *Inside Higher Ed News* (November 10, 2010).

Jentz, Barry C., and Jerome T. Murphy. "Embracing Confusion: What Leaders Do When They Don't Know What To Do." *Phi Delta Kappan*, 2005.

Jobs, Steve. Commencement Address, Stanford University, June 12, 2005. Available online at http://news-service.stanford.edu/news/2005/june15/jobs-061505.html.

Joeckel, Samuel, and Thomas Chesnes. *The Christian College Phenomenon: Inside America's Fastest Growing Institutions of Higher Education.* Abilene: ACU Press, 2011.

Keyes, Corey L. M., and Jonathan Haidt, eds. *Flourishing: Positive Psychology and the Life Well-lived.* Washington, DC: American Psychological Association, 2003.

Kezar, Adrianna. "Expanding Notions of Leadership to Capture Pluralistic Voices: Positionality Theory in Practice." *Journal of College Student Development* 43.4 (2002): 558–578.

Kezar, Adrianna, Rozana Carducci, and Melissa Contreras-McGavin. *Rethinking the "L" Word in Higher Education: The Revolution of Research on Leadership.* San Francisco: Jossey-Bass, 2006.

Kezar, Adrianna, and Jaime Lester. "Leadership in a World of Divided Feminism." *Journal about Women in Higher Education* 1 (2008): 49–73.

King, Martin Luther, Jr. *Where Do We Go from Here: Chaos or Community?* Boston: Beacon Press, 2010.

Kouzes, James M., and Barry Z. Posner. *The Truth about Leadership: The No-fads, Heart-of-the-Matter Facts You Need to Know.* San Francisco: Jossey-Bass, 2010.

LaCelle-Peterson, Kristina. *Liberating Tradition: Women's Identity and Vocation in Christian Perspective.* Grand Rapids: Baker Books, 2008.

Lakoff, George, and Mark Johnson. *Metaphors We Live By.* Chicago: University of Chicago Press, 1980.

Lamott, Anne. *Plan B: Further Thoughts on Faith.* New York: Riverhead, 2006.

———. *Traveling Mercies: Some Thoughts on Faith.* New York: Anchor Books, 2000.

Laughlin, Patrick, Erin Hatch, Jonathan Silver, and Lee Boh. "Groups Perform Better Than the Best Individuals on Letters-to-Numbers Problems: Effects of Group Size." *Journal of Personality and Social Psychology* 90.4 (2007).

Laytham, Brent D. "The Membership Includes the Dead: Wendell Berry's Port William Membership as *Communio Sanctorum.*" In *Wendell Berry and Religion: Heaven's Earthly Life,* eds. Joel James Shuman and L. Roger Owens. Lexington: University Press of Kentucky, 2009.

LeDoux, Joseph. *The Emotional Brain: The Mysterious Underpinnings of Emotional Life.* New York: Simon & Schuster, 1996.

———. *The Synaptic Self: How Our Brains Become Who We Are.* New York: Viking, 2002.

Lencioni, Patrick. *The Five Dysfunctions of a Team: A Leadership Fable.* San Francisco: Jossey-Bass, 2002.

L'Engle, Madeleine. *A Stone for a Pillow: Journeys with Jacob.* Wheaton: Shaw, 1986.

———. *A Wind in the Door,* revised edition. New York: Square Fish, 2007.

Lewis, Thomas, Fari Amini, and Richard Lannon. *A General Theory of Love.* New York: Vintage Books, 2001.

Linley, Alex. *Average to A+: Realising Strengths in Yourself and Others.* Warwick: CAPP Press, 2008.

Linley, Alex, Janet Willars, and Robert Biswas-Diener. *The Strengths Book: Be Confident, Be Successful, and Enjoy Better Relationships by Realising the Best of You.* Coventry: Capp Press, 2010.

Lobe, Bert. "Begin with the End in Mind." In *Setting the Agenda: Meditations for the Organization's Soul.* Scottdale: Herald Press, 2011.

Longman, Karen A., and Patricia Anderson. "Gender Trends in Senior-level Leadership: A 12-year Analysis of the CCCU U.S. Member Institutions." *Christian Higher Education* (2011): 1–22.

Longman, Karen A., and Jolyn E. Dahlvig. "Women's Leadership Development: A Study of Defining Moments." *Christian Higher Education* 9.3 (2010): 238–258.

Longman, Karen A., and Shawna Lafreniere. "Looking Back and Looking Ahead: A Review of the History and Impact of the CCCU's Women's Leadership Development Institute." CCCU White Paper (Nov. 2009).

———. "Moving Beyond the Stained Glass Ceiling: Preparing Women for Leadership in Faith-Based Higher Education." *Advances in Developing Human Resources* 14.1 (2012).

Lounsbury, John W., and Daniel DeNeui. "Psychological Sense of Community on Campus." *College Student Journal* 29 (1995): 270–277.

Lucado, Max. *Cure for the Common Life: Living in Your Sweet Spot.* Nashville: Thomas Nelson, 2005.

Lundberg, Ulf, and Cary Cooper. *The Science of Occupational Health: Stress, Psychobiology, and the New World of Work.* Hoboken: Wiley-Blackwell, 2010.

Luthans, Fred, Carolyn M. Youssef, and Bruce Avolio. *Psychological Capital: Developing the Human Competitive Edge.* Oxford: Oxford University Press, 2007.

MacTaggart, Terrence, ed. *Academic Turnarounds: Restoring Vitality to Challenged American Colleges and Universities.* Lanham: Rowman & Littlefield, 2007.

Martin, James, James E. Samels, and Associates, eds. *Turnaround: Leading Stressed Colleges and Universities to Excellence.* Baltimore: Johns Hopkins University Press, 2009.

McKay, Heather A. "Gendering the Body: Clothes Maketh the (Wo)man." In *Theology and the Body: Gender, Text, and Ideology,* eds. Robert Hannaford and J'annine Jobling. Exeter: Short Run Press, 1999: 84–103.

McKee, Robert. "Storytelling That Moves People." *Harvard Business Review* (June 2003).

Menand, Louis. "Live and Learn: Why We Have College." *The New Yorker* (June 6, 2011).

Merton, Thomas. *Contemplation in a World of Action.* South Bend: University of Notre Dame, 1988.

Metaxas, Eric. *Bonhoeffer: Pastor, Martyr, Prophet, Spy.* Nashville: Thomas Nelson, 2010.

Miller, Arthur, Jr., and Bill Hendricks. *The Power of Uniqueness.* Grand Rapids: Zondervan, 1999.

Moir, Anne, and David Jessel. *Brain Sex: The Real Difference between Men and Women.* New York: Delta Books, 1991.

Moore, Kathleen Dean. "The Eternal, Beautiful, Fearsome Mundane." *Oregon Quarterly* (Autumn 2004).

Morse, MaryKate. *Making Room for Leadership: Power, Space and Influence.* Downers Grove: InterVarsity Press, 2008.

Muller, Wayne. *A Life of Being, Having, and Doing Enough.* New York: Harmony, 2010.

———. *Sabbath: Finding Rest, Renewal and Delight in our Busy Lives.* New York: Bantam, 2000.

Mullin, Shirley A. "Leadership: It's Not About Us." Leader's Lectern, *Fuller Focus*, Fuller Theological Seminary (Winter 2011).

Norfolk, Donald. *The Stress Factor.* New York: Simon & Schuster, 1979.

O'Connor, Flannery. *The Habit of Being: Letters,* ed. Sally Fitzgerald. New York: Farrar, Straus, Giroux, 1988.

O'Neil, Deborah, Margaret Hopkins, and Diana Bilimoria. "Women's Careers at the Start of the 21st Century: Patterns and Paradoxes." *Journal of Business Ethics* 80 (2008): 727–743.

Ortberg, John. *The Me I Want to Be.* Grand Rapids: Zondervan, 2010.

Padilla, Arthur. *Portraits in Leadership: Six Extraordinary University Presidents.* Westport: Praeger Publishers, 2005.

Palmer, Parker. *The Courage to Teach.* San Francisco: Jossey-Bass, 1998.

———. *Let Your Life Speak: Listening for the Voice of Vocation.* San Francisco: Jossey-Bass, 2000.

Peterson, Christopher, and Martin E. P. Seligman. *Character Strengths and Virtues: A Handbook and Classification.* Oxford: Oxford University Press, 2004.

Pink, Daniel H. *Drive: The Surprising Truth about What Motivates Us.* New York: Riverhead Books, 2009.

———. *A Whole New Mind.* New York: Riverhead Books, 2006.

Plantinga, Cornelius. *Engaging God's World.* Grand Rapids: Eerdmans, 2002.

Price, Terry. *Leadership Ethics: An Introduction.* Cambridge: Cambridge University Press, 2008.

Rath, Tom. *Vital Friends: The People You Can't Afford to Live Without.* Washington, DC: Gallup Press, 2006.

Rath, Tom, and Barry Conchie. *Strengths Based Leadership: Great Leaders, Teams, and Why People Follow.* Washington, DC: Gallup Press, 2008.

Reis, Harry, and Shelly L. Gable. "Toward a Positive Psychology of Relationships." In *Flourishing: Positive Psychology and the Life Well-lived,* eds. C. L. M. Keyes and J. Haidt. Washington, DC: American Psychological Association, 2003: 129–159.

Reivich, Karen, and Andrew Shatte. *The Resilience Factor: Seven Keys to Finding Your Inner Strength and Overcoming Life's Hurdles.* New York: Broadway, 2003.

Reyes, Robert, and Kimberly F. Case. "National Profile on Ethnic/Racial Diversity of Enrollment, Graduation Rates, Faculty, and Administrators among the CCCU." Center for Intercultural Teaching and Learning, Goshen College, January 2011.

Robinson, William P. *Incarnate Leadership: 5 Leadership Lessons from the Life of Jesus.* Grand Rapids: Zondervan, 2009.

———. *Leading People from the Middle: The Universal Mission of Heart and Mind.* Bloomington: iUniverse, 2010.

Roethke, Theodore. "The Waking." In *The Norton Anthology of American Literature,* Vol. 2. New York: W.W. Norton, 1979.

Rosener, Judy B. "Ways Women Lead." *Harvard Business Review* (Nov.–Dec. 1990): 1–10.

Ryff, C. D., and B. Singer, B. "Flourishing under Fire: Resilience as a Prototype of Challenged Thriving." In *Flourishing: Positive Psychology and the Life Well-lived,* eds. C. L. M. Keyes and J. Haidt. DC: American Psychological Association, 2003: 15–36.

Sample-Ward, Amy. "Telling Stories." Stanford Social Innovation Opinion Blog, April 23, 2008. Available online at http://csi.gsb.stanford.edu/ telling-stories.

Sanaghan, Patrick and Susan Jurow. "Fostering a Risk-Taking Culture." *Business Officer* (May 2011).

Schein, Edgar H. *Organizational Culture and Leadership,* 2nd edition. San Francisco: Jossey-Bass, 1992.

Sebba, Rachel. "Girls and Boys and the Physical Environment." In *Women and the Environment,* eds. Irwin Altman and Arza Churchman. New York: Plenum Press, 1994: 43–72

Secrest, William B. *Perilous Trails, Dangerous Men: Early California Stagecoach Robbers and their Desperate Careers, 1856–1900.* Sanger: Word Dancer Press, Inc., 2002.

Seligman, Martin E.P. *Flourish: A Visionary New Understanding of Happiness and Well-being.* New York: Free Press, 2011.

———. *Learned Optimism: How to Change Your Mind and Your Life.* New York: Pocket Books, 1998.

Senge, Peter. *The Fifth Discipline: The Art and Practice of the Learning Organization.* New York: Doubleday, 1990.

Serratt, Olivier. "Managing by Walking Around." *Knowledge Solutions* 37 (April 2009): 1–2.

Sertillanges, A. G. *The Intellectual Life.* Washington, DC: Catholic University, 1946.

Sheehy, Gail. *New Passages: Mapping Your Life Across Time.* New York: Random House, 1995.

Showalter, Shirley H. "Discovering an Anabaptist Voice." *Teaching to Transform: Perspective on Mennonite Higher Education.* Goshen: Pinchpenny Press, 2000.

———. Presidential Inaugural Address. Goshen College, April 29, 1996.

Shulman, Lee S. "Taking Learning Seriously." *Change* 31.4 (July/Aug. 1999): 10–17.

Simmons, Annette. *The Story Factor: Inspiration, Influence, and Persuasion Through the Art of Storytelling,* revised edition. Cambridge: Basic Books, 2006.

Simon, Caroline. *Mentoring for Mission: Nurturing New Faculty at Church-Related Colleges.* Grand Rapids: Eerdmans, 2003.

Sinek, Simon. *Start with Why: How Great Leaders Inspire Everyone to Take Action.* New York: Penguin Group, 2009.

Smith, Christian. *Souls in Transition: The Religious and Spiritual Lives of Emerging Adults.* Oxford: Oxford University Press, 2011.

Smith, Gordon T. *Courage and Calling: Embracing Your God-Given Potential.* Downers Grove: InterVarsity Press, 1999.

Snyder, C. R. "Hope Theory: Rainbows in the Mind." *Psychological Inquiry* 13 (2002): 249–275.

Stafford, William. "Ask Me." In *The Way It Is: New and Selected Poems.* St. Paul: Graywolf Press, 1988.

Steger, Michael F., Natalie Pickering, Joo Yeon Shin, and Bryan J. Dik. "Calling in Work: Secular or Sacred?" *Journal of Career Assessment* 18:1 (2010).

Stockett, Kathryn. *The Help*. New York: Amy Einhorn/Putnam, 2009.

Stoesz, Edgar. "Scaling Mountains." In *Setting the Agenda: Meditations for the Organization's Soul,* eds. Edgar Stoesz and Rick M. Stiffney, Scottdale: Herald Press, 2011.

Sullivan, William M., Matthew S. Rosin, and Gary D. Fenstermacher. *A New Agenda for Higher Education*. San Francisco: Jossey-Bass, 2008.

Sykes, Bryan. *Adam's Curse: The Science that Reveals Our Genetic Destiny*. New York: W.W. Norton, 2004.

Thompson, Thomas R. "Ungrasping Ourselves." In *The One in the Many: Christian Identity in a Multicultural World*. Lanham: University Press of America, 1998: 9–24.

Thoreau, Henry David. *Walden and Resistance to Civil Government*, 2nd edition, ed. William Rossi. New York: Norton, 1992.

Tichy, Noel M., with Eli Cohen. *The Leadership Engine: How Winning Companies Build Leaders at Every Level*. New York: Harper Business, 1997.

Tolkien, J. R. R. *The Lord of the Rings: The Two Towers*. New South Wales: Allen & Unwin, 1954.

———. *The Tolkien Reader*. New York: Ballantine Books, 1966.

"2010 Census Shows Nation's Hispanic Population Grew Four Times Faster Than Total U.S. Population." U.S. Census Bureau. Report available at http://2010.census.gov/news/releases/operations/cb11-cn146.html.

Van Denend, Mike. "Heart in Hand: The Journey of Stephen Okeyo." Calvin University website. Available online at http://www.calvin.edu/news/archive/heart-in-hand-the-journey-of-stephen-okeyo.

Van Leeuwen, Mary Stewart. *Gender & Grace: Love, Work, & Parenting in a Changing World*. Downers Grove: InterVarsity Press, 1990.

Van Norstrand, Catherine Herr. "Words, Space, and Sexism: How Males Enforce Entitlement through Language and Location." In *Gender-Responsible Leadership: Detecting Bias, Implementing Interventions*. Newbury Park: Sage Publications, 1993.

VanZanten, Susan. *Joining the Mission: A Guide for (Mainly) New College Faculty*. Grand Rapids: Eerdmans, 2011.

Veysey, Laurence R. *The Emergence of the American University*. Chicago: University of Chicago Press, 1965.

Wheatley, Margaret. *Finding Our Way: Leadership for an Uncertain Time*. San Francisco: Berrett-Koehler Publishers, 2005.

Wolfe, Thomas. *I Am Charlotte Simmons*. New York: HarperCollins Publishers, 2004.

Wright, Walter. *Relational Leadership: A Biblical Model for Influence and Service*. Philadelphia: Authentic, 2009.

Wrzesniewski, Amy, Paul Rozin, and Gwen Bennett. "Working, Playing, and Eating: Making the Most of Most Moments." In *Flourishing: Positive Psychology and the Life Well-lived,* eds. Corey L. M. Keyes and Jonathan Haidt. Washington, DC: American Psychological Association, 2003: 185–204.

Yukl, Gary. *Leadership in Organizations*. Upper Saddle River: Prentice Hall, 2002.

Zander, Rosamund Stone, and Benjamin Zander. *The Art of Possibility*. New York: Penguin Books, 2000.

Zyman, Sergio. *Renovate Before You Innovate*. London: Penguin Books, 2004.

CPSIA information can be obtained at www.ICGtesting.com
Printed in the USA
LVOW10s1120250914

405836LV00003B/6/P